TO BE
DISPOSED
BY
AUTHORITY

THE BIGGEST
ASPIDISTRA
IN THE
WORLD

The aspidistra is a useful and decorative plant that thrives in parlours, sitting-rooms and the like; it prospers in temperate conditions and reproduces itself by division.

THE BIGGEST ASPIDISTRA IN THE WORLD

a personal celebration of fifty years of the BBC
by Peter Black

British Broadcasting Corporation

Published by the British Broadcasting Corporation,
35 Marylebone High Street, London W1M 4AA

ISBN 0 563 12154 8

First published 1972

© Peter Black 1972

Printed in England by The Broadwater Press Limited,
Welwyn Garden City, Hertfordshire

CONTENTS

INTRODUCTION

While this book was in the making I went to one of those huge parties given by the communications industries to their own kind. The rooms were filled with the men and women who shape the country's opinions – MPs, newspaper editors, television tycoons, public relations consultants, fashionable clergymen, disc jockeys, the composers of TV jingles, interrogators on current affairs programmes. Soon I found myself jammed next to the interviewer Robin Day, who bawled above the hubbub: 'Where does it leave your image as a critic, writing a book puffing the BBC?' I shouted back that my critical image might indicate that this was not to be a book puffing the BBC. We were then swept apart by a burly female columnist and her bodyguard.

The following pages attempt no puff. Nor do they seek to tell the history of the BBC. The intention is to celebrate the first half-century of the house that Reith built. That it should be undertaken by a man who has earned most of his living by writing about broadcasting as a newspaper critic ought to puzzle and affront nobody. Having lived through the fifty years of the BBC's life I regard such a birthday anniversary as an event well worth celebrating. Anyone who does not must be a dull or crafty person; and to suppose that I am disqualified from taking part in the celebration is to misunderstand the function of criticism. To those whose objections persist I wish the best of luck, coupled with a cordial invitation to them to fill their pockets with heavy weights on the next dark night and take a stroll in the direction of the nearest river.

Although abusing the BBC is one of our most popular national traditions most of us are glad to have it and wish it well. Such is certainly my attitude, though readers who like to hear it abused should not altogether lose heart. They will find themselves catered for somewhere along the route.

Not writing a history it followed that I had to find a formula that would allow me to select. The one that struck me as best was to choose a theme that seemed to mark the style of broadcasting most relevant to the three periods Prewar, War and Postwar, into which the story conveniently divided, and to illustrate it with accounts of programmes and people that I thought were characteristic of those styles. The Prewar and War sections more or less sorted out themselves. The Postwar, in which I had to deal with the rise and fall of radio as a mass entertainment, and the rebirth, growth and rise of television into a huge national industry, presented difficulties before which the author of *The*

Decline and Fall of the Roman Empire would have recoiled exclaiming 'You must be joking'.

To select requires omissions. Here my guides were my personal taste and the opinion that the frame ought to include only domestic radio and television services. A long and absorbing book could be written about the BBC's external broadcasts, which began in 1932 with the Empire Service, spread into Europe as war threatened, became comforter and counsellor to the enslaved continent, and in 1971 were broadcasting forty different services round the world and round the clock. They are the only propaganda service in the world to be financed by the Government (the Grant-in-Aid for 1971/72 was £14m) but independent of it. (The Government's control is limited to prescribing the languages used and the time each language gets on the air.) The BBC's wartime broadcasts to North America and its service to Europe were certainly equal in importance to its service to the home front; indeed it was in the North American service that the BBC began to learn how to be important without being stuffy. But the readers for whom this book is written heard none of them. Neither did I. So I bow towards them and pass on.

Nor have I written as much about music as the size of the BBC's contribution seems to call for. Of course music entered broadcasting naturally and inevitably. It formed the largest proportion of programmes from the first year of the old British Broadcasting Company's life; the BBC became the biggest patron of music the world had known since the medieval church and the heyday of the nobility and the American oil and corned beef millionaires. It saved the Promenade concerts in 1927 by accepting the financial responsibility for them. It did better than save them; it liberated them from the need to plan their season with too sharp an eye on the box office. By 1935 its own Symphony Orchestra was on Toscanini's list of the world's great orchestras. Today it spends £5m a year directly on music and employs a third (580) of all the orchestral players in Britain who can hope for full employment. It has sustained Britain's musical life for half a century. Without the BBC most of us would never have heard a great symphony orchestra, never have heard opera from Covent Garden and Glyndebourne, might never have discovered music, certainly would have had less opportunity to develop understanding and enjoyment of it. Without the BBC young composers and musicians might have lost good years looking for an outlet.

But it is reasonable to say that broadcasting has been the great provider, the communicator of music more than the creator; so, although references to its achievements are scattered through the following pages, there is more detail about the Scrapbooks than the symphony concerts, just as there is more about Children's Hour than the services for schools.

There are other appalling omissions. I see I have said nothing about Morecambe and Wise. But it proves my point that to select is to omit. If I can avoid mentioning my favourite double act, whom can I not avoid mentioning? The object is to remind myself and others of some of the pleasures of its company the BBC has provided. If there seems to be disproportionately more about radio than television, it is because there is always more magic in the past than the present.

July 1972

THE HOUSE THAT REITH BUILT

1

LIKE SPEARS AGAINST THE SKY

I am a few years older than broadcasting as an entertainment, having been born the same year that H. J. Round of the Marconi company demonstrated the gadget that made it all possible. This was his three-electrode gas-filled valve embodying an oxide-coated filament, which greatly improved the quality of broadcast speech. I can remember what leisure was like without radio only as a child observer in a middle-class home. People went to the theatre, the thriving music hall, the silent movies, and could get a good restaurant dinner for five or six shillings. There was a lot of horse-drawn traffic about; our doctor wore a top hat and a spade beard and drove around in a one-horse carriage. At home people made their own entertainment. They read not very good books, knocked up shelves and put down linoleum, played the gramophone, darned and knitted, and amused each other in the ways imperishably described by Mr Pooter in *The Diary of a Nobody*. You might think that even with the price of drink as low as it was (a bottle of scotch cost 12s. 6d.) some of these evenings would be heavy going, but they were not. I dare say I should laugh now if I heard my aunt playing a medley of Great War tunes called *Remember Louvain*, with terrific noises in the bass to evoke the sound of battle; but I didn't then. It was thrilling. These evenings were not dull, they were only normal. Meanwhile broadcasting waited to change all that.

In 1919 the Marconi company managed to get a licence to broadcast experimental transmissions of speech and music from Chelmsford. In June 1920 Lord Northcliffe's *Daily Mail*, which had quickly grasped radio's huge possibilities, promoted with Marconi a concert by Dame Nellie Melba. Her voice was heard by listeners all over Europe and as far away as Newfoundland, and from that hour can be dated the beginning of broadcasting as an entertainment. But at once the dismal howl of militant puritanism was heard, denouncing the concert as a frivolous misuse of a national service. The services objected that a later concert by the Danish tenor Lauritz Melchior had interfered with aircraft communication; and in November the Government gave in to pressure and cancelled Marconi's licence. That was the kind of thing broadcasting had to put up with. The Post Office's ban delayed the start of broadcasting by almost a year, long enough to give the Americans a precious start in the race for world markets. It could be laid to its credit that its cautious control of radio, enforced from an instinctive distrust of entertainment, kept its growth logical and orderly at a time when, in the United States, free enterprise radio was falling into anarchy. It took the whole of 1921 for the industry and the societies of amateur enthusiasts to persuade the GPO to allow speech and music broadcasts once more. But an irresistible tide was bearing radio on. In February 1922 began the first of the weekly half-hours from Writtle, joined in May by the new 2LO station on top of Marconi House in the Strand. Arranged by Arthur Burrows, Marconi's publicity manager, these broadcasts were supposed to be demonstrations and were not publicly advertised, but between them they notched an astonishing number of 'firsts'. Writtle did the first radio play, *Cyrano de Bergerac*, passing the microphone from actor to actor, and planted the seed that would grow into Children's Hour. Writtle's best achievement, though it took another generation to catch on, was its demonstration by Captain Peter Eckersley, its organiser and chief performer, that broadcasting could be informal. His funny, unpredictable, irreverent half-hours fulfilled the Post Office's worst fears by creating a terrific public interest in broadcasting as an entertainment, and Eckersley's little station would probably have had its licence revoked for frivolity if the 2LO broadcasts had not redressed the balance by going in for more serious stuff. 2LO was on the air for an hour a day, and broadcast among other firsts the first running commentary (of the Kid Lewis–Georges Carpentier fight). These events could not be concealed from the public. Indeed these broadcasts, transmitted before broadcasting had officially begun, created a difficulty that has not been solved yet. The audience that heard Writtle and London – almost all keen members of amateur wireless societies – preferred Writtle's fun to 2LO's sobriety but wanted to hear both and between 8 and 8.30 pm on Tuesdays, when Eckersley's half-hour went out, they could not. Burrows had to acknowledge letters requesting him to avoid the clash by closing his station while Writtle was on the air.

Once the possibilities of radio had become imaginable, they could no longer be held back. Thereafter events began to move fast. In early summer the GPO invited applications to run a national service. In July the leading companies in the electronic communications field agreed to the GPO's suggestion that they should form a single British Broadcasting Company; and on 14 November 1922 the BBC took over 2LO's transmissions. Birmingham and Manchester stations opened the day after; within four months a broadly nationwide service was putting out 4–5 hours of broadcasting daily.

Before all this began the BBC had had its biggest stroke of good luck. On the morning of 13 October 1922 the eye of John Reith, a determined and successful Scottish engineering manager of thirty-three looking for a job which would fulfil his premonition that the Lord kept a sharp eye on his future, rested on an advertisement in the *Morning Post*. It was by the BBC; it invited applications for the jobs of General Manager, Director of Programmes, and Chief Engineer, to Sir William Noble, chairman of the committee of founder-members of the company. Reith wrote out his application for the general managership in the Cavendish Club. Then, having looked up Noble in *Who's Who*, he retrieved his letter from the hall porter and added a postcript: 'No doubt you would know some of my people in Aberdeen.' This appeal to tribal loyalty – Noble was himself an Aberdonian – was a curious departure from Reith's austere code of self-reliance, but he had no doubt that this postscript, coupled with the hand of God, had done the trick. And his first meeting with the board of the BBC, his first acquaintance with the possibilities of broadcasting, convinced him that he had found the work which the Lord had in mind for him.

The kind of man he was looks out from the pages of a book he wrote in 1937 but did not publish (his friends said people would laugh at him) until 1966.[1] It was an account of his time in France with the 5th Scottish Rifles, based on the diary that he scrupulously kept and posted home to his parents in big chunks. A shy, solitary, cussed, obstinate character takes shape, of infinite interest to the student of broadcasting. When he left for France he asked the eighteen-year-old Kitty, daughter of a presbyterian minister whom he had known slightly for some years, if he might kiss her goodbye. 'She nodded. I kissed her on the cheek. I knew no better, nor did for long years after that.' Later on, when another eighteen-year-old sent him her photograph, he thought of the embarrassment it must cause his parents should he be killed and it found among his effects. He then sacrificially burned it. He was at this time twenty-six years old.

He was not a good mixer. He supposed he had been born intolerant, reserved and aloof. When he was thirteen his father told him it seemed he would have to live on a desert island. As Transport Officer he characteristically performed his task with unbridled efficiency and, characteristically, got on with those he was responsible for much better than with his brother and senior officers. 'There were various dinner parties but all company affairs, and I was not bid to any.' As an ardent teetotaller his presence might not have been keenly competed for. He fell foul of his commanding officer and adjutant, and deemed it important to risk his life to score off the latter by walking above him on open ground while his enemy crawled along the trench sap. In Glasgow months later he saw his CO advancing towards him with smiles and an outstretched hand. Reith cut him dead. 'Are people so forgiving or so oblivious of the need of being forgiven that they expect the same in others?' he asked himself. He added that this was one of the occasions when he regretted being a teetotaller, for the encounter had left him

[1] Numbered footnotes refer to bibliographical references beginning on p. 232.

feeling that he could have done with a pick-me-up. There was something very characteristic about his insistence on teetotalism even while his common sense was reminding him that in the Flanders of 1914–15 it was a dangerously unhygienic observance. He nearly killed himself by drinking a quart of water drawn from a farmyard pump which later enquiries showed to have been connected to the manure heap. He revelled in giving German snipers opportunities to score off him. Eventually, in the battle of Loos, he drew attention to himself by visiting a redoubt wearing his best tunic and riding breeches and light-coloured shirt. A sniper accepted the challenge and shot him in the side of his face. He felt first surprised, then tired, then foolish, and finally angry; but his wound took him out of the front line and probably saved his life.

He was essentially a romantic Roundhead, who felt that he was fulfilling the purpose for which he had been born only when he was working himself half to death leading a cause that did the public good, in a bracing kind of way. That such a man, pre-eminently equipped for a big task, should have been knocking around London looking for something to do at the moment when the BBC was looking for a chief executive is a coincidence extraordinary enough to make you suspect that Providence may have had a hand in it, after all. But it is misleading to imply that he cuffed and kicked and badgered broadcasting into going the way he wanted. The team he steered, the directors he served, thought as he did.

They thought it an enormous piece of luck to have such a marvel put into their hands and this response, the pitch of enthusiasm that could only be felt once, is preserved in the books they wrote. Reith thought that the glory of blazing a trail through virgin forest, overcoming disease and danger, opening up and developing what had been barren and desolate, was more wonderful still when the opposition came not from the blind force of nature but from the indifference, ignorance or hostility of man.[2] Arthur Burrows shuddered when he imagined what broadcasting might have become had it fallen into the hands of persons lacking in ideals.[3] Captain C. A. Lewis, deputy organiser of programmes, defending the monopoly, thought public criticism would have much the same effect as competition and in a rather fine phrase set out the company's view of the audience. 'We shall always be the losers matched against an ideal.' To him wireless continued to be a marvel; he wrote about the broadcasting of symphony concerts as though the music was being physically carried about the country in stage coaches – 'along the roadsides, over the hills, through towns, brushed by trees, soaked by rain, swayed by gales'. He held it unthinkable that this medium should ever fall into the hands of a single man or group of men. Some would say that that is exactly what happened to it, but what Lewis meant was a man or group that did not have the ideals of Reith and his group.

At this stage Reith's influence was chiefly political and economic, bent towards organising the facilities and chasing revenue. He laid down the programme policy, ordered the percentages of music, religion, variety, etc., but took little interest in the material except when it infringed his moral code. One day he entered Lewis's office and threw a copy of *The Times* on his desk. 'I see Daisy Kennedy's performing tonight.' Lewis was working six weeks ahead and had forgotten. 'Oh, is she?' 'Yes.' 'Anything wrong with that?' 'Haven't you seen the papers? She was divorced yesterday. We can't have a divorced woman performing.'

They were all totally untrained for the work they were doing, Lewis recalled half a century afterwards, but saw that the thing about broadcasting was that everything under the sun, not just entertainment, could be brought to it. Everyone was interested in it. One day Shaw turned up; somebody spotted him in the waiting-room playing among a group of children. Lewis grabbed him and promptly invited him to produce one of his plays, to read one of his plays, to talk, do anything he liked. Shaw worked out that at a royalty of five shillings per listener his fee ought to be about £10,000, but when Lewis said the most they could afford was £100 Shaw said he would read *O'Flaherty, VC* for nothing. The broadcast was arranged; Shaw did it perfectly, and afterwards Lewis went to the pictures with him feeling, he said, exactly as some Tudor spark must have done walking with Shakespeare.*

Reith knew very clearly the sort of thing he wanted, and though as a Roundhead he expressed himself in terms of a romantic vision in which broadcasting was a drawn sword cleaving the darkness of ignorance his vision was only another way of putting across what was sound common sense, like the voices of Joan of Arc. He saw that broadcasting could only fulfil its huge promise if it were run by a single service which was free of state control and did not have to make profits (the old British Broadcasting Company's dividend was limited to $7\frac{1}{2}$ per cent). He grasped immediately two of the things that made broadcasting unique. Because it was a live communication mistakes were not only probable but certain, and they would be impossible to retrieve or even to limit. And unlike the theatre and cinema the wireless did not offer the customer a choice between a score of different plays and films but made his choice for him. It was, said Reith, exclusively a table d'hôte menu.

He also saw that this created problems of control, and laid down a principle that guided broadcasting policy for two generations. He decided that whereas a theatre manager or an editor was dealing with a public that had

* Creative writers then as now were undervalued compared with interpretive artists. A year later Lewis handed Chaliapin, the Russian bass, a cheque for £1000: it was the largest sum of money young Lewis had ever seen in his life.

come to buy what he was offering, a broadcaster had to consider the public that did not want it – 'the unwilling audience, the people who if the matter were, say, performed in a hall would not be there'.[4] He thought too that he had to consider that even for the willing audience material quite proper in a theatre or newspaper might be objectionable in a family group. 'This is not Philistinism but common sense.' Here he put his finger on what was to be an incurably tender spot in the BBC's relationship with its public. It took forty years of modifications to establish a rather more sensible principle by which audiences were encouraged to have certain expectations from certain programme slots, which they might then attend as willing buyers; if they disliked a drama series for its frankness but watched it in order to complain they placed themselves in a position in which nobody could do much to help them.

As for the BBC's duties, they were so obvious to him that they scarcely needed clarifying. It had to offer the best of what was available without waiting to be asked. He saw the public as the whole population of the kingdom, a collection of groups of varying age, sex, taste, education, religion, politics, wealth and status; and broadcasting addressed itself to the totality.

Some of his colleagues were entranced by the potential of broadcasting far beyond their power to see things straight, and confused what audiences could hear with what they would like to hear. The 'shepherd on the downs, the lonely crofter in the farthest Hebrides, and what is more important the labourer in his squalid tenement, equally the lonely invalid on her monotonous couch, may all in spirit sit side by side with the patrons of the stalls and hear some of the best performances in the world.'[5] Lewis predicted that before long a Beethoven symphony would be as popular as dance music. Reith thought this more possible than probable, and knew as well as his critics that what he called 'grand' music had to be kept within reasonable bounds; but he knew that without nourishment taste died, and that it was his privilege and duty to use the ease and cheapness of broadcasting to supply a service that could never be done in terms of local profit. As for instruction, the mere fact that the medium was there, able to override distance, overcome inequalities of teaching ability, to broadcast seed on a wind that would take it to every fertile corner, imposed the duty of taking advantage of it. In spite of the crofter in his hut and the labourer in his squalid tenement the broadcasters unselfconsciously took it for granted that in addressing everyone they were addressing their own kind. Lewis, listing the distractions that called the listener's attention from 'the concert', included the maid entering with coffee.

On the whole the public shared the belief that there was something special about radio, until they got used to it. I think this was because it was mysterious as well as extraordinarily cheap and simple to make. I built several crystal sets, all of which worked quite well without my having the slightest idea how, or what I was doing. It was difficult not to wonder if we were tampering with some powerful force. Late one night, I remember, in about 1924, my brother and I in our bedroom and my parents in theirs were listening to the Savoy Orpheans on headphones. We were dumb-founded to hear my mother's voice imposed on top of the band: 'George. It's time the boys went to sleep.' My elder brother caught on quicker than I to what was happening; the headphones acted as microphones as well as earpieces. He called back: 'Just another ten minutes.' This reply, apparently responding to a remark he could not have overheard, caused a sensation in my parents' room. My father, a man of habitual uncertainty where any-thing mechanical was concerned, shouted to turn the thing off before it blew up in the face of this provocation, and as far as I recall we never again communicated in this way.

One of the best attempts to explain how broadcasting worked, in terms that could be understood by any clever man of under thirty, was written by Burrows, the BBC's first director of programmes. The first essential for wireless telephony was a very rapid, unbroken wave-ripple across the ether, spreading outwards at 186,000 miles per second, and at a frequency of between 1,007,000 and 605,000 per second. On these ripples was super-imposed an electrical counterfeit of the sounds from the studio; by changing the pattern of the ripples, these created new formations. Burrows managed to sum it up in a paragraph. 'The complete process of wireless telephony, we may say, consists of producing an electrical counterfeit of a sound, of throwing this counterfeit across space on top of a high-speed ripple, and in reconverting the impulses from that ripple as received at a distant point into a direct electrical current, such as will set in motion, through the medium of small electro-magnets, the diaphragms of a pair of headphones. These diaphragms, beating the air in sympathy with the microphone at the transmitting station, reproduce sounds exactly equivalent to those made by the voice or instruments in the studio.'

To hear them, though, you needed a 'detector' which would sort out the changes in the wave pattern produced by throwing electrical sound on top of it. These could be valves but in the earliest days were mostly crystals. You placed a metal wire, called a cat's-whisker, in contact with a lump of crystal about the size of a large pea. The BBC advised that a crystal set would give quite good reception within four miles of a main station, or up to 20 miles from the high-powered 5XX transmitter at Daventry. But, as I recall, trying to pick up 2LO in Thames Ditton, fifteen miles away, was a matter of favourable conditions. The strength of signal we received depended on where the wire touched the crystal. If we found a good spot the sound came magically whispering in; but contact was tenuous, liable to be broken off by the banging of a door or too heavy a tread. Then we would have to hunt for the spot again.

There were never enough sets of headphones to go round. My brother and I learned that you could amplify the sound by putting a single headphone into a jug, thereby converting it into a kind of loudspeaker; but this was a makeshift more desperate than practical. The thing was to get hold of a set of headphones. The peculiar exasperation of those days was that the occupants of any room divided into those who had headphones on, and could hear the wireless, and those who had not and could not. On the other hand, if they spoke to those who were listening they completely drowned the sound in the headphones, so you had exchanges like this: 'Anyone seen my brown boots?' 'Listen!' 'How can I listen, you've got the earphones?' 'Shush! – Listen!' etc.

Looking back on those days in 'These Radio Times'[6] Anthony Armstrong, one of the early broadcasters, insisted that nobody ever had better and clearer reception than the old cat's-whisker used to give them. What is beyond argument is that nothing in broadcasting will ever sound as wonderful, nor can while the earth lasts, as those first sounds that came out of the air. C. A. Lewis described hearing the first opera from Covent Garden, broadcast in January 1923. Suddenly the loudspeaker on the table came alive. 'At first indistinguishable it became apparent that we were hearing the talk and the rustling of programmes in the auditorium. Finally there was a burst of clapping which died down to dead silence and was followed by two sharp raps; a second later the huge orchestra had leapt into its stride, swelled into a great crash of brass and cymbals which could be heard all down the corridor.'[7] Thus Mozart's *Magic Flute* entered the new dimension. It gave Lewis and others a revelation of what the future of broadcasting might be, carrying their imagination forward to the days when the BBC would have great orchestras and conductors in their own studios. The myth that the millions out there were only waiting to hear to enjoy began to work. 'Many people imagining opera to be a dull or dreary thing were converted in an evening; many others who had never heard or expected to hear opera had it brought to their hospital or bedside.'[8]

The tremendous novelty and the wonderful sense of opportunity were two of the things that gave broadcasting its unique opening status. Probably the fifteenth-century British never felt quite like this about printing, which they could see for themselves was an obvious step forward from carving, once Caxton had shown that it was. But whereas the first books were costly, wireless was extraordinarily cheap. Its cheapness was the third ingredient it needed to exploit novelty and opportunity.

The BBC was financed in part by half the licence fee of ten shillings and

in part by royalties on receivers and components sold, payable to the manufacturers who comprised the BBC. But the royalty system soon ran into a
muddle, for the Post Office had underestimated the public's interest in
running up their own sets; it believed they would be content to buy them.
The market was quickly flooded with home construction kits that were
possibly less efficient than those marketed by the BBC but could be made
at a fraction of the cost. Percy W. Harris, in the first number of *The Wireless
Constructor*,[9] told his readers how to make up a simple crystal set from a
pound of No. 16 DCC wire, a sixpenny piece of crystal, and a pair of headphones, a piece of dry wood, a piece of tinfoil, a few screws and a hexagonal
pickle bottle round which he wound the wire to make a coil. (That was the
coil that got you 2LO. To get Chelmsford, Harris recommended wrapping
a length of wire round a bottle of tonic elixir.) How cheaply it could be
done can be measured by the cost of buying a crystal set. You could buy a
BBC one from £2 – £4, including two pairs of headphones.

Power meant quality. The BBC always gave the same advice. We were
recommended to buy the most powerful set we could afford to avoid having
to work it flat out. The aerial ought to be 100 feet of copper wire or copper
alloy; it was secured at its free end by a thirty-foot-high mast and preserved from contact with its supports by porcelain insulators. An earth wire
was soldered to a zinc or copper plate which you buried in the ground
outside the window. You had two sets of coils, one for tuning in to London
or other medium-wave bands, the other for long-wave stations such as 5XX
and Radio Paris. Because distance equalled power and power equalled
wealth there was intense rivalry in tuning in to foreign stations. An early
H. M. Bateman cartoon drew 'The man who boasts he can get Timbuctoo
on one valve'.

The coils looked like stiff knitting. You tuned by plugging in the correct
one, then turning the control knob of the variable condenser until the
station came in. At the same time you had to keep the reaction coil away
from the tuning coil. If you did not, your set would turn into a transmitter
and emit the frenzied howls and whoops known as oscillation. The BBC
campaigned ceaselessly against this offence, even, in the early informal days,
broadcasting requests to guilty areas: 'Will residents in Acacia Avenue,
Brixton, look to their sets, as they are causing severe interference to their
neighbours.' As late as 1928 it was still receiving 15,000 complaints of
oscillation in a year, and Bateman drew another cartoon of men shunning a
fellow commuter on a suburban railway platform above a caption: 'Suspected! Frigidity on the 9.15.'

I was on comfortable terms with the crystal sets, which needed no batteries
of any kind, but withdrew from the manufacturing side when they were
swept away by the development of valve sets. These required a mastery of

such dangerous appliances as soldering irons and a certain amount of confidence in the handling of electricity. They were powered by high-tension batteries, which were dry and lasted for months, and low-tension batteries which were wet and called 'accumulators' and ran down fairly soon. They were, however, rechargeable, and the households learned to maintain two, one in use and the other on charge. To take back one accumulator and pick up the charged one was a regular domestic chore, usually shared in turn. The charging place was a room at the back of a garage in which scores of these batteries, each labelled with the name of their owners, silently and mysteriously absorbed energy, exuding a peculiarly sharp, metallic smell like the taste of the liquid that sometimes spilled on to your fingers. Separate coils soon gave way to a single coil, the batteries to power from the mains. A host of gadgets and accessories appeared. The Hailglass Shades and Globes company addressed itself in a full-page advertisement to The Women Of Britain. 'The radio has undoubtedly helped to keep your husband and boys away from the club and kept them at home where they thus experience the benefits of your gentle charm and influence; but you must now go one step further and make your home comfy and cheerful by having Hailglass Shades and Globes on your lights. Your menfolk, as they listen to the radio in a home made bright and comfy by our charmingly coloured glassware, will indeed feel that they are in a real Heaven on Earth.' C. S. Dunham, who left the BBC to set himself up as a manufacturer, in 1928 advertised a three-valve set (at 35s 6d down plus 25s a month, or 21 guineas cash) that had everything enclosed in a cabinet that could be locked; the only thing that could be stolen was the cabinet, with the set inside it. A radio alarm, advertised as an automatic programme selector, appeared in the same year; you connected it up with your receiving set and low-tension battery, plugged it in to a clockface at the time required and waited for the set to turn itself on. It failed to please the market, probably because it was more fatiguing to operate it than to remember the time of the programme one wanted to hear. But the component that was to stay unchanged longest, altering the look of back gardens all over the country, was the aerial, visible sign of the spread of wireless. C. A. Lewis used to see them as he walked home late at night after his day's work, 'the aerial posts standing like spears against the sky'. They did not look in the least like spears, only like poles; but the romantic image fitted the notion Lewis and his co-pioneers had of broadcasting.

2

THE END OF THE BEGINNING

In so far as it had no public money behind it broadcasting was entirely dependent on the public's response to its programmes. But it was quickly obvious that progress was unstoppable; if the BBC had put out nothing but weather forecasts and hymn tunes the rise in listening would probably have been only slightly affected, such was the strength of public interest. It was clear too that the licence-fee system was going to be enough to pay for wireless without the help of the cumbersome and difficult royalty system; and that the licence system was the best possible one for enabling a service to develop without having to watch the box-office returns. What the listener paid ten shillings for was the right to operate a wireless receiver; within that right one listener's claim to be entertained was as good as, but no better than, another's; wireless was, said Lewis, the most democratic entertainment ever devised.

Because Britain was a compact island with an advanced trunk telephone system the business of establishing a national network was done within three years. By September 1925 forty million people were within what the BBC called 'uninterrupted service' range of a BBC station broadcasting an average of $6\frac{1}{2}$ hours a day. The growth of the audience was harder to check. By March 1923 the Post Office had issued 80,000 licences, but probably four or five times that number of sets were in use.[1] By September 1924 the number of licences was reaching towards the first million; assuming that the proportion of listeners like my brother and myself, who certainly intended to get round to buying a licence one day, remained unchanged there were probably 4m – 5m sets in use.

During the first year the BBC's staff multiplied by twelve times from its beginnings in Kingsway, where Reith commanded the policy and direction of broadcasting from a cubicle in one overcrowded room. Lewis wrote nostalgically about the hectic, exciting and always expanding atmosphere of enthusiasm and overwork, of the brilliant improvisation, the microphones tied up with string, the switches that needed to be coaxed by mechanics who knew their ways – 'there is something very attractive about unorganised methods when handled by intelligent people' – and mourned his foreknowledge that the disciplines of age and experience lay waiting for all.

The opening up of the regional wireless stations raced ahead of the development of a national network, and for a few months broadcasting in Britain had a local autonomy it was never to know again. They arranged and broadcast their own programmes; only the evening news bulletins came from London, telephoned and then read. But the growth of landlines quickly connected every station to every station, and the company had to learn how to build the complicated programme mosaic, planned centrally but fitting local contributions from the provinces into what some of the broadcasters continued to refer to as 'the concerts'. It was learned very soon that the regional listeners preferred London to their local station, though if you had a set with valves you could sometimes tune in to the local opt-out as well as the networked programme. But it was not until July 1925, when the high-powered long-wave transmitter at Daventry began to broadcast the London programme over Britain, that this simple pleasure became generally available. Most of us heard one programme only.

The BBC's first attempt, inevitably, was to please everyone. It produced some quaint patchwork effects. One September evening in 1923 the evening began at 7.30 with an orchestral concert, broke off the music for John Henry's Tour, went back to the concert, this time playing light music, and ended with John Henry singing. John Henry entered the radio immortals by being the very first wireless comedian. He was a Yorkshireman who presented himself with a flat, lugubrious voice in the character of a henpecked husband. He had a wife named Blossom whose peremptory 'John Henry, come here,' and his own 'Coming, Blossom,' became the first radio catchphrases to replace conversation. Like all comedians he had to work from written scripts – a condition which the BBC admitted deprived comedians of their special craft of spontaneity and improvisation. But there it was. A script had to be written, submitted, accepted, checked for advertising, libel, bad taste (Reith hated jokes about drunkenness or mothers-in-law) or 'anything that was likely to cause offence to our vast audience'.[2] The performer undertook to deliver it without any additions or alterations, and if, after passing all these checkpoints, he had enough spirit left to attempt such a breach, the announcer on duty would have immediately thrown his microphone out of circuit. The announcer had all manner of extra work of this sort. He bashed a set of tubular bells to give the time signal, helped move the furniture, steered artists among the trailing lengths of wire, and warned them not to sneeze.

The incontestable fact that not one of the BBC's chief administrators and programme creators knew much about show business, and had had no practical experience in it whatever, worked on the whole to the infant broadcasting's advantage. It expanded wireless's horizon. Variety in the music-hall sense suffered; but variety without the capital letter blossomed. The broad policy was to keep on the upper side of public taste but to cater for the majority about seventy-five per cent of the time, though if any programme, no matter now unappealing to the majority it might be, were reckoned to be in the national interest it went out as a matter of course between 9 and 10 pm. The broadcasters addressed themselves to the nation, and had a very high opinion of it. Burrows thought that vulgarity, had the BBC wished to offer it, could not have lasted ten minutes; it would have been scorched by the blast of public opinion.

The company began to open out the field of broadcasting, developing programmes that could sometimes be fitted into a category but as often could not; they were merely broadcasts, interesting because they were interesting and because they could be done. On Burns' Night in 1923 the microphones went to Princes Restaurant to hear the after-dinner concert and G. K. Chesterton propose 'The Immortal Memory'. Ian Hay gave the first broadcast appeal. The wireless brought evensong from church and Edgar Wallace into the studio to give the first eye-witness narrative of the (1923) Derby. It broadcast the Armistice Day ceremony, spreading the silence – that strange compound of pride, grief, nostalgia and remorse – across the nation as no other communication could. It reminded us to put the clocks forward the day summer time began. It invented the request programme. Some famous and legendary names began to appear. Some, like Monsieur Stephan, came to the microphone because to use broadcasting to give French lessons was an obvious plank in the BBC's structure. Another of these was Sir Walford Davies, who became the first and most famous of the popularisers of music when he started talking to schoolchildren in 1924. The names call back the voices: I can still remember the hard, firm timbre of Stephan and the melodious, fluting tones of Davies. The extraordinary quality these people shared was their ability to talk to a microphone as though it were another person smoking a pipe in a chair opposite. They were unself-conscious because the wireless was new enough for everyone to be novices together. Another of them, though he was a highly self-conscious performer, was A. J. Alan. He sprang into prominence as a born radio storyteller after his first broadcast – 'My Adventure in Jermyn Street' – in January 1924. He told intricate, malicious mystery stories in a light, knowing, bantering manner that subtly flattered the listener by suggesting that he was on the same level of worldliness. Although his stories read well in print their special merit lay in the artistry with which Alan told them on the air. Far from objecting to the rule about scripts, Alan prepared his in extraordinary detail. He pasted the pages on to cardboard so that the illusion of a man making it up as he went along would not be shattered by rustling noises. He inserted his own production notes – 'cough here', 'sigh', 'pause', etc. – and he relied on them to the point of taking matches and a candle to the studio with him in case the light failed. What sounded so casual must have strung him up fairly tight, for Stuart Hibberd told how Alan would never take a drink or smoke for a week before he broadcast. Partly from a shrewd sense of showmanship, probably to appease some deep-seated need for anonymity, he created a mystery about himself. He was a civil servant whose real name, a well-guarded secret until his death, was Leslie Harrison Lambert. He stoked up the public's curiosity by broadcasting only two or three times a year, increasing each time the atmosphere of a special occasion and giving rise to some of the sort of speculation about his real identity that was called up by the name of Jack the Ripper.

What Alan, Davies and the others had grasped was that though their audience might be anything from ten thousand to ten million the utterance was from one person to another, as Sir Walford Davies explained in an article he wrote for the BBC's 1929 *Handbook* on how he did it. 'Unaffected simplicity of utterance alone gets over.' But it would be misleading to claim that talkers were the nation's favourite entertainment. What Davies did was to please very much those who wanted to hear him, and those who enjoyed the romantic experience of feeling that a new vista was opening before them. The majority preferred a good laugh.

By 1928 the BBC was producing 60,000 hours of programming a year for audiences never below a million and often as high as fifteen million. Its programme policy was summed up in a sentence from its review of that year: 'It would be a derogation of duty for those placed centrally, in a position to know what of cultural interest is available, not to give the great public the opportunity of knowing for itself, without waiting for anything in the nature of an indication that it was wanted.' Or, as Reith's succinct working rule put it: Offer the public something better than it now thinks it likes. A section on music illuminates the confident expectations of the early broadcasters. 'Broadcasting, that magical agent, has made available by means of comparatively simple apparatus and at next to no cost the finest things there are to hear in music. . . . Literally millions of people have heard for the first time in their lives the simple, youthful and sparkling tunes of Papa Haydn or the elegant Mozart and the joyful early quartets of Beethoven and realised that therein lies a wealth of melody undreamed of. Hosts of bright, impressionable children whose music had consisted mainly of snatches of music-hall ditties inflicted by itinerant executants in the bar entrance, or sobs of the worst type of sentimental slop played in the local cinema at the weekly popular Saturday performance, have heard over the broadcast such music as must have had a great and good influence on the sensitive unfolding mind.' The desire to do good, accompanied by the conviction that everyone would want to be done good, gleams, as a beam of light strikes a domed forehead, from the programme details of those years. It would be foolish to deny its nobility.

3

THE LONG FOXTROT

The beginning of broadcasting coincided with an extraordinary craze for dancing, as though the nation were trying to drown its memories of the war years in the bray of the saxophone and the plonk of the ukulele. I have described earlier the fun of lying in bed and listening to the Havana Band and the Orpheans from the Savoy. That must have been about 1923, when dance music was first broadcast from a hotel – not, as it happens, the Savoy, but the Carlton. It stayed an enormously popular staple item in the schedules (by 1931 it took up twenty per cent of time on London Regional and ten per cent on the National Programme) until, in the nature of things, it was overtaken by other entertainments.

In the early years the bands played mostly in clubs and hotels, and so were part of outside broadcasting (an outside broadcast was defined as anything that did not come from a studio, and could include variety, opera, talks, music and every other section of broadcasting's output). The BBC's technique was fairly simple. When C. A. Lewis handled a relay from Covent Garden in 1923 he would arrange with Stanton Jefferies in the opera house the point in the opera at which the relay would begin, go to the transmitting room, telephone Jefferies and with his own hands throw the switch connecting the transmitters to the opera. For dance music relays the engineers would sling a microphone above and in front of the band and would telephone Savoy Hill to let them know the players were ready to go.

One reason why outside broadcasts were so popular was their creation of atmosphere. The BBC's engineers had tried – reasonably enough – to create a studio in which the sound would be as free from artificial and unpredictable resonance as heavy curtains and other damping devices could make it. To this pure sound they would then be able to add the effects they wanted. In time this worked very well, but performers hated it. Speaking in no. 3 studio at Savoy Hill (although called no. 3 it was the first to be built) was almost like hearing a voice disembodied from one's self:* it was the contrast to these dead conditions that made the hotel broadcasts sound so

* The actor-producer Nigel Playfair, listening on his monitor headphones to what his cast were saying in Studio 3, asked, 'What's wrong? There's nothing there.' So he ordered everyone out into the corridor, where the sound was livelier, and produced the play from there.

thrilling. You can still recapture the sound by listening to *Grand Hotel*, for not all the light music relays were of dance music. There were always midday lunchtime relays from London hotels or theatres. Albert Sandler from the Park Lane hotel and Tom Jones from the Grand, Eastbourne, were regular Sunday-evening fare; for Reith believed very much in relaxation on Sundays. This music, quiet and genteel, for which even the applause sounded elderly and respectable, was for many years the lightest thing listeners got to hear on Sundays.

It was the atmosphere of a night out among people who were enjoying themselves (and paying good money to do it) that the dance band relays captured so appealingly. The studio announcer introduced the band and the place, and wished the nation good night as though ending broadcasting for the day. But there would then be up to ninety minutes of dance music. The leaders might say a few words, to the extent of naming the tunes; the other sounds were of music, shuffling feet, an occasional overheard fragment of talk, applause, and the by no means regular singer.

Up to 1925 the only bands to broadcast regularly were from the Savoy, but the fame these relays brought to Debroy Somers and Carroll Gibbons was not lost on other groups. The BBC gave way to pressure in favour of spreading their patronage a little wider, and in November new names began to appear. For the pleasure it will give some older readers, here are some of the bands who so pleasantly idled the end of the days away between 1925 and 1928: Teddy Brown's from the Café de Paris (Teddy was a fat, lightfingered xylophonist); Ray Starita's at the Ambassador Club; George Fisher's at the Kit-Kat; Bert Firman's at the Carlton; Ronnie Munro's at the Florida Club; Ambrose's at the Mayfair; Alfredo's from the New Princes; Herman Darewski's at Covent Garden; Jack Payne's at the Cecil. And some of the tunes folk danced to, played on gramophones on the thick and fragile 78 rpm records of the time, and bashed out for their own entertainment on the piano were 'The Sheik of Araby', 'Margie', 'Ain't We Got Fun', 'Carolina In The Morning', 'Horsey Keep Your Tail Up', 'Yes, Sir, That's My Baby', 'Three O'Clock In The Morning', 'It Had To Be You', and the deliciously melancholy Irving Berlin waltzes, 'What'll I Do?', 'All Alone', 'Always'.

In those days the music industry made as much money from selling sheet music as gramophone records. Those were for the richer fans. A single record cost three shillings and wore out, whereas sheet music cost from sixpence to two shillings and lasted, if not for ever, certainly longer than the six-week life of the average song. Printed in two to three colours, the sheets bore on the front cover a likeness of the singer or the band associated with the tune. You got for your money a simplified piano arrangement plus the lyrics and an accompaniment for banjolele and ukulele. This amounted to sets of chords which were in harmony with the piano, if both players were reading their notes right, and if it did nothing much for the song it did nothing much against it.

The attraction of large sales plus the wide exposure offered by radio led to the vexatious and, as it turned out, insoluble plague of song-pluggers, for the wily fellows in the industry knew that repeated exposure held the key to sales, and the sensible way to ensure constant repetition was to pay band leaders for it. When the bands happened to be broadcasting a minor but serious social nuisance emerged, for as the BBC justly complained dance music programmes were being selected not on merit but according to the desires of the music publishers. Programmes therefore tended to contain the same tunes day after day. As the publishing industry's interest lay in the selling of songs, and it knew that a good one sold better than a bad one, the direct influence of the plugging system was probably less than the BBC supposed. It is doubtful if it ever turned a poor song into a smash hit; and to kill a good tune by denying it air time because nobody would pay for it would have been as silly as if a chef, having created an appetising and lucrative dish, would throw it down the rubbish chute rather than tell anyone about it. It was true that some dance bands refused to play music which had not been paid for; the casualties were not among Tin Pan Alley's songs but those – usually much better ones – from the musical shows in the theatres.

The BBC tried to persuade the publishers that plugging was not in their best interests. The publishers insisted that it was, whereon the BBC acted unilaterally and forbade the announcement of all titles in dance band programmes except those provided by Jack Payne. Older readers will remember these strangely spooky sessions, which were made unnecessarily annoying by the BBC's failure to tell listeners why it was doing it. The BBC had to drop it soon and look for other means. It appointed a special watchdog over dance music with power to warn or suspend, but the pluggers kept the initiative by inventing the request item. This was popular with listeners and almost impossible to identify as a proven plug. Chafing in its role of unwilling accomplice the BBC said it was taking steps to end the practice. It first tried to buy some control over bandleaders by paying them; until then the BBC and the bands considered that the publicity of a radio engagement was enough fee; but the craftier leaders merely added their BBC fee to their plug money. Although it had the only outlet for broadcasting there was little more the BBC could do against the pluggers short of cancelling all dance music programmes except those of its own band, and trying to persuade offenders that the BBC's wrath ought to be feared more than the sales were coveted. The song-plugging wave did not recede until 1948, when the BBC and the publishers managed to draw up an agreement which contained stiff penalties to be used against the guilty. This was fairly effective until gramophone records began to take over from sheet music and presented fresh temptations over which the feet of the crafty were only too willing to stumble. Plugging re-emerged under the name of payola.

Two newcomers to the dance were Jack Payne and Henry Hall, who realised about the same time that the thing to do was to get into radio. I admired Jack very much as a schoolboy, I cannot remember why. I told him how much I'd enjoyed his broadcasts when we first met; I was then a TV critic and Jack and I were members of a little group that used to meet for lunch once a month. He was aghast at being remembered so well by such an aged fan and said, in the tone of voice that old-fashioned writers used to describe as 'nettled': 'You make me feel as old as God.'

Jack came from the Midlands. After the war he passed through a phase undergone by many young officers who did not quite know what to do with the lives that had been handed back to them. He thought farming might suit him, or the manager's job on a tea plantation. Finding nobody to give him a start in these crafts he faced the fact that the only thing he had to sell was his ability to play a piano fairly well. He formed his first band with two friends from before the war, a drummer and a banjolinist (the banjoline sounded not quite like a banjo but was easier to play) and worked up quite a profitable little circuit of engagements at dances in private houses. He averaged £8 – 10 a week for himself, not bad for 1920. He broke up his little group to take a job as pianist with a band at the Birmingham Palais (the huge public-hall fashion of dancing was spreading outward from London); then he took a second band (himself and three others) to the Grand Hotel, Folkestone, and a year later cast himself with his savings into a London where a piano-player could pick up ten guineas a night and more if he played in a band that was praised by the Prince of Wales.

Jack Payne made his own luck by going to see the management at the Hotel Cecil and suggesting that if ever the resident band should leave he would like his own to be considered. The Cecil has been gone for so many years that I must describe it a little. It was a huge, luxurious hotel on the Embankment close to its fiercest competitor, the Savoy. It took its share of the postwar spending spree, but adapted much slower to changing times than the Savoy, and lacked fashionable snob appeal. At a time when, for instance, the Savoy was putting a third tap (for icewater) in its bedroom to placate the American visitors there were still some rooms in the Cecil that had no hot and cold water. The stuff was brought up in the grand old way by grand old chambermaids. It had a marvellous atmosphere of gilt chairs and leather-padded doors, of family parties up from the country. The Prince of Wales used to dance at the Cecil (as where did he not?) but this could not save the place. The management decided, too late, to hire Gelardi, the former manager of the Savoy, to remodel and modernise the hotel, but the shareholders ran out of nerve halfway through and sold the site to Shell-Mex. Jack got the job, and with it what he wanted, a showcase for his band. But he was already broadcasting, and pestered the BBC so relentlessly that, as they had never had much of a case for limiting the relays to the Savoy, they had to give way. On Boxing Day 1925 Jack and his band made their first broadcast in Children's Hour. He was introduced as Uncle Jack, but did not mind a bit. He was in.

He quickly became a favourite, for the public liked the image they and the newspapers formed of him as the ex-officer turned bandleader. He seemed to typify that perennially popular hero, the amateur who beats the professionals at their own game (H. C. McNeile, 'Sapper', was currently writing his Bulldog Drummond best-sellers based on a group of ex-officers who went about doing good by bashing Bolshies). There was, however, nothing of the amateur about Jack. He was an exceptionally tough, determined and ambitious young man. In February 1928 he brought his band formally into the BBC as The Dance Orchestra, and introduced the variation he had long planned: dance music that you could listen to.

The BBC certainly got its money's worth out of him. In one year his band supplied 650 hours of broadcasting, and put up a record which was never to be beaten of playing sixty-five tunes in a day's work of four and a half hours actually on the air. Crowds of autograph seekers hung about to greet him outside Savoy Hill, and his fan mail climbed to a staggering 50,000 letters, postcards and telegrams a year, most of them requests for tunes.[1] He had with him a number of players who became as well known. Jack Jackson was his trumpeter; Bob Busby played the piano. Ray Noble was his arranger. Billy Scott-Coomber was one of his singers in the numbers described as 'special arrangements'. These were mostly comic dramatisations in which the singer would discharge the chorus in different voices, possibly as an Englishman, Irishman and Scotsman, accompanied by appropriate variations from the band. 'Riding On A Camel In The Desert', 'Swinging On A Five-Barred Gate' and 'All By Yourself In The Moonlight' were some of these. Jack also undertook more serious works. One which touched my boyish susceptibilities was 'Sergeant Flagg and Sergeant Quirt', based on the feuding marines of one of the best Hollywood films about the Great War, *What Price Glory*, as played by Victor McLaglen and Edmund Lowe.

In 1932 Jack ended his contract with the BBC; and as he stepped out the much less flamboyant but no less shrewd Henry Hall stepped sprightly in. Henry had gone into the music hall about the same time Jack formed his first three-man band. He formed an unsuccessful variety act with two other musicians, then, after hearing Harriet Cohen play at the Queen's Hall, changed course and enrolled as a student of piano at the Guildhall School of

Music. He entered the extravagant and lucrative dance band era by taking on a Christmas relief engagement as deputy pianist in the band at the Midland Hotel, Manchester, one of a group of hotels run by the old London Midland and Scottish Railway Company. In those years the railway hotel business was still expanding and Henry's career blossomed with it. By 1924 he was musical director of the group's hotels; but what brought his name before a wide public were the relays of the band he led in person from the LMS's new luxury hotel at Gleneagles. Henry, who had a sharp eye for publicity, was the first bandleader to think of introducing his relays with a signature tune: he wrote 'Come Ye Back To Bonnie Scotland', reasoning that it would help to establish the name of his band among listeners who could remember the tune but not who played it. He was also creating a recognisable Henry Hall sound, aiming carefully at the sweet rather than the hot.

By 1932 he was at the top of his profession in the provinces, but when the BBC invited him to replace Jack he jumped at it. Because the styles of the bands were so different his appointment was as sensationalised by the newspapers as Jack's resignation had been; but Jack wanted to cash in on his radio fame and try the promotional side of show business, and the BBC wanted to replace him with a band that was immediately noticeable as different. Henry aimed for a light touch that was an obvious contrast with Jack's show band style. At the microphone Henry's manner was so hesitant he sounded nervous, a fault which for some reason always arouses the blood lust in audiences. Roger Eckersley told him he must not do his own announcements, so for a time Henry's manager introduced the numbers. But his voice was so like Henry's that Henry could practise announcing without anyone noticing, and gradually acquired the confidence to make a virtue of his apparent defects. He thought that even if listeners did not like it they would recognise it, and worked hard to professionalise his natural tendency to pause before words and sometimes stumble over them. It proved one of the most successful of all radio gimmicks, and is still the one by which most aged listeners remember him.

Henry soon became a very solid success in broadcasting with a flair for picking winners and spotting trends. He found 'Teddy Bears' Picnic' and 'Goodnight Sweetheart', the crooners Les Allen and Phyllis Robins (but missed Vera Lynn, whom he apologetically told after an audition that she was unsuitable for radio). He brought a resident comedian, Oliver Wakefield, into his band session, and found Jeanne de Casalis's famous ditherer, Mrs Feather. His best and simplest idea – he thought it the greatest of his career – struck him one Saturday morning at the Columbia recording studios in St John's Wood whither Henry and his band had gone to record 'Underneath The Arches' with Bud Flanagan and Chesney Allen. Lupino

Lane, Elsie and Doris Waters, and the musical comedy star billed as 'June' were there fulfilling their own engagements. It happened that Henry was looking for some novelty for his broadcast that evening to celebrate the second anniversary of his arrival at the BBC. He thought of asking them along to join the party. Later that day he invited Anona Winn along to complete the bill; and thus began *Guest Night*, a series that was to run for seventeen years and establish Henry as an impresario. It combined the appeal of regularity and surprise with the great merit of presenting a much wider range of entertainment than any other single programme had so far accommodated. As Henry said, it was essentially simple but capable of enormous development.

He left the BBC in 1937 to follow his fame into the music halls. He had stayed longer than any other of the resident bands, and in spite of his natural aversion to dance-band leaders Reith said some nice things about him; and the Hall era was officially ended with a grand *Guest Night*. His music-hall tour demonstrated the appeal that had begun to cluster round the name of a famous broadcaster. He was a sell-out wherever he went, and when he gave away Kitty Masters at her wedding (she was one of his singers; her best-known number was a glutinously sentimental ballad called 'Little Man You've Had A Busy Day') the crowd would not go away until he appeared on the balcony and threw them his hat.

Meanwhile the dance bands played on, ending the day's broadcasting for the BBC from the night clubs and hotels. I had supposed that they gradually faded out of public affection. In fact they lasted until the war broke out and the clubs and hotels were forced to close down the lighter side of their business for a few weeks. After sixteen years on the air the music stopped.

4

BIRTH OF A DRAMA

INTERLUDE III. *The rhythmic puffing of a train accompanies the dialogue.*
Many Different Voices: Tickets, please, show your tickets, please . . . Season, sir? All right! . . . She's late again. I have to run to the office as it is . . . Do you mind if we have the window *open*? . . . Care to see the paper, sir? . . . Do you mind if we have the window *shut*? Tickets please, all tickets ready, please. Season, sir? All right . . . Do you mind if we have the window *open*? . . . It simply means I'll have to go on the 8.10 . . . Do you mind if we have the window *shut*?

The passage comes from *Squirrel's Cage*, with which radio drama as an independent medium can be said to have arrived. It was written by Tyrone Guthrie in 1929 and, with his 1930 *The Flowers are not for You to Pick*, became the first wireless plays to make a lasting impression on me, probably because they were both sad. *Squirrel's Cage* dramatised the monotonous futility of most lives, and the social pressures that forced on people an apathetic acceptance of defeat. *The Flowers are not for You to Pick* was about the solitary loser in a world of winners, for all of whom the flowers were theirs to choose and grasp. The hero, Edward, stammered and wore spectacles, was always bumping into things, became an ineffectual clergyman, fell ridiculously and unrequitedly in love, and drowned by falling overboard on his way to China to become an incompetent missionary. His last words, accompanied by the sound of lapping waves and remembered by me for forty years, were: 'I'm glad I went down in my dog collar.'

Guthrie's depressed view of the human situation echoed my own at seventeen. I felt he had got it about right. But what made these plays outstanding at the time and historically important in the story of radio was their skilful use of the machinery that radio plays now had at their command. Notice how the symbol of futility in *Squirrel's Cage* became the sound of the commuters' train. The passage I have quoted from went on in the same strain, gathering speed and volume, all the while paralleling the train's monotonous rhythm, the two words 'open' and 'shut' a counterpoint to the clicking of the wheels. The play's symbolism was criticised as platitudinous, and I dare say it was. But it showed a mastery of the wireless play's new-found ability to handle sound literally and impressionistically.

After *Flowers* Guthrie abandoned radio drama, to its great loss. But although among the best, he was not the first. Radio's D. W. Griffith was Lance Sieveking, and its *Birth of a Nation* was his remarkable *Kaleidoscope*, done a year before *Squirrel's Cage*.

Radio drama had been struggling from the first to break away from the theatrical form, for though the first producers' training applied theatrical conventions to radio, the instinct that had led them into radio told them it would not do, that radio must create its own forms. The first radio drama department was established in 1924 with R. E. Jeffrey as its head and Howard Rose, one of the central contributors to the art, as his chief assistant. In the next four years they thought of at least the beginnings of what drama would grow into. They commissioned plays written for radio, adapted stage plays and novels to it (the first adaptation was a seventy-minute version of *Westward Ho!* in 1925) and produced the first series; it dramatised episodes in the histories of famous regiments. But the theatre influence stayed. As late as 1926 radio plays observed the convention of musical overtures and entr'actes.

Early developments were a matter of thinking how best to put across what could be put across on the equipment of the day. One of the earliest problems was how to suggest distance and emphasis. It was solved by the simple wheeze of opening or shutting doors between the microphone and the source of the sound. The equivalent of the cinema close-up was invented in 1925. They brought the speaker close to the microphone to deliver the speech and moved him back when they no longer wanted the emphasis.[1] To get the muted effect of background music that accompanied Shakespeare (as an out of copyright author he was very popular with the BBC) they played it in a room off the studio with the door open a couple of inches. Sometimes, however, natural sound would not do. They quickly learned that the microphone was an unpredictable transmitter of certain noises. A pistol shot sounded like a cork leaving a rather flat bottle of champagne and was a danger to the equipment. The swaying of trees in a breeze sounded like the shovelling of coal on steel floors; the play of water at a fountain like the continuous crash of broken glass. One of the few times that natural sound was right and came in on cue was during a 1923 play from the Glasgow station. To suggest that a dog had barked, the author wrote a line: 'Listen! Isn't that a dog barking?' The weather was hot, the studio windows were open, and from the square below an unknown and uncaring dog gave a bark that was received all over Scotland.

The young broadcasters had much fun finding out how to manufacture the right noise. In *The Merchant of Venice* the sound of Shylock's knife-whetting was done by scraping two pieces of angle iron across each other. Wind and storm noises (the shaken sheet of tin) were adapted from the theatre; others were the fruit of necessity and invention. A large drum, covered with buckshot, reproduced most faithfully when tilted the sound of waves breaking and receding. A pair of roller skates pressed against the skin of a drum could sound like a railway carriage bumping over the joins in the track. The early effect of seagulls was made by tightening bands of elastic round two pieces of wood. Sand falling on paper sounded exactly like a sharp and drenching shower. The crumpling of paper and the crushing of a matchbox reproduced perfectly the acceptable likeness of an airplane crash.

Producers deplored the attention that their ingenuities received, but the public was and is fascinated by sound effects. A cartoon of the time showed a producer shouting at the effects man: 'I said a warm, wet wind from the *south*!' For producers the creation and use of effects were concerned increasingly with the conjuring up of moods as well as pictures – in *Squirrel's Cage* the combination of voices and effects produced a crescendo of frustration and tedium. And if listeners gave a play a chance, and listened to it without distraction, they were rewarded with a curiously heightened realism. Because radio's pictures were solely of the mind, as Guthrie put it in his introduction to the published version of his plays,[2] they were less substantial but more real than the stage scenery. 'From the author's clues the listener collects his materials and embodies them in a picture of his own creation. It is therefore more real to him than the ready-made picture of the stage designer.' Guthrie picked moonlight to illustrate his point. Stage moonlight was the designer's moonlight; but the listener's picture was of his own personal, private brand of moonshine, like no other in the world.

For some listeners the effects created a kind of counter-response. A psychologist told Sieveking that he could not experience the illusion because he knew that effects were producing it, adding: 'I can *see* the man knocking the coconut shells together.' Sydney Moseley, one of the early newspaper critics of radio, thought radio drama was wildly out of line in trying to make sound suggest the visual scene. He thought the ideal play for listeners was one that did not demand 'picturisation' but was built of music and speech, poetry and prose. He did not say how far he would permit the words to make pictures. He was of course voicing the critic's proper resentment of effects for their own sake, which was shortly to menace radio drama. But until 1928 the medium was still caged by technical limitations; plays were confined to a single studio with rarely more than one microphone. In that year Captain A. G. D. West, one of the BBC's research engineers, put into drama's hands the device it had besought the technical side to hurry up and perfect. It came from the obvious need to separate one source of sound from another and mix them as required; Lewis had got the engineers to build him a lash-up job and wrote a little piece set in four different studios to show how it might work. West's refinement was the tool that set drama free. Called the Dramatic Control Panel, it was the size and shape of an old-fashioned inter-office communicator, with a row of knobs and buttons, and with it the producer could listen to what was coming from the studios, talk to the cast through his own microphone, and cue them with light signals. Studio sound could be cut, mixed, faded, wiped, superimposed, given deadness or an echo – reproducing, in effect, all the basic grammar that gave the cinema such fluidity. Speech, music and effects lay under the producer's hand as an orchestra is under its conductor's. Such, then, was the instrument; and one evening in 1928 Lance Sieveking put on his white tie and tailcoat and drove to Savoy Hill to play *Kaleidoscope* on it.

Sieveking was an actor and writer who had joined the BBC in 1925 as assistant to the Director of Education and switched to drama. (There was a good deal of this switching around in the Savoy Hill days. Val Gielgud became head of drama from editing readers' letters in *Radio Times*, and Eric Maschwitz joined as an assistant in outside broadcasting, became editor of *Radio Times* and moved back to production as head of variety.) He conceived the idea of taxing the control panel to its limit by writing a kind of aural panorama of man's life, presented (to condense it to its barest) as an allegorical tussle between good and evil. Its subtitle was: 'A Rhythm, representing the life of man from Cradle to Grave'. Over a hundred performers – actors, effects men, orchestras, etc. – took part. The production ran for ninety minutes, occupied eight studios, featured John Gielgud as the Voice of Good, and was by far the most stupendous adventure broadcast drama had so far undertaken. Sieveking's account of it – remember that all these productions were live – compared the moment when the red light came up and the enterprise began to move forward with the desperate excitement and tension of his first solo flight. His is still an extraordinarily vivid description of what it felt like to sit at the panel:

The first two or three pages passed in a trance. I faded in one studio after another. I flicked cue-lights at certain points – all in a state of suspended consciousness. It was not until the top of page 4 that I came out of my trance and heard what was coming out of the loudspeaker. They were at the school scene. Football on playing fields in distance behind a voice describing wet autumnal afternoons, with an occasional fading in of a singer in the middle background singing *Ich Liebe Dich*. Ah! So that's where we were! My fingers knew well enough, even if my head did not. Without consciously reading the directions on my script I faded the tiny football matches out off the horizon, wiped the narrator off with the singer, and then cut the music off sharply. Now it was play, play, play the instrument if ever you did anything in your life. Hold it up, hold it up! Nicely now! Gently up the long crescendo of one orchestra in perspective behind another. Now flick Studio 2. Now Studio 4. Now 1. Cross fade. Ah! That's the way. He's *got* it. . . .

Then came the third phase. Suddenly I was perfectly cool and businesslike. I observed the faces about me in the half-light. I would play this thing to *them*. They should be representative of the millions of unseen hearers. There – hold it a second longer – now *click!* Caught you! Good! That made 'em laugh. . . . How's the time going? Ah, running well, made up that minute already. . . . So now give them their cues and one after another fade them up. The big orchestra, one of the singers, the musical box, the marching feet, the untuneful voices singing Tipperary, the Quintet, the Dance Band!

The play was never published because only about twenty per cent of it was ever written down. The rest was sounds. His climax used bits of Beethoven's Fourth and Fifth Symphonies (Beethoven represented man's noble side and jazz his weak and backsliding one), Dowson's *Cynara*, Chopin's 17th prelude, a quintet, a dance band, Tennyson's *The Lotus Eaters* and a negro spiritual. Phew! The papers said *Kaleidoscope* was an extraordinary feat of broadcasting, real wireless drama, and a strange experience, all of which was true. The general public's response was probably reflected by the critic who said the flow of images coming out of his speaker recalled his sensations under gas in the dentist's chair. Val Gielgud, who was one of Sieveking's studio managers in the production, thought the theme had been perhaps grandiose and trite as well as grand;³ but it fired his imagination with the possibilities of radio drama, and convinced him that far from being a makeshift attempt to do what the theatre could do better, radio drama could and would become exciting and important in its own right. Its historic achievement was to demonstrate that radio drama was not speech and hoofbeats and gunshots and slamming doors. Its employment of music and effects justified Sieveking's contention that the craft called for a musician's instinct as much as a writer's, and many of his novelties were quickly absorbed into the technique of radio production.

Sieveking stayed in the vanguard of production, turning out a succession of plays distinguished for their inventive and extravagant use of sound. The critic Moseley could not bear them and attacked the BBC for letting him waste public time and money on productions that were either too clever or too muddled to appeal to listeners.⁴ But there was nowhere outside normal programme hours for Sieveking's and other experimental drama to go, and Reith accepted the argument that programmes must at all costs avoid becoming enclosed within the conventional. Meanwhile listeners continued to clamour for adaptations of stage plays and strong yarns.

The first play to win wide public and professional acclaim was Compton Mackenzie's *Carnival*. Eric Maschwitz, still editor of *Radio Times*, wanted to write radio scripts, and as the custom was not to pay staff for their writings no obstacles were put in his way. He and Val Gielgud, by then head of drama, took Mackenzie to lunch and over oysters at Wheelers sold him the idea of transforming his story of Jenny Pearl, the Edwardian chorus girl, and her artist lover, Maurice Avery, into the longest radio play so far mounted. It lasted over two hours, contained one hundred scenes, two orchestras, a doubled sound effects staff and an unprecedented number of extras for such scenes as Jenny's twenty-first birthday party. The producer, Peter Cresswell, used so many studios that, as Maschwitz happily recalled,[5] they practically tied Savoy Hill into knots. It ran far too long, of course, and Gielgud wondered what Reith would have to say about its undoubtedly Bohemian flavour and a sequence that described, admittedly in expressionistic terms, the birth of a baby. However, all went well on and after the night. Compton Mackenzie himself read the linking narration and Harman Grisewood, later the head of the Third Programme, played Maurice. Jenny was played by Lilian Harrison, the leading radio actress of her day. To write about it recalls for me the things for which, I think, most of us remember *Carnival*; the exuberant and fragile gaiety of the birthday party, and the extraordinary success of the sound effects – the artificial echo, the jingling of the harness and the clip-clop of horses' hooves as the hansom cabs of 1910 London sped through the nation's listening parlours.

If *Carnival* captured the public's imagination, Guthrie's plays, each running under an hour, using all resources of sound to dramatise a clear story line, indicated the way drama would probably go. But the intoxicating opportunities opened up by the dramatic control panel led some writers to create plays that served the machinery better than the listener. Actors hated them because they felt that they were losing status as flesh and blood and being turned into humanoid 'effects'. The overall impression, said Gielgud, was one of a complicated mechanical toy with which a few odd young men were having fun. The impression was not accurate, but it was undoubtedly damaging. Gielgud himself, in whom there was a by no means invisible strain of arrogance, further depressed the actors by decreeing that cast lists of plays or photographs of the players were not to be printed in *Radio Times*. The names of the actors who had appeared would be read on the air only when the play was over. He thought the illusion of reality would be heightened if the audience was not reminded that it was only a play. His reasoning was pretty shaky, for one of the major pleasures of watching or hearing a good play is the knowledge that actors are pretending to be people. It enhances enjoyment of their skill. Nor had it occurred to him that the actors would take to the withdrawal of their credits as happily as they would have agreed to hand over their fees to the Red Indians. He weakened his case further by allowing the *Radio Times* to print the names when the production was important enough or when it was a broadcast of a stage play featuring actors well known for their performances in it. This seemed a distinction based on a snobbish unwillingness to annoy those who were powerful enough to make their resentment felt, and probably explained the furious attack on Gielgud by the newspapers. He was accused of obstinately and dictatorially flouting public opinion. He in turn resented the newspapers' misrepresentation of his case. What he called 'the experiment' was maintained in the teeth of the actors and the newspapers for nearly two years and then quietly dropped, having done no little damage by reinforcing the public's opinion of the BBC's growing arrogance.

Gielgud was appointed BBC Productions Director, with responsibility for drama, features and variety, on 1 January 1929, and ran the drama side for a quarter of a century. Maschwitz pretended to believe that Reith gave him the job after being directed by Gielgud in the BBC Dramatic Society's production of *Tilly of Bloomsbury*, in which the BBC's awe-inspiring chief played Mr Stillbottle, the bibulous broker's man. Thanks to Gielgud's severity Reith turned in a magnificently comic performance. Gielgud thought that Reith had taken the longest of long shots in choosing him. His only connection with radio drama, apart from helping in *Kaleidoscope*, had been to listen to a lot of it and use his privileged place as letters editor to write pseudonymous letters to the *Radio Times* criticising the work of his predecessor Jeffrey. But he came from a famous theatrical family and had the business in his nerves and bones. His chief qualifications were that he badly wanted to produce plays, had strong ideas about what radio drama should do, and was capable of standing up to opposition. He had a remarkably free hand; he had no Lord Chamberlain to persecute him and Reith's practice was not to interfere in his experts' fields unless they crossed his convictions as to what was proper for broadcasting. Gielgud said that apart from having to observe the amber warning lights at the crossroads of Sex, Religion and Politics he could drive ahead with reasonable confidence.[7] The fact that a Philistine censorship was often too innocent to know when it was being flouted helped him. Soon after his appointment he sought official clearance for a production of Ibsen's *Ghosts*, at that time still thought by some to be the ultimate in a dramatist's self-degradation. The Deputy Director-General, Vice-Admiral Charles Carpendale, reported after reading the script that though he could not imagine why Gielgud wanted to do such a long and dull piece he saw no reason for fuss. Later on, when a decree forbade adultery as a subject for plays, Gielgud simply ignored it, relying on the fact that its promulgators would have to acknowledge that radio could not represent drama if it had to do without sex. Operating within a monopoly he was free from interference from the kind of commercial pressure which in America had already turned drama into a showcase for commercials (a version of *The Prisoner of Zenda* cut the story to twenty-eight minutes and allowed Rupert of Hentzau one line). One valuable Gielgud rule was that the time allowed for a play should be the length of the play; the needs of production, not the stopwatch, would determine length.

In so far as anyone knew what the public liked (there was no audience research to tell them) its tastes in plays was stoutly conservative. What it wanted from radio in the twenties was what it would clamour for from TV in the fifties: adaptations of current stage hits, or revivals with West End stars in them, or adaptations of popular novels. It hated Shakespeare as implacably then as now, and resented and despised most new writing for radio as attempts by smart young men to show off in front of their own little coterie. Gielgud set about building an audience for a wide range of radio drama without conceding too much to popularity too quickly. By 1930 he was presenting some fifty plays a year, made up of stage vehicles, adaptations of books and original works for radio. The most notable of the last-named apart from the two Guthries – Gielgud thought it marked the peak of dramatic achievements so far – was *Brigade Exchange*, a war play by the German Ernst Johannsen created by the pre-Nazi German radio. The controlled imagination of the writing and the disciplined use of sound produced a shattering impression of the helplessness of men trapped by war, though for most listeners the Armistice Day production of R. C. Sherriff's *Journey's End* probably touched more personal chords. Its sentimental middle-class attitude to the Western front, so difficult to hear without impatience now, seemed to ring pitifully true in 1930 – though I must add that my young Uncle Bob, himself a subaltern in France, always said he'd never met anyone like Sherriff's officers in his life.

Radio drama was aimed not so much at the cultivated as the intelligent. It did *Twelfth Night*, *Henry V*, *A Midsummer Night's Dream* and *Antony and Cleopatra*. It did three Shaw plays – *Saint Joan*, *Captain Brassbound's Conversion*, *The Man of Destiny* – and works by Molière, Chekhov, Wilde, Arnold Bennett. It adapted Anthony Hope (*Rupert of Hentzau*), Stevenson (*The Wrecker*), Conrad (*Typhoon*), Buchan (*Huntingtower*), and A. E. W. Mason (*The Four Feathers*). It presented Masefield and Synge's modern poetic dramas, *Pompey the Great* and *Deirdre of the Sorrows*. It broke new ground with *Roland* and *Robin Hood*, dramatised versions of Middle Ages romances. But the impermanence and appetite of broadcasting were already shaping the direction radio drama had to take. By 1931 the BBC was reflecting wistfully on the suggestion that a good play should be broadcast every night for a week.

Within two years of Captain West's perfected control panel the microphone play had become a branch of drama capable of serving as the only national theatre the nation seemed likely to get, and had discovered an idiom as individual and artistically interesting as the theatre and the movies. The trouble was that not enough writers who could write believed in radio, a difficulty they had in common with writers who could not write; a high proportion of the manuscripts submitted had obviously been written for and rejected by theatre managers. Although radio was a fascinating medium to work in it was not as satisfying to writers as the novel or the theatre, in which success was not only more solid but paid better, for the BBC could not compete financially with the rewards of a long run and a multitude of editions. There was also the obstinate distrust among the audience of anything that threatened to be experimental or was by a name it could not recognise.

As a monopoly the BBC had nothing to lose financially by ramming unpopular plays into the public's jaws; but it was a monopoly supplied by artists, and artists needed applause. As Gielgud put it, while it could perhaps be maintained that the listener should be given what he ought to like, it was difficult to suggest with confidence that he should be consistently given what he actively disliked, and impossible to deny that a public service had to supply accepted popular standards of entertainment.

The consequence was a narrowing of drama in one way and a wide broadening of it in another. Gielgud had to admit the impossibility of pleasing all his listeners with all his plays and thus was begun the departmentalisation of drama – the fragmentation, if you prefer it – that comes to all broadcasting systems sooner or later. The function of the original radio play became openly acknowledged in 1937 with a series title, *Experimental Hour*. Round about the same time three famous and immortal forms of drama were developed; the classic serial, the series written round recurring characters, and the family serial.

The first classic serial was a twelve-part version of *The Count of Monte Cristo*, with Terence de Marney as Edmond Dantes. From the Birmingham studios Francis Durbridge sent Paul Temple into the world. In London Mabel and Denis Constanduros wrote *The English Family Robinson*, about which I recall only the title. Gielgud was uneasy about the coming of the family serial (already stigmatised across the Atlantic as 'soap opera') but on the whole departmentalisation was a big and lasting success. The heat was taken off the minority drama and though *Experimental Hour* could not attract enough writers who could fill it adequately, experimental drama had already been reborn, so to speak, in the form of one of radio's finest achievements: the feature. The story of features' development awaits a later chapter (pp. 128ff.). Their first and most widely memorable success was the Scrapbook.

5
THE SCRAPBOOKS

Almost everything on radio – music, talks, variety, the news, stage plays – showed radio as a pipeline carrying stuff from other media. The only true radio was in the creation of arranged sound, as in the microphone play and the feature programme, defined by Lance Sieveking as 'an arrangement of sounds which has a theme but no plot'. He had also noticed that, in its use of sound, radio had the unique ability to borrow from the real thing. He showed this in *Kaleidoscope*, but in the general dazzle of the production it passed without much attention. In a later play he positively inserted a recording of Stanley Baldwin making a speech, using the politician's voice as an artistic tool exactly as he had used Beethoven's Fifth. When he could not get the reality he reconstructed it.

Thus the pioneers opened up new lands; for in Sieveking's work was engendered the feature programme, and among the work it led to were the famous Scrapbooks, in popularity and appreciation the most successful dramatised radio series ever produced in Britain. They began in 1933, were an instant and tremendous success, and by 1937, when they had become a looked-for series outside Britain as well, were playing to thirty million listeners. The BBC, as was its tendency with popular successes, ignored the Scrapbooks in its official reviews of the year until 1937, when it tried to cover up with a bland and wide-eyed paragraph: 'The "Scrapbook" programmes have become such an institution that it is surprising to recall how recently they began.'[1]

One explanation for the late acknowledgement was the admittedly extraordinary fact that the Scrapbooks were produced by the fertile Eric Maschwitz and his Variety Department. Its creators were Leslie Baily, a journalist from the North, and Charles Brewer, a producer in the BBC's Birmingham station. Baily said that one characteristic feature of the Scrapbooks, the introduction of real celebrities into entertainment programmes, began as early as 1926 in Leeds in a programme called 'Hello, Yorkshire!' He invited to the studio George Hirst, the Yorkshire cricketer, and W. Riley, author of a then renowned book entitled *Windyridge*; this idea was such a novelty that the studio was filled with reporters who wanted to write it up.

The title Scrapbook first appeared in *Radio Times* in 1932. Baily's programme, by then coming from Manchester, was still only a light-hearted medley of music, prose and verse. The idea of reconstructing actuality was born when he wrote a couple of scripts for Gielgud's drama department; in these, called 'As it might have been', he tried to show what radio programmes might have been like if the BBC had existed thirty and 150 years ago. The further idea of combining the two styles came to him when Maschwitz was demanding programmes to fill his expanded allotment of time for variety. (Variety in those days meant what it said; vaudeville was only vaudeville.)

Baily brought to the series an experienced and resourceful journalist's talent for spotting news and working at high speed. He was also a very good popular writer for the ear. Brewer had been reared in a house saturated with good music (his father was Sir Herbert Brewer, organist of Gloucester Cathedral and conductor of the Three Choirs Festival) and grew into an infatuated follower of the pre-1914 musical theatre. The first Scrapbook, 1913, recalled that period. Brewer and Baily thought it a crude piece of work, but it contained all the ingredients that made the series so popular: the reconstruction of reality (they dramatised the rescue, largely through the efficient use of ship's wireless, of the *Volturno*'s passengers from mid-Atlantic); the recollections of events by the famous (Lt Col. Moore-Brabazon, the first Englishman to pilot an airplane, and Mrs Lambert Chambers, the tennis champion); music of the year; and above all a powerful whiff of nostalgia for times lost.

The series took enormous trouble to get things right. It tracked down the actual participators in an event wherever it could, never used the budding recording systems if it could get live speech; for 'Scrapbook for 1914' Brewer found not only the original singer of the recruiting song 'On Sunday I walk out with a Soldier' (she was Gwendoline Brogden and the show was *The Passing Show of 1914* at the Palace Theatre, London), but got the original full score from Herman Finck. Because of their provincial background they deliberately avoided metropolitanism, aware that the central Londoner, with a fairly wide choice of public entertainment, probably followed radio a good deal less than the folks out in the regions. It reconstructed sound so vividly that puzzled listeners wrote in to say they had not known the scene had been recorded and to ask where could they buy it. Brewer thought one of their best successes was to reproduce the sound of the Giant Racer at Wembley ('Scrapbook for 1924'); they mixed a record of an underground train passing through a station with the sound of an office chair on castors being moved about on a thundersheet; on top of this they imposed appropriate giggles and shrieks from two girls in the cast.

Artistically the formula was the well-tried classical one of punctuating serious bits with light interludes, or alternating hard fact with sentiment and good humour. It made everything sound as if it had been much better then.

Events of which this could hardly be said, such as the Great War, were made
to sound at least a worthwhile experience which had shown the nation in a
pretty good light. It was expressed in its absolute unimprovable essence by
the deep, reassuring voice, as safe and comforting as that of a trusted family
doctor, of the actor Patric Curwen, a voice for which adjectives such as
rich, fruity, or mellifluous were hopeless understatements. It embodied
nostalgia like an Elgar symphony.

Nostalgia was certainly the most popular ingredient of the Scrapbooks,
and the one that makes it hard to listen to them now. It was expressing for
one thing the attitude of one class only: the middle. I did not notice this at
the time, probably because I was middle-class myself. It never occurred to
me that the Scrapbooks were not reflecting the life of the whole nation.
There was nothing about the General Strike in the early Scrapbooks; and
the pre-1914 ones lingered in what they called the golden Edwardian afternoon without looking past the regattas and pierrots to the slums and the
unemployment that drove great waves of British out of their homeland by
denying them a living in it. But nostalgia was part of the mood of the time.
Another source of the Scrapbooks must have been Noël Coward's *Cavalcade*, which had been overpowering audience's emotions at the Theatre
Royal, Drury Lane, since October 1931. Its curtain speech, in which the old
woman and her husband drink a toast – 'Come, dear, let's couple the past of
England to the present of England – let's hope that this country of ours,
which we love so much, will find honour, dignity and peace again' – said
what people deeply felt. The fact that I can quote those words from memory
shows how they bit. A curious thing about the appeal of the past, and the safe
times therein, was by no means confined to those who had survived it.
Young people cried as hard as their parents over *Cavalcade*, and gulped no
less over the Scrapbooks.

One of the most famous and quotable endings to a Scrapbook was the
one celebrating the 'Edwardian summer' of 1905. It was broadcast on
Derby Day 1935, and the final item contrasted the motorised modern Derby
with the horse-drawn one. It is translated into print very effectively in *The
BBC Scrapbooks*, published by Hutchinson in 1937. The compère (Curwen)
began:

as the last motor car in the procession from the Derby roars away homewards, you
may hear – if you stand by the roadside ever so quietly, as the twilight creeps over
Epsom Downs tonight, the sound of another throng...

Distantly, ghostlike, creeps the crunch and tinkle of coaches and carriages and
coasters' carts, and the clopping of hooves ... not the black gleam of tarmac, but a
white dusty road; not the reek of petrol fumes but the scent of May blossoms in the
hedgerows – and from some wayside hostelry the sound of...

Voices stealing back to us, voices singing, gay, tired, alcoholic, sentimental...

'With a heart that is true I'll be waiting for you, In the shade of the old apple tree'. . .

They swell, they harmonise, they fade away into the past which is theirs, and the pleasant clatter of the horse-vehicles ambles on:

This Cockney carnival! – long and leisurely into the night it jingles, with rumbling wheels, and dust clouds drifting in the light of the swaying lanterns. . . A people who have yet to catch the craze for speed. . .

One of the critics called this picture painting by sound a masterpiece. One can see why it was so effective; Baily's script used the kind of language – 'twilight', 'white dusty road', 'into the night', etc. – that the listeners would have used themselves if they could have thought of it. I well remember being stirred by it. I knew nothing whatever about 1905, and was no more possessed by the craze for speed than most of the listeners, who like me could not afford a motor car; but it seemed to evoke a lost world of peace and quiet. It was a time (one must not forget) when the nation, with two million unemployed, the north-eastern industrial towns so idle that they had begun to look clean, Hitler already troubling the weekends, was having to face the bitter truth that the sacrifices of the war had been got out of them by promises as unrealisable as shares in a dud mine. This was the common chord the Scrapbooks touched. It explains why they rose above their beginning as a variety item into a national event.

But it would be unfair to put too much emphasis on nostalgia. The truth was that the programme had two voices. The popular one was the equivalent of Shakespeare's comic interludes – 'Faith, we may put up our pipes and be gone' – and was carefully aimed to touch the bulk of its audience's emotions. It has been much parodied, and you cannot wonder. Here is an extract from a beach scene in the 1911 Scrapbook:

The voices of two holiday-makers are heard in the foreground:
WOMAN: Aren't you interested in the pierrots this morning, Tom?
MAN: I'm more interested in the paper.
WOMAN: What's the news?
MAN: There's a queer report about a German naval landing at a place called Agadir.
WOMAN: Where's that?
MAN: Oh, I don't know – somewhere on the African coast . . . what on earth the Kaiser wants in a place like that –
WOMAN: Oh, well, it doesn't matter to us, Tom. Here, put your old paper down and listen to the pierrots. . . .

It spoke in quite a different style when it was reconstructing authenticity or using the famous to recollect it. Baily and Brewer were two of the first to realise that words alone could induce the sacred shiver down the listener's spine as potently as music if they were the real thing and spoken well. If you heard it, you will not have forgotten its evocation of the trial of Mrs Pankhurst and Dorothy Holmes-Gore's declamation of her famous speech from the dock – '. . . I should not be here if I had the same kind of laws that the very meanest of men have. . .'. They were able to draw from their own reading the line or two of poetry that would perfectly round off a passage, as in their reconstruction of Shackleton's death. Sir Ernest Shackleton, the explorer, was a great hero of what the compère called 'the stay-at-homes in that easy-going age' (he was talking about 1909). He died in South Georgia, in January 1922. The programme quoted the last entry in his diary. 'Now we must speed all we can, but the prospect is not too bright, for labour is scarce. It is a wonderful evening. In the darkening twilight I saw a lone-star hover gem-like above the bay.' There was only one quotation that could cap this, and Baily and Brewer found it. 'Twilight and evening bell, And after that the dark, And may there be no sadness of farewell, When I embark. . . .'

Their difficulty was that often they had to mix the two styles within a single scene, and for some critics never managed it without producing the effect of a fingernail being scraped along a pane of glass. But most listeners were unconscious of it, and took what the programme offered with huge enjoyment. It was fundamentally a serious programme which respected the truth of what it was presenting. If it had not been it could hardly have got J. L. Garvin, probably the most serious journalist in Europe, to have appeared on it. If one judges the quality of a programme by the names that take part – the best test on any level of broadcasting – the Scrapbooks deserve honour as radio's most successful early attempt to produce serious material in an entertaining way. I am glad to acknowledge my gratitude to them.

6
UNCLES AND AUNTIES

Most middle-aged listeners, asked what a pair of headphones reminded them of, would name Children's Hour and the Reithan Sunday. The first Children's Hour was broadcast on 23 December 1922, in the first month of the BBC's service, and jumped at once into a permanent place in the nation's life. As the provincial stations opened they followed London in developing their own children's programmes. They ran for forty-five minutes daily and became the most regular feature of the somewhat pragmatic programme schedule of those days.

It began, like most programmes, because to begin it was an obvious thing to do. It became hugely popular because it struck from the start a note of unpatronising and unselfconscious gaiety and enthusiasm. No doubt it was in part a kind of therapy for overworked programme staff. In the Birmingham station under Percy Edgar (Uncle Edgar) the whole office staff stopped their work when children's hour arrived, adjourned to the studio and let go in a kind of office romp – 'not a romp of incoherent noise,' commented Arthur Burrows, 'but a sort of communal outpouring of happiness'.[1]

'Worried all day by a thousand things, fighting opposition, overcoming obstacles, pushing like fun for the success of the British Broadcasting Company, we join together at 5.30 to forget the quarrels, the difficulties, the vested interests, because here, at least, we are free of them.' Thus Uncle Caractacus (C. A. Lewis) pitching it a little strong again. They were all young uncles and aunts. Burrows, the first of the wireless uncles, was Uncle Arthur. Rex Palmer, director of 2LO, was Uncle Rex. Kenneth Wright, director of the Manchester station, was Uncle Humpty Dumpty, presented as a mysterious being who was wrapped in cotton wool, sat on a stool before the microphone, and was kept from falling off by an elephant (Uncle Jumbo). Later Wright became head of BBC TV music. The head of music in London was L. Stanton Jefferies (Uncle Jeff).

Reith defined the aim of Children's Hour as 'to provide an hour of clean, wholesome humour, some light music and a judicious sprinkling of information attractively conveyed.'[2] He liked to think of it as a satisfying entertainment at the end of a happy day, but he saw it as he saw the whole of broadcasting, a light beating down the darkness of poverty and ignorance. He thought that to the children of the well-to-do wireless listening would take its place among their carefully supervised routine of lessons, recreations, pastimes and hobbies; but for the children of the poor broadcasting could be a kind of antidote to the harm done to them by their living conditions. 'To these children, therefore, the Children's Hour must come as a wonderment, truly a voice from another world.'

In making this special effort to win the children the BBC was following a path well beaten by the circulation managers of the great dailies, who knew that a pound spent on promoting Pip, Squeak and Wilfred, Teddy Tail, and Rupert the Bear was a shrewd investment. The Birmingham station quickly built up a radio circle of 10,000 children with membership badges and arranged functions at which the uncles and aunties would appear, making the word flesh. Uncle Edgar once kissed 800 Birmingham children in an hour. Uncle Caractacus used to receive 150 letters a day, all of them acknowledged on the air until this courtesy provoked a stream of letters past the programme's power to handle. The Uncles were extremely sentimental about children; they called them kiddies, babies, and girlies, and summoned such adjectives as chubby, angelic, sweet, to describe them.

The picture they had of their audience resembled the shining-haired, cleaned and polished boys and girls of their own milieu, and it was no mere coincidence that the lines of poetry that came into their minds when they thought about it was a poem by Longfellow called 'The Children's Hour'.

> Between the dark and the daylight,
> When the night is beginning to lower,
> Comes a pause in the day's occupations,
> That is known as the Children's Hour.

The poem goes on to describe how the poet, sitting in his study, is rushed by his three daughters who devour him with kisses and hugs. It was one of the poems they made you learn at school.

> From my study I see in the lamplight
> Descending the broad hall stair,
> Grave Alice, and laughing Allegra,
> And Edith with golden hair.
> A whisper, and then a silence:
> But I know by their merry eyes
> They are plotting and planning together
> To take me by surprise. . . .

At first it was no single person's job to plan and supervise the programmes; they did good work because the people broadcasting had the kind of minds that knew what, in this context, good work was. As usual Lewis put his finger on it, describing the atmosphere of children's hour as one where 'one can be foolish without being a fool, where a good story, a jolly song, or wholesome backchat are taken on their face value with no arrières pensées.' The atmosphere projected was that of the bright, intelligent middle class talking to itself, and inviting anyone else to join in.

When the volume of letters grew too great to be answered individually over the air they decided to limit these acknowledgments to children who were sick or were celebrating birthday and other parties. The uncle on duty would read out the names; when he came to a multiple birthday there would be a pause and then a catchphrase that everyone learned to wait for: it passed into general currency and is still used by grandparents who were then children: 'Hello . . . Twins' or 'Hello . . . Trrrriplets!' Sometimes parents tipped off the uncles that a birthday present had been hidden somewhere in the room, and these lucky children would have the enormous thrill of hearing the wireless guiding their hunt to find it. My family did not belong to the type that wrote letters to public bodies; listening to this section of Children's Hour I felt what, perhaps, some other children felt; that a party was going on to which I had not been invited.

Uncle Caractacus used to sign off by wishing his nephews and nieces pleasant dreams and a nice hot bath – this at a period when probably half the population had no bath to get into and were supposed by some of the middle classes to keep coal in them should they be given them by some misguided benefactor. There was some criticism of Caractacus for this, to which he defiantly replied that he would like to offer the same wish at the close of the evening programme as well. 'Everyone loves pleasant dreams, and as for a nice hot bath, well – I mean to say – well, after all, why not?'[3]

Fairly soon Children's Hour lost its quality of office romp. It became clear that it had to be systematically organised. Mrs Ella Fitzgerald was created Central Organiser of Children's Hour programmes, with Auntie Geraldine (Miss E. Elliott) as her assistant. By 1924 the programme had its own national advisory committee, weighty with several famous students of the child mind and representatives of such approved bodies as the Boy Scouts and Girl Guides. They began to consider the variations of age, mental attainments, personal tastes, experience and environment. Music, for example, had to span the entire range between nursery rhymes, part songs, instrumental music, ballads, classical and modern works, chamber music and opera. But the accepted principle remained. The purpose of Children's Hour was mainly recreational and not to provide instruction or moral improvement. Standing instructions laid down that 'if the organisers keep in mind the creation of the atmosphere of a good home and the presentation of real beauty, in song, story, music and poetry on a plane attractive to the young, they will inevitably, without self-conscious efforts, raise the standard of culture in their young listeners, and the result will be educative in the best sense.' The level of wisdom illustrated therein, read half a century after it was written, reminds one very forcibly of the most important spin-off of the Reith attitude to broadcasting. It attracted talent and character.

As time passed, and what was spontaneous hardened into routine, the informality of Children's Hour was questioned. In November 1926 the uncles and aunts disappeared as such from the programmes. Still, the management had to agree that no better usage seemed to be discoverable and they continued to be used, though less extravagantly, as courtesy titles.[4] And the spirit of the uncles, kindly, civilised, convinced that every child needs must love the highest when it saw it, that the King and Queen were at the apex of an establishment striving with the help of honour and conscience to do its best according to the Scout Law, continued to pervade the spirit of Children's Hour. The object was always to offer a complete children's BBC. The sensible and bright men and women who ran it, tending to stay for many years, could take advantage of the willingness of children to accept the unfamiliar eagerly instead of suspecting it as they would when they had grown up. There was no need to divide the programme into a small Home, Light and Third. A catalogue of the best things Children's Hour created or found would be delightful to read but extravagant to print here; let it be said that there is no person who had access to a wireless set between 1922 and 1964 whose life as a child was not enriched by the Toytown stories, the talks by Romany, the Zoo Man, and Commander Stephen King Hall, the Worzel Gummidge stories, the plays of L. du Garde Peach, the serialisations of books by Arthur Ransome, Noel Streatfeild, Rosemary Sutcliffe, and a thousand others whose names ought to be set down. Let two that everyone remembers speak for all.

'Out with Romany' was a piece of pure radio magic distilled by the Reverend Bramwell Evens. The Bramwell stood for his family's friendship with the founder of the Salvation Army, but his grandfather had been a pagan gipsy until a revival meeting converted him to Christianity, whereon he became a noted converter of other gipsies and, with rather less obvious logic, burned his beloved violin. This ancestry gave Romany an obsessive, mystical love of outdoors, communicated to a number of local country papers in the north as a contributor on nature. It was the BBC's north region that discovered his talent, as it discovered so many others, as a broadcaster.

What listeners seemed to hear was a man taking two children for a walk with his dog, showing and explaining things encountered on the way. They saw what he described so vividly that one has to wonder if his voice – it was a very quiet, soothing one – had some hypnotic quality that stimulated the inner eye to supernormal perception. Laidman Browne, the radio actor, told how he listened to a broadcast in which Romany was describing an old dog otter teaching the cubs to dive. 'For five minutes I watched the father otter pushing his youngsters in and out of the water, nudging the timid one, cuffing the quarrelsome one, darting after the adventurous one who had headed out midstream. It was Raq* that broke the spell. His bark, as he came bounding towards us over the fields, alarmed the family. There was a sudden flurry of water, and when the ripples stilled against the muddy bank there was no sign of the otters.' Browne felt annoyed with the dog and vexed with Romany for bringing him. Then he remembered he had been listening to a studio broadcast. 'But – was it a studio broadcast? I listened again. The explorers were now in Romany's caravan. It couldn't be from a studio. This was too real. The microphone must be hung in the caravan. . . .' Then a glance at his clock cleared all doubt. There could be no outside broadcast at 5.35 on a dark, cold November evening.

The early Romany programmes contained musical interludes, for the BBC had never pretended that the programme came from outside. But when they discovered the power of the illusion Romany was creating they stoked it up to the extent of leaving the piano behind. The programme was introduced like this: 'And now, children, we are going out with Romany.' There would be a pause before the voices were faded in, and at the end they were faded out, with no announcement of cast. It was all carefully scripted as narrative, questions and answers, and sound effects. The children were a couple of Aunties, Muriel (Levy) and Doris (Gambell) who by some lucky chance could present the young, fresh, difficult to imitate voices of childhood. As a southern listener Herbert Farjeon, the writer, had never heard of Auntie Muriel and Auntie Doris and asked himself in his critical review in the *Listener*: 'Have the voices of two children with their spontaneous wonderments, their broken exclamations, unfinished sentences, half laughs, interrupted interruptions, ever been and will they ever be more perfectly presented?'

The spontaneity was real enough in those live days, for though Romany was supposed to work from a script like everyone else his producers well knew that a magic too strictly disciplined might run away. A very great factor in completing the extraordinary illusion he created was that he was totally unconscious of the microphone. He would begin from his script, but was liable to break away from it after a few minutes and never get back to it; or he would rise and walk about or turn away from the mike and Nan Macdonald (who ran the programme for seven years) and others would have to grab him and pull him back to it. In their role of children Muriel Levy and Doris Gambell simply asked the questions that occurred to them as Romany spoke. The sound effects were as extraordinary as he, in their own way, for they were done live and on the spot. The effects men, Terry Cox and Jack Hollingworth, were called on to provide such sounds as of walkers climbing

* Romany's spaniel.

a cliff, of hiding with Raq, of the beat of the wings of a plover, of the irregularity of the hoofbeats of Romany's horse. All of these had to satisfy Romany's ear. Birdsong was recorded, but when no appropriate record was available Romany would describe the sound and say, 'Listen'. His listeners would have given evidence in court that they had heard it. It is a thousand pities that only one recording of a talk was ever made.

Romany was always presented on Friday afternoons. Sunday would have been better but it was a good principle of Children's Hour that on Sunday it should be essentially different from the weekday edition. However great their popularity none of the regular weekday programmes ever appeared on Sundays. That it was five years before London heard him must be attributed to the jealousy and envy that spoiled relations between BBC London and BBC Northern, the former resenting the north's claim to independence, the north resenting London's metropolitanism and airs. Derek McCullough, the renowned Uncle Mac, was very different in his administrative capacity as head of children's programmes from the gentle, friendly voice the children heard. He had been terribly knocked about in the war (he lost an eye, a leg and a lung) and suffered intermittently much pain. He had one of those peculiarly violent irrational dislikes of northern England that often crop up among the southern upper class. He was also in the naturalist line himself. However, in 1938 Romany was brought south and consoled and delighted wartime audiences until a dreadful day in November 1943, when he collapsed in his garden and died within the hour like one of his beloved creatures, without fear or foreknowledge. The children felt his loss more deeply than anyone could have imagined, mourning not in grief for themselves but in touching compassion for the dog Raq. They were afraid he had been left alone in the caravan. He had given, as one of the obituaries said, the purest kind of pleasure.

Toytown too was discovered by a happy accident. May Jenkin, Aunt Elizabeth, came across the stories in a book called *Tales of Toytown*, first published in 1928. The first dramatisation, of a story titled Proud Punch, was broadcast in 1929, but it was the other five that established the enchanting child's world which everyone shared – the Mayor, the policeman, the magician, the bad-tempered old gentleman, the inventor, and the animals – on equal terms. Larry the Lamb was as good as a sea captain except that he couldn't write. (The script explained that he couldn't hold a pen in his hooves, and had to get his friend Toby the dog, later Dennis the dachshund, to blow his nose for him.)

After broadcasting the six Miss Jenkin invited the author to call to discuss a further series. A very shy book illustrator named S. G. Hulme Beaman came along, and in the next two years brought in a fresh Toytown story every three or four weeks. He used to work out his stories from little models of his characters in a cardboard theatre. Soon his town had 300 inhabitants, all recreated by the actors with a simplicity and rightness that always left me speechless in that condition of deep satisfaction that comes from experiencing a work of art done as perfectly as it could be. Once he invited the cast and staff to his studio to help him produce one of his tales in the puppet theatre. His son helped him with the gramophone effects and he conducted all the manipulations himself. May Jenkin recalled it from forty years further on as one of the funniest and most exquisite shows she ever saw.

Then calamity struck the pretty, charming little world. In 1932 Beaman took pneumonia and died swiftly. By then his stories had taken imperishable hold. For the next thirty years the thirty-six stories he left were never out of the top half-dozen favourites asked for in the annual Request Weeks. They were performed in London by a vastly distinguished cast: it included Ralph De Rohan as Mr Grouser, Felix Felton as Mr Mayor, Norman Shelley as Captain Brass, and Derek McCullough as Larry and the narrator. Children who lived in the North and Midlands heard a different cast; they disliked the southern voices because they sounded so unlike those they heard every day; so although they voted for the programme in Request Week like everywhere else they stuck out for the version prepared by their own people. This civilised variation did not survive the ending of Children's Hour in 1964 but Toytown did, and six stories were broadcast in Story Time in 1966. But if another Romany or another Hulme Beaman appeared there would be nowhere in broadcasting for them to go, for their magic depended upon the mind's eye and ear.

7
RADIO BECOMES SHOWBIZ

After insisting for some years that the amount of variety in the schedules was just about right, and that any increase would be sharply resented by the bulk of the audience, the BBC decided in 1933 to double the output and create a new department responsible for it. The success of the continental stations beaming in commercial radio from Luxembourg, Toulouse, Fécamp, etc., could not be ignored. Looking round for the right man to run it, Reith did not hesitate. He sent for the editor of the *Radio Times*. It turned out to be one of the most successful appointments that Reith ever made.

Eric Maschwitz's family originated in Lithuania and by the time he was born had become solid Midland middle-class – so he said, though there never was a man who had less patience with that kind of distinction. He was a born Bohemian who regarded his life as a roller coaster of ups and downs, most of which could be laughed at. His account of his early life, sometimes broke, sometimes writing a bestseller, sometimes in publishing, sometimes carrying off and marrying Hermione Gingold, at times so hungry that his first pay check from a new job all went on food, could have fitted without embellishment into one of the light operettas he was to write. He joined the BBC because he happened to run into Lance Sieveking at a time when he was unemployed and broke. When they heard of his publishing experience they moved him from outside broadcasts to be managing editor of the infant *Radio Times*, and he became editor a few months later when the existing incumbent dropped dead. These were the days when the dizzying expansion of radio presented limitless opportunities. A man who said he could do a thing generally found himself called on to do it. Maschwitz wrote scripts under the name of Holt Marvell, and it was as Marvell that in 1932 he created with George Posford 'Goodnight Vienna', the first smash hit musical in radio's brief history and forerunner of innumerable operettas about soubrettes called Mitzi, Fritzi and Pitzi. The BBC paid him nothing for it, of course, but the morning after the broadcast Herbert Wilcox, the film producer, rang him up and offered £200 for the film rights. The Wilcox production, with Jack Buchanan and Anna Neagle in the lead, was the first British musical talking picture. It ran for fourteen weeks in the West End and a stage version, much beloved by amateur operatic societies, brought

Eric a steady income in royalties for years after his hasty acceptance of Wilcox's offer.*

Operetta was part of variety, along with light music, feature programmes and what was then still called vaudeville (dance music remained part of outside broadcasts until 1935). Vaudeville had always been troublesome for, as the BBC admitted, British audiences had never much liked purely verbal wit and broadcasting could not transmit the violent and irresistible appeal that devices such as the false nose, the slipping trousers, the crushed top hat, or the upset chair, possessed for the eye.[1] Nevertheless entertainers who addressed themselves only to the ear had come along. One of the funniest of them was Mabel Constanduros, who in 1925 introduced the Buggins family. She used to do all the voices herself and wrote the first sketches to amuse her mother and sisters (thereby aiming without knowing it at the entire radio audience listening in its own family groups). She rode to fame and fortune on the character of Grandma Buggins, a crotchety old lady who always got the better of everybody, always had the last word, and had a very funny line in the style of damp melancholy created by Dickens's Mrs Gummidge. Grandma proved an extraordinarily durable character, for she was called up, so to speak, as a wartime auxiliary in 1940 to help the nation by broadcasting recipes. Another of these early stars was Ronald Gourlay, a war-blinded pianist and whistler whose act always ended with an impromptu fantasy which blended together a handful of tunes nominated by the audience. The careful listener, said Tommy Handley, who toured with him, could hear as many as three tunes being played at the same time. Tommy, destined to become the biggest of all radio's stars, made his own début in 1926 as a member of Radio Radiance, one of the first wireless concert parties for which the producer, James Lester, conceived the startling novelty of including six tap-dancers in the cast. A photograph of the girls, looking rather older than their years, with shingled hair, rather stout legs and in dancing gear that looked liked Little Lord Fauntleroy suits, preserves their likeness.

Tommy Handley was already well known in music hall principally for his 'The Disorderly Room', which set a medley of Great War tunes to fit a farcical court-martial. Tommy made a very good thing out of it for many years, and so did its author, who went on to play butlers in Hollywood under the name of Eric Blore. Tommy appeared in many of the revues that the BBC favoured at this time. He was a very resourceful, quick-witted comedian with a flair for coining absurd words and phrases which was to prove the making of him later on; in 1929 he was already a radio personality

* A theatrical tour was less successful, according to Maschwitz. 'How are they liking it?' he asked the manager of the Theatre Royal, Huddersfield. 'About as well as they'd like a musical called Goodnight, Huddersfield in Vienna.'

of enough popularity to have his wedding to Jean Allistone described as a
RADIO ROMANCE on the newspaper posters.

Another oldtimer of equal fame was Leonard Henry. He entered radio
from the flourishing world of concert party (they had names like the
Mountebanks, The Cooptimists, The Bow Wows, etc.) and quickly made a
name as one of the very few comedians who could meet radio's demands for
fresh material. (The days when a good song would last a comic two or three
years were ending.) He was so confident of his ability to make, or at any rate
remember, an impromptu joke that he used to incorporate the feat into his
turn with The Bow Wows. It worked because a poor joke delivered quickly
was as good as a better one he had to think about. He was stumped one
night, curiously enough, by being asked for a joke on 'beer'. His mind went
blank and he had to be rescued by Davy Burnaby, who leant out from the
wings and shouted, 'Here, you'd better *hop* it!' Henry had the comic spot
in a lot of the popular radio revues of the early twenties (the BBC used to
invite well-known revue impresarios, Philip Ridgway, Albert de Cour-
ville, Andre Charlot, to present their own half-hours) and has the distinction of having invented the gong with which radio simulated the
black-out that signalled the end of a sketch in the theatre. His 'hollow'
triumph, he called it. In his time he was the most prolific of radio comedians
and with Handley the most popular.

In radio, of course, the impromptu was forbidden, but he had a chance to
display his gifts one night when just before he was due to appear he could not
find his rehearsed and censored material. He fished some blank sheets of
paper out of his pocket, turned them over at what seemed the right moment,
and made up his show as he went along; nobody, he recalled, knew the
difference. Another of his distinctions was to take part in the first outside
broadcast from Alexandra Palace (in September 1936) and to make perhaps
the first bad joke in the new medium. When the make-up girl painted a comic
moustache and eyebrows on him he rose to the situation by remarking that
the new entertainment was very "ighbrow'.

One of the most original of them was Stainless Stephen, at whose name I
smile and hear his signature tune – 'At daw-hawn the la-hark sings i-hin the
sky, The nightingale at even'. Stainless Stephen came, as you could deduce,
from Sheffield. His real name was Arthur Clifford Baynes and, like nearly all
the first radio entertainers, he was a thorough music-hall professional. His
patter was quite amusing, but what lifted it from the ruck was his 'gimmick',
as we would have called it had we known the word. He verbalised its
punctuation like a reporter telephoning his copy. 'At my sister's boarding
house all the windows have stained glass comma stained with the soup the
visitors throw at them exclamation mark.'

Perhaps because my own humour was of a literary turn I laughed more at him than at any other, though now I come to look at that joke I believe it was not one of Stainless's but of Julian Rose's, a famous Jewish comedian of the same period. Rose appeared frequently in what most old listeners remember as the best of all the variety from the pre-Maschwitz era, the weekly visits to the London music halls. Up to 1928 the opposition of the theatre managers to broadcasting had been no less sharp than obtuse, but led by George Black of the Palladium and Sir Oswald Stoll from the Coliseum and the Leicester Square Alhambra (now the Warner Theatre) they began to see that the advertisement was good for business. From 1929 we could count on one broadcast a week from the bill at these theatres, where the art of variety was celebrating a clear and brilliant evening.

The BBC hit upon a very effective method of presenting these visits. At a minute or two before switching to the theatre Jack Payne and his orchestra struck up. At the appointed moment the engineers superimposed the stage sounds on the dance band, fading the former up as the latter was faded down – the result being to transport the listener's mind's eye from studio to packed auditorium with a highly stimulating effect on the livelier imaginations. Sometimes the listener's mind's eye would have to concentrate itself fearfully, for a relay would run into a turn that had to be described, such as a juggler's; but these were rare accidents of timing. Mostly the relays were of acts that the ear could enjoy by itself, with a little explanation from the commentator when some funny visual business was going on. Through these broadcasts I first heard Harry Tate's motoring sketch and was reduced to a choking haze of laughter by Will Hay's schoolmaster act. The illusion of a night out, the fame of the performers, more than made up for their inadequacies as radio acts, of which we were unconscious anyway.

But radio vaudeville could not exist on music-hall relays, and the BBC found it a puzzle to know how to find the acts to fill the hours. By 1930 it needed 150 vaudeville programmes a year, compiled from those acts that were available (roughly two of every six asked) and had not been on so frequently that their material was worn out. To complaints that it was not finding fresh talent the BBC replied that it did not exist, claiming that of about 2000 aspirants auditioned yearly less than twenty reached the standard the BBC required. It is possible that this standard was too high, certain that it was higher than the public would have accepted; whatever the cause by 1930 there was a proposal inside the BBC, fortunately defeated, to solve the difficulty of finding acts by cutting down the number of vaudeville programmes. In the end the problem was to be solved as the BBC had already prophesied, by moving vaudeville away from the music-hall format into something more flexible and free ranging.

This was the system Maschwitz was to elaborate in variety. He took over three very successful shows, John Watt's *Songs From The Shows*, *Music Hall* and Harry S. Pepper's *Kentucky Minstrels*. Pepper was the son of Will C. Pepper, the founder of the White Coons concert party, and as an old music-hall man had his own way of accommodating himself to the atmosphere of the BBC. At the statutory interview everyone had to have for a staff job Admiral Carpendale asked him how old he was, to which Harry, gratified by this personal touch, answered: 'Forty-four. How old are you?'[2] However, he got the job: no doubt the admiral liked the cut of his jib. Watt, one of the great originators of radio entertainment, had been found by Val Gielgud in, of all places, Belfast, where he was producing rather good, original shows on almost invisible budgets. Gielgud brought him to London where his zestful delight in showbiz created in 1931 the first Music Hall. It was done from Studio Ten, formerly a warehouse on the south bank of the Thames near Waterloo Bridge. It was bigger than any studio in Savoy Hill, and Watt used its size to present BBC variety for the first time as though it came from a genuine music hall. The performers wore stage make-up. Watt and the band were in white tie and tails. They imported a stage (borrowed from the BBC's amateur dramatic society) and used, for the first time inside a studio, an invited audience, unleashing thereby one of the longest and most fatuous controversies in radio history. Some listeners resented the studio audience as a body unfairly privileged, and especially hated it when it laughed louder than itself thought appropriate or at something itself did not think was funny. Sydney Moseley denounced it as 'a sycophantic claque'. He had a strange puritan objection to effects that might suggest to the listener that an entertainment was coming from a theatre or a night club instead of a studio, holding the quaint notion that as the true function of broadcasting was to please the ear anything that created atmosphere, such as studio audiences and costumed performers, offended against purity. He seemed to suppose that the ear's response to sound was not connected to the imagination of the ear's owner and demanded, as though introducing an argument that must settle it, what was the use of showing something that millions of listeners could not see? He objected to the dancing girls on economic as well as moral grounds, pointing out quite accurately that all the listener could hear was a rhythmic tapping that could have been supplied at much less cost by an effects man. 'There were many friends of broadcasting to whom the tap-tap of the unseen chorus came as a shock because it seemed so much at variance with the lofty ideals proclaimed in the BBC's earlier days.' I confess that this flight of indignation soars higher than my power to follow it. Anyway, to Moseley the wastage of public money was a serious matter; and when the BBC increased the offence by allowing the girls to sing a few choruses in addition to dancing, he rebuked its continued flouting of public opinion. But however vexatious the studio audience was thought to be it was clearly essential, and survived through *Music Hall's* run of twenty years.

These three series shows had been exceptions rather than part of the rule. Maschwitz had to fight hard to persuade his chiefs that the American system of programming – same show, same channel, same time, same night every week – was acceptable. According to Watt they thought it was vaguely ungentlemanly to entice the listeners so blatantly; this may have been so, but perhaps a better motive was their instinctive reluctance to harden broadcasting into a pattern. With flexibility and the impromptu in mind there had been a weekly space in the programmes for some years called Surprise Item. Its raison d'être was quite deliberately to encourage listeners to tune in out of curiosity. They never knew what they'd get: one week it was the drama critics Hannen Swaffer and James Agate discussing a broadcast play, next week it was Jack Hobbs, the England batsman, introducing the England XI on the eve of its sailing for Australia. Once it was a broadcast from the signal box at King's Cross and, on a weekend in April 1929, a selection of gramophone records played backwards. There *must* have been more to that particular broadcast.

That surprise should itself become channelled into a series was one of radio's inescapable ironies. Eric conceived the idea of collecting together a number of these last-minute items and presenting them at the peak time of 6.30 on Saturdays under the title of *In Town Tonight*. It ran for twenty-three years, even making the transition (in 1954) to television as a simultaneous broadcast. I suppose the opening of this show – the sounds of London's traffic rumbling below the Piccadilly flower girl's 'Violets! Lovely violets!', gradually being overlaid by the infectious excitement of Eric Coates's Knightsbridge march, swelling to a crescendo of noise that the reverberating shout of 'Stop!' (the shouter was Freddy Grisewood) instantly silenced – became the most famous and evocative of all programme openings, to be remembered with sighs and tears by those who would hear it separated by the war from the familiar noises of home. Maschwitz picked Coates's march from an armful of records of music with a London theme. It made London sound a glittering city of light and gaiety and turned Coates from an obscure if well-regarded composer into a public favourite, able to fill concert halls as conductor as long as his march was in the programme.

Evocative sound proved radio's power over the imagination with Café Collette, designed to present continental dance music as a change from Anglo-American jazz. Like the music from the hotels and night clubs it communicated the sounds of a night out. Corks popped, snatches of conversation (in French) intervened, waiters were heard shouting supper orders down the service hatch. The orchestra was Magyar in style and though the leader's name was never mentioned it was generally supposed that he was an émigré count. Nothing was easier to imagine, as you listened to it, than the charming café, with its little round tables under the lime trees, among which the leader moved with his fiddle under his ear. But it was all a cleverly contrived illusion, the fruit of Maschwitz's romantic temperament and the dramatic control panel. The café was a basement studio in Broadcasting House, the orchestra was British to a man, and the leader was Walford Hyden, a distinguished-looking musician who looked like the Abbé Liszt but was from Hanley in the Potteries. Traces of Hanley clung to his speech, but as he did not speak it did not matter. Without meaning to the BBC had accomplished a big wireless hoax or, to put it more respectably, the first mass suspension of disbelief. So many listeners thought the café was a fact that for several weeks the French post office had to return to the BBC batches of letters addressed to Café Colette, Paris, France, and in London the BBC had to deal apologetically with hundreds of requests for table reservations.

Maschwitz was exactly what light entertainment needed. He had tireless energy and enthusiasm, was a boon companion, one of those rare life-enhancing spirits in whose presence everyone felt younger, wittier and better-looking. He was marvellously unstuffy. He greatly admired and revered Reith and Reith liked him, paying variety the compliment of occasional visits to rehearsals at which he loomed over the awestruck performers like a pike in a tank of tropical fish. Maschwitz was a leader who could do it as well as run it, with an inspirational flair for show business and a talent for lyric writing which suddenly flowered into one of the undying songs from the thirties, 'These Foolish Things'. (He wrote it on Sunday morning for a late-night BBC revue. The broadcast caused no stir whatever, but Leslie Hutchinson, the West Indian singer 'Hutch', recorded it and the song was made. Thirty years later Eric was still drawing £1000 a year in royalties from it.) In 1937 Hollywood offered him a contract he could not refuse and he left the BBC as gaily as he had entered it, accompanied by a presentation fountain pen in gold which he tried to pawn in Marseilles two years later when he was trying to reach home in time for World War Two.

By 1939 radio was the big patron. The time came, as John Watt had said it would, when practically every top of the bill performer on the music-hall circuit was an artist who had made his name in radio. Radio was the star-maker, able to explode a little-known performer into stardom almost overnight, as it did with Claude Dampier, Richard Goolden and Arthur Askey. Dampier fluffed his lines in a broadcast from the Argyll Theatre, Birkenhead, and adlibbed by pretending he had caught sight of his lady friend, Mrs Gibson, in the audience; he promptly had more work than he could handle. Goolden was a little-known actor until he had been playing the title role for a week or two in *The Strange Adventures of Mr Penny*. Suddenly everyone wanted to know more about him and crowds formed to watch him enter and leave Broadcasting House. The brightest glare illuminated Askey; a modestly successful comedian when *Band Wagon* began, he could command £600 a week on the halls before it ended its first run.

Band Wagon was typical of the series that had evolved out of the need to find fresh material every week. It ran for an hour and offered a variety of peculiarly radio entertainment. One of its happiest ideas was to have a tale told each week by an actor named Syd Walker in the character of a wandering junk man. Each episode presented a human problem and ended with a question that joined the growing list of catchphrases with which people could replace conversation if they so wished: 'What would you do, chums?' The show had sketches, music, a discovery spot; the longest regular section was left for a comedian, who had 7½ minutes out of the hour. The first series was committed to run thirteen weeks, an unprecedented length which was held to require a comedian of exceptional stamina. Watt and his producer Gordon Crier toured the concert parties and narrowed the field to two candidates. Askey was plucked out of concert-party work and within a few weeks was famous. His affectionate and funny relationship with Richard Murdoch, as supposed caretakers of the six time-signal pips in a flat over the BBC, became one of the best of all the prewar comedy partnerships.

Harry S. Pepper had an equal success with *Monday Night at Seven*, devised as more of an entertainment magazine. It too had regular features: a singing commère, a detective sketch ('Inspector Hornleigh Investigates') presented as a problem which listeners could share, and the famous 'Puzzle Corner', which was to survive the long life of *Monday Night at Seven* (later it became *Monday Night at Eight*) and translate into television.

As Maschwitz's successor Watt became one of the most powerful men in show business, and in the restaurants and pubs round Portland Place shop talk was as much about radio as about the second-hand car and the dress trades. Watt and Pepper had a permanent table reservation in Paganini's restaurant, where they held court with their retinue of producers, agents, artists and song writers. By 1938 the BBC had become the nation's biggest source of light entertainment (except on Sundays) and there was no more talk of sending for C. B. Cochran to take over variety, as some of the newspapers had once suggested.

8

SUNDAY FOR THE PEOPLE

If you had walked down a residential street on a fine Sunday morning in a summer of the 1930s you could have heard, floating through the open windows, the sounds of all the wireless sets; and the sounds that reached your ear would have been of Radio Luxembourg, Radio Normandie, Radio Toulouse, Radio Fécamp and, from Ireland, Radio Athlone. Such was the curious nature of the Reithan Sunday.

The public's hopes for a full and varied weekend programme of broadcasting had begun to stir as soon as the new medium became nationally established. After the Company became the Corporation in 1927, and the nation became accustomed to the wonder of wireless, Reith had to deal with a determined and widespread attempt to rouse public opinion against the pervading religious character of his Sunday programmes and in favour of an alternative choice that would offer 'entertainment'. Reith's answer to this was that careful examination of the problem provided no evidence of any substantial dissatisfaction with existing arrangements. On the contrary, it confirmed the opinion that the services and concerts on Sunday represented the most highly and widely appreciated part of the work of the BBC. This could have meant nothing more than that listeners who wanted the Reithan Sunday appreciated it very much. But it was true that the attempt to change it had little articulate public backing, from other than some newspapers. The Victorian Sunday was firmly in the tradition of British humbug, and could not have been seriously opposed politically unless enough MPs could be found who had the courage to point out that it was humbug.

Radio Times for the week beginning Sunday 29 March 1925 showed the day beginning at 3 pm with two hours of chamber music from London. At 5.30 Children's Hour was transmitted from Birmingham. The service closed down until a religious service at 8.30. At 9 o'clock De Groot and his Piccadilly Orchestra played an hour of light, but not flippant, music. The news at ten was followed by some piano music and at 10.30 the service closed down for the night. The high-powered station covering most of the country from Daventry on 1600 metres opened at stated times during the day to take a light orchestral programme from Manchester and De Groot from London.

During the whole of Jack Payne's time with the BBC he was forbidden to accept any outside engagements on Sundays. Reith believed he was guarding not just a religious observance but doing listeners a favour. He explained his motives in *Broadcast Over Britain*: 'The surrender of the principles of Sunday observance is fraught with danger; even if the Sabbath were made for man the secularising of the day is one of the most significant and unfortunate trends of modern life. Apart from any puritanical nonsense the Sabbath should be one of the unviolable assets of our existence, quiet islands on the tossing sea of life.' He never showed any awareness of the different attitudes to Sunday that might be held by a man like himself, fully stretched in a challenging and exciting job, and the huge majority of his countrymen whose work hardly used them and whose Sundays were boring islands in a flat sea. 'The programmes which are broadcast on a Sunday are therefore framed with the day itself in mind. There need be nothing dull in them. If they are dull, or thought so, something is wrong somewhere. It may simply amount to this: that certain things are not done on Sundays that are done during the rest of the week.'

The value of religious services on Sunday was never questioned; for Reith's claim that they had returned the 'privileges and delights of attendance in the house of God' to many shut off from them was unanswerable. So was his reflection on the influence of the services on backsliders who chanced to hear them. 'There are tens of thousands who would not go to any sort of church but to whom are now brought the influences of a straightforward and manly religion. I know that even the singing of once familiar hymns has brought back the remembrance of happier and better days. There is no telling the effect when, for this brief period in a busy week, the lamps are lit before the Lord and the message and music of eternity move through the infinities of the ether.'[1]

There was no true alternative to the Reithan Sunday even after the division of broadcasting into the National and Regional patterns was in full swing. In April 1935 programmes began at 10.30 with the time signal and weather, at 11 am the National Programme broadcast Bach's *St Matthew Passion*, its two parts separated by a curiously secular interval of two hours filled by the Luton town band and the Gershom Parkington quintet. At teatime Children's Hour offered Bible Stories; Heroes of the Free Churches; Treasures of the Bible; and How to Read an Epistle, by the Rev. A. C. Dean. From 5.30 to 7 pm there was a production of Sheridan's *The Rivals*; and then an hour of piano and cello music took listeners up to the religious service and the first of three half-hour talks by Canon Charles Raven on 'The Way to God'. After the Grand Hotel orchestra from Eastbourne and the Alfredo Campoli trio, the Epilogue ended the day at 10.45. The Regions offered alternative church services and music.

The Sunday schedule had evidently become a subject for discussion in *Radio Times*, for an American listener, H. Tosti Russell, was wondering about it. He testified that though he admired the way religion was handled he invariably tuned in to continental stations on Sunday in order to liven up his day off. He did not, however, complain. He coined the word 'decency-ship' to describe the kind of self-imposed censorship that he believed listeners were willing to accept. 'There are many in this country who would enjoy livelier programmes on Sundays but they undoubtedly approve of decency-ship rather than demand of those in control of programmes alterations that would offend other listeners. So on Sundays they philosophically tune in the continental dance music.' Most of us now over forty-five can admit that Russell described the situation correctly. In a mainly irreligious and hypo-critical nation Reith's trump card was that no politician would ever find party backing for propaganda against Sunday observance; and his Sunday was in the national tradition whereby social legislation is enacted by those who do not want the pleasures they are legislating for.

Change was forced in the end from outside. Insipid, trivial and repetitive, aimed unblinkingly at the least discriminating layer of taste, the programmes from the continental stations gave a great many listeners a feeling they'd never had from the BBC: that the people running the broadcasts were chumps like themselves. By 1937 the BBC was losing half its Sunday audi-ence to them. On that day, therefore, the unified structure of broadcasting in Britain, the planned alternative under single control, ceased to exist. Faced with this unacceptable truth the BBC decided to lighten its Sunday programmes, while pretending that it was doing no such thing. The word it preferred was 'extend'. An important point about this surrender was that it was made by Reith, as one of his last policy-framing acts before his resigna-tion in 1938.

The last peacetime Sunday began in the morning with light music, gramophone records, Troise and his Mandoliers, and included a talk on gardening, more music from Falkman and his Apaches, the Leslie Bridgwater Quintet, God in Common Life, more music, a religious service, and closed down at 10.30. The Regional programme opened at four and was drawn from the same band of material. It was only with the outbreak of war and the necessity for the Forces Programme that the BBC broke finally with the past and offered a secular alternative to the Sunday-evening religious service. As the war had brought more and more listeners nearer to meeting their maker a rational procedure would have stepped up radio's religious obser-vances rather than cut them down, but by then national morale had become too important to be left to religion; by the summer of 1940 the British people, who had never been asked for their opinion, were exposed on Sunday nights to the profane appeal of cinema organists, variety from the Coventry Hippodrome, and *Hi Gang*.

The Reithan Sunday was in several important ways a disaster which he

E

saw as a triumph. Broadcasting was exempt from the law of the land controlling Sunday entertainment; in imposing it Reith appeared to be acting out of disinterested puritanism and against the flow of general opinion, for in 1932 the Government's Sunday Entertainment Act liberalised the day to some extent, chiefly by permitting cinemas and concert halls to open. His obstinacy ensured the success of the commercial stations (Moseley reckoned that had they been allowed a share of the licence fee in proportion to the number of their listeners the BBC would have gone out of business) and allowed the British to become used to hearing commercials. It deepened a feeling among the inarticulate working class that the national broadcasting service was for Them rather than them. The *Daily Mail*'s Collie Knox, surmising that the BBC's chief often pepped himself up on Kipling's *If*, reflected that there was not much credit to be claimed out of treating triumph and disaster just the same if you could not tell which was which.

9
BIRTH OF THE NEWS

If there was one thing on which the newspapers, theatres, cinemas, concert halls, authors' and musicians' associations, lecturers, preachers, booksellers and publicans had agreed on back in 1922 it was that broadcasting threatened their interests. Reith, as usual, got it right, and promised them that broadcasting would give all of them (except the publicans) the best boost they ever had. But they continued to stare at the short-term threat. The first result of the broadcast of *The Magic Flute* from Covent Garden was a ban on future relays from theatres. The managers could not imagine that radio would create its own programmes. They thought it would rely solely on excerpts from theatre plays. The immediate response of some of the concert organisers to a new outlet which, fairly obviously, would use music to an extent hitherto undreamed of, was to threaten artists with exclusion from the concert circuit if they took part in it. The newspapers at first refused to print the details of programmes, changed their minds when they saw that they were rejecting a powerful aid to circulation, and then tried to have the new *Radio Times* stopped on the ground that broadcasting had no right to enter the publishing business. Most of the restrictions imposed were so daft that, as Reith put it, 'absurdity has so offset injustice that no defence is required'. But in news he had to accept that the newspaper industry had the whip hand. Because it was the only supplier of news (the BBC had no sources of its own, nor was it in a position to build them) he had to agree to the terms of the Newspaper Proprietors' Association: no news bulletins before 7 pm and no live descriptions of events. The microphones were allowed to transmit only the sounds they picked up. Oddly enough the effect on the imagination was liberating; when the listener could hear only the sounds of horses' feet and marching men and wheels rolling from the Lord Mayor's Show his imagination was free to paint a scene as richly as it could colour it, with no third party to overlay his picture. It imparted a kind of expanding magic to a night in May 1924, when the BBC took its microphones to a wood in Surrey to broadcast the nightingale and listeners in the north of England and Scotland heard for the first time in their lives the overrated but undeniably romantic song that they had read about in Hans Andersen.

Earlier news bulletins, running commentaries and eyewitness accounts had to wait for the changeover from Company to Corporation, and a charter embodying the recommendations of the 1926 Crawford Committee. Once given a free rein the sporting and ceremonial broadcasts entered the nation's life as quickly and permanently as Children's Hour. The peculiarly urgent resonance of John Snagge's voice describing the University Boat Race was carried from the launch to the nation in 1927, the year of the first Derby commentary by Geoffrey Gilbey and George Allison. Allison's hurrying, breathless, authoritative voice came to seem a perfect parallel to the swiftly changing excitements of football. The catch-phrase 'back to square one', still on the lips of people who probably could not say where it came from, was born out of the football commentaries; the *Radio Times* used to assist listeners' imaginations by publishing a picture of the playing area divided into squares which the commentator's assistant would identify when Allison paused for breath. The fact that some sports were less suitable for commentaries than others immediately struck the BBC. Cricket and golf were reckoned too leisurely and were allotted eyewitness accounts until, in the early thirties, Howard Marshall began his famous cricket commentaries, proving that the trick was to find a speaker who could adapt the pace of his commentary to the pace of the game. Wimbledon tennis was a success from the start, though the commentators found the instant transfer of fast movement from eyes to mind to lips a frightful strain.

All sport was popular, for the fact that the listeners could see nothing was redressed by the commentators' skill in conjuring atmosphere and the competitive element. But broadcasts of ceremonial were more popular than anything. The BBC believed these were the only one of its activities to attract audiences from all grades of the listening public, though as it had no properly organised means of measuring audience opinion it could not be sure. It is certain that those that liked them liked them very much, though younger readers must wonder what on earth we got out of events that seem to them purely visual, such as the storming of Badajoz from the 1928 Searchlight Tattoo at Aldershot and the flypast from the RAF pageant at Hendon. The explanation is that the BBC did them very well and listeners' imaginations were not blunted by habit. In about 1935 I was taken to Rushmoor Arena to watch the Aldershot Tattoo, and was disappointed to find how small the spectacle seemed compared to the stupendous thing my mind's eye had seen.

The live outside broadcast, transporting the listener to some place he would like to be, was the very stuff and essence of broadcasting; the Prince of Wales at the Mansion House, the Promenade Concerts, a sale of old masters at Christies, the opening of the Ypres memorial – the subject disseminated the same magic whatever it was. The nightingale broadcasts captured so many imaginations that they nearly died of it, for the locality of them became known. In 1927 the twitterings of the immortal bird were overborne by a background of motor horns and gear grindings; the following year the BBC cautiously announced the broadcast as coming from 'somewhere in Berkshire'.

Listeners soon became sufficiently accustomed to the commentators to begin criticising them (the very word troubled pedants, who pointed out that a commentary was an expository treatise whereas the BBC's describers of scenes never in fact offered any opinion of them), for though not everyone can read and write, everyone can speak, and so took the extraordinarily difficult feat of describing events on the wing as something they would probably do much better than the commentators if they could penetrate the conspiracy of nepotism and be given a chance.

News and the running commentary were basically the same kind of broadcasting – the broadcast of an event on the wing was in itself the most immediate form of news – and when the BBC was given freedom to cover such newsworthy events as sport it acquired a very strong bargaining counter in its battles with the newspapers, for no paper could compete with its immediacy; and in Gerald Cock, head of outside broadcasts, and his successor S. J. de Lotbinière, it had two men well able to exploit it.

But news languished in the sense that the BBC continued to rely on Reuters, the Press Association, the Exchange Telegraph and the Central News – four titles stamped indelibly on listeners' memories by the constant repetition of them the BBC was obliged to make in acknowledgment of the copyright. The style and spirit carefully excluded the personalities of the news reader and any news judged to be sensational or unsavoury. There was no betting news, and lurid murder cases of the day (the newspapers used to drive themselves into a competitive frenzy over them) were not mentioned until the jury had returned a verdict.

The success of the news bulletins in neutralising personality can be judged by the strength of the popular belief that there was only one news reader (there were several). But certain one-off broadcasts suggested the shape news would take. On Budget Day in 1932 the journalist Wickham Steed observed the scene in the House of Commons until the last possible moment, dashed to Savoy Hill in a taxi and went on the air at 6.50, speaking from the notes he was still sorting out when the green light came on. This was the first up-to-the-minute reporting by radio of the Budget.

Topical talks had become established, and by 1933 were occasionally promoted to a place close to the subject they concerned, instead of following the bulletin. Moreover they were concerned with the events of the day, rather than of three days earlier, and from further afield, from the provinces and from overseas; the topical talkers were giving place to a new title of special correspondent. Vernon Bartlett, whose *The Way of the World* broadcasts on international politics had been running since 1928, was appointed foreign correspondent in 1932. How vulnerable the BBC was to charges of intruding opinion into the news was shown when Bartlett went to the microphone one October evening in 1933 and defended Germany's decision, announced that day by Hitler, to leave the League of Nations. Bartlett suggested that as the Allies had not kept their Peace Treaty commitment to disarm, Germany had at least a case to be examined. The *Daily Telegraph* was outraged that one of the BBC's talkers should present an opinion at variance with its own and the Foreign Office's and Bartlett had sixty-three phone calls and 700 letters mostly agreeing with the *Telegraph*. The incident showed how careful the BBC had to be; that Bartlett had been broadcasting for years as an independent commentator was overridden by the placing of his talk at the close of a news bulletin.

These developments were pulled into a single programme in 1933, a late news bulletin extended from twenty to forty-five minutes presented in a crisp, newsreel style that today's listeners to *The World at One* would not have found extraordinary, though they might have been impressed by its literacy. It included live broadcasts from Paris on the World Economic Conference, from Manchester on the opening of the new Liverpool airport and, for the first time in a home news bulletin, material recorded earlier in the day (it was of a Davis Cup tie from Wimbledon). Its most adventurous stroke was to incorporate the technique of radio features into the presentation of small magazine-type stories which were not part of the hard news. Thus a recollection by Derek McCulloch of the first day of the battle of the Somme was boosted with some sound effects as of trumpet calls. The whole complicated broadcast went without a hitch and the Prince of Wales sent congratulations. The experiment was declared a success and from October extended bulletins of the same sort, aimed to present the news in this more varied and vivid form (they were forerunners of *Radio Newsreel*) were broadcast every Saturday night until, in December, they had to be taken off through lack of staff, money and equipment. But the territory won was not lost. Reith was determined to have an independent news service, and before he left the foundations of it had been solidly laid.

News had been part of Talks until 1934, when it acquired independence under Professor John Coatman, taken on as Senior News Editor from the London School of Economics. With his appointment news began to expand. He brought in a number of professional journalists, led by R. T. Clark of the *Telegraph* and *Guardian* and Kenneth Adam of the *Guardian*, who began a long and important BBC career as home news editor. Their jobs were to supervise the sub-editing of the agency tapes, but this was an unsatisfying and inadequate business and Coatman set himself to improve it. But just as drama had needed the control panel to set it free, so news needed its own technical liberator.

The arrival of reliable and portable recording techniques was important to every aspect of radio but absolutely essential to news. Only by using recordings could it meet its obligations to go on the air at fixed times every day. I pause here to honour the memory of Louis Blattner, who in 1931 gave the BBC his device for recording magnetically on steel tape. Blattner was not, as his name suggests, an expatriated middle-European scientist; he was the director of the Gaiety Cinema, Manchester. His steel tape ran at three feet per second (compared with the modern tape-recorder's 1¼ inches) but had its descendant's merit of reproducing recordings an infinite number of times without any loss in quality. Much early material was recorded on it, including such curiosities as the 1931 victory in the Schneider Cup trophy.

As an aid to programme producers it was invaluable, but for recording actualities, such as a horse-race, the gramophone record was better. By 1934 the engineers had extended the playing time of a 12-inch record to nine minutes, by slowing the turntable speed to sixty r.p.m. compared with the normal seventy-eight and using a fine cutting device that cut 150 grooves to the inch compared with the standard record's eighty. One of these, fitted into a converted laundry van, became the BBC's first mobile recording unit; and one day in September 1936 sound engineer L. F. Lewis drove it to the model engineering exhibition at the Royal Horticultural Hall to meet a stout young man who was anxiously and enthusiastically waiting to clasp his destiny. This was Richard Dimbleby.

Dimbleby had got himself into news by the expedient – still the best there is – of asking the head man. He wrote to Coatman in May 1936, respectfully suggesting that it might be possible to enliven the news to some extent, without spoiling the authoritative tone for which it was famed, if reporters were held in readiness to cover unexpected news for that day. In the event of a big fire, strikes, civil commotion, railway accidents, pit accidents, or any other of the major catastrophes 'in which the public, I fear, is deeply interested', the 22-year-old Dimbleby craftily added, a reporter could be sent from Broadcasting House to cover the event for the bulletin, not just in his own words but by securing eyewitnesses. As for the name of the reporter, he would be happy if he was able to play a part. He was pushing at a door that if not actually open was ajar. Dimbleby at this time was news editor of the *Advertiser's Weekly* – 'I have, I believe, the doubtful honour,' he wrote, 'of being Fleet Street's youngest editor.' His father was also a journalist, for many years the political correspondent of the *Daily Mail* until the pro-Fascist politics of the first Lord Rothermere began to infect the paper. He resigned to run the family newspaper business in Richmond, and the change in fortune put paid to Richard's hopes of becoming a surgeon. He joined his father at Richmond and broke out on his own in 1934, when he joined the *Bournemouth Daily Echo*. He must have been exceptionally bright, for he was soon making money out of 'lineage' for the London papers. Behold him, then, at 22, a bachelor in a Bloomsbury bedsitter with a beaten-up old Morris Oxford which had cost him £3, a fairly fluent command of French and a smattering of German, waiting for Lewis outside the Royal Horticultural Hall.

His piece went in the 9.30 news and made an immediate impression on Reith. He rang down to ask the reporter's name and said he never wanted to hear it again. But the news organisation protected him and he was allowed to broadcast his first interview. It was admittedly only with a cow, a champion named Cherry who had broken a milk-yield record. Dimbleby went down to Amesbury with the recording van and the cow mooed into his microphone as co-operatively as though aware of assisting at the birth of a broadcasting legend. But his troubles were not over, for the gramophone turntable in the Bournemouth studios, from which the recording was to be fed into the news, broke down just before transmission time. Dimbleby was in despair, but Arthur Phillips, then a programme assistant with the van, saved the situation by turning the record on the turntable with his finger. From then on Dimbleby developed quickly, and his rise is really the story of the development of news as a fast and worldwide reporter of events in which bulletins and outside broadcasts were part of the same stream. This was the form that Reith from the start had laid down as desirable: the bulletin should give clear, accurate, brief and impartial news in a form that would not pander to sensationalism yet would arouse a continuing interest. They should be vitalised by outside broadcasts with commentaries and topical talks by the man of the moment or an expert.

As radio's second news observer Dimbleby went everywhere with the laundry van. He rarely wrote down a script. Ralph Murray, who was to enter the Foreign Office, become Ambassador to Greece and wind up as Sir Ralph and a governor of the BBC, was in charge of the news talks section and responsible for subbing Dimbleby's stuff.* He recalled that he had a rolling fluency but at a terrible stylistic price. He spoke the clichés with such relish and conviction that they seemed freshly minted. Murray slashed his adjectives and begged him to think about his use of language. He must have learned fairly quickly, for by March 1937 his reporting of the Fenland floods showed the beginnings of the style that could make the listener see what Dimbleby saw: '. . . down the stream the moving pinpricks of light that are the lanterns of men working to close the cracks in the bank.' He learned that there was no substitute for homework before a broadcast, and how to accommodate the facts to the time he had to tell them. He was joined by

* Murray was the first of the BBC's news observers. He described the arrival of British troops in Calais on their way to the 1934 Saar plebiscite. His work as observer with the League of Nations led to the creation of a squad of such observers.

Charles Gardner as news observer and the two young men and their accompanying engineers began to enjoy the delights of competing with Fleet Street and often beating it, for they discovered very quickly that people would respond better to the novelty of being asked to talk to the BBC than to a similar invitation from the newspapers, which were comparatively humdrum. They even had scoops; Gardner in 1937 found the America's Cup challenger *Endeavour* (she had broken her tow on her return journey and was missing for days) and interviewed her captain while the newspapers were still looking.

They always wanted to do more than they were allowed, and begged the engineers for a recording apparatus that would record adequate sound and could be fitted into the back of an ordinary car instead of the seven-ton truck that now accompanied the laundry van. The skirmish was as old as broadcasting, between engineers who put sound reproduction first and the newsmen for whom what mattered was to get the story on the air fast and preferably first. There were occasions when the official policy was not to put the story on at all. One of the dark patches in the BBC's record was its refusal to allow its news to carry a word about the divorce of Edward VIII's Mrs Simpson even after the newspapers had broken their self-imposed silence. The News department threatened to strike unless that night's bulletin referred to the affair but that day Baldwin brought it into a statement in the House of Commons that the BBC could not ignore.

Dimbleby had his share of depression and frustration and he and his sound engineer, David Howarth, once seriously thought about trying to sell themselves to Ed Murrow, who had just reached London as European director of CBS News. What Howarth called the breakthrough for radio reporting came on the night of 30 November 1936 when the Crystal Palace caught fire, at a time that could not have been more convenient for radio news: the evening papers had closed down and the morning papers awaited the morning. The crowd round the blaze was so thick that the recording van could not break through it to return to the studio. De Lotbinière sent Dimbleby down. Engineers wired him up to a telephone and he broadcast direct, surrounded by the roar of crowds, the clash of firebells, the shouting of commands, and the sound of the Palace burning. De Lotbinière felt he had proved his point; that the story came first and the sound quality second.

By 1939 listeners were becoming aware of Richard Dimbleby as a reporter of individual style. He became the first man to report a royal tour (of Canada), with such distinction that the BBC governors recorded their appreciation of it. But his most memorable broadcast was from the roadside at Le Perthus on the Spanish-French frontier, as the fugitives of the broken Republican armies poured past him out of Spain. In my memory this broadcast is inextricably linked with the growth of radio news, with the fear, relief and shame of the Munich settlement, with the curious change of mood in the ensuing twelve months, and with one of Hitler's speeches relayed from a Nazi gathering in the Berlin Sportpalast. This voice, charged with a raging hate and an exultant consciousness of power, marked one of the moments when we realised that war was inevitable and would be horrible; it seemed to foreshadow the evil things that Chamberlain would commit the nation to fighting against; and young Dimbleby's broadcast from Spain, carefully neutral because the BBC news had to be neutral, nevertheless aroused something to which its hearers had to respond: the stirrings of dread, disgust, anger and determination.

10

AMONG THE STUFFED SHIRTS

On 1 January 1927 the Company formed by the original consortium disappeared to be reborn as the Corporation. The directors became the board of governors, the Director General remained the chief executive of an unchanged organisation; but Reith had got what he wanted – independence of financial and political control, duly established by Act of Parliament. The transfer was celebrated with a grand ball in the Hotel Cecil, still remembered by survivors for the monumental hangovers that ensued. Maurice Gorham, then a young and sprightly assistant editor of *Radio Times*, was one of many who committed the strategic error of assuming that the party would be teetotal and stoked himself up beforehand, only to find that Management had approved not only a bar but a bar where the drinks were free. With this event the infancy of the BBC can be said to have come to an end. Like other infants it had survived the threat of an early death. During the General Strike it came within inches of being commandeered by the Government. Caught between its duty to tell the nation what was happening and its need to consider a government armed with dictatorial powers, the BBC survived by doing most of what the government wanted. The unanswerable question for Reith – then aged thirty-six – and the board was whether, if so young a concern were taken over by government, it would ever recover its freedom. Reith placed its survival first, and preserved it, but the price was high. The strike unquestionably established radio as a fully fledged communications and propaganda medium. John Snagge, who had just joined the company in Stoke on Trent, remembered how, every evening at six o'clock, Reith would talk from London to the provincial stations; it was during these days that for Snagge the wireless ceased to be an occupation in rather uncomfortable surroundings and became something of self-evident importance.

Reith seemed to Snagge totally in command of the situation, but it called for continuous and delicate compromise and in fact the company's use of radio deepened the division within the nation. (Reith, perhaps sensing that some reuniting gesture was called for, recited 'Jerusalem' over the air when he personally announced the end of the strike.) Labour maintained that more than any other weapon radio was the one that broke the strike, and that it had been unfairly used to present only one side. The feeling that the BBC represented the middle class and was not for the masses undoubtedly dated from this event, though it existed without an outlet until the monopoly was ended nearly thirty years later.

Another punctuation mark in the BBC's history came in 1932, when Reith, who enjoyed these romantic gestures, was photographed locking up behind him on the night Savoy Hill closed, and the next day striding across the entrance hall of the newly opened, purpose-built Broadcasting House. The move dramatised the vast physical and artistic expansions within the BBC, but the romantics hated it. Eric Maschwitz walked round the cavernous rooms and studios of Savoy Hill after all the furniture had gone, recalling the times that were no more, when the programmes had an air of lively improvisation and the atmosphere was that of an exciting club whose members never wanted to go home. For him Broadcasting House, with its slightly Teutonic décor characteristic of the early thirties, seemed to be reminding him that broadcasting was a serious matter.* Gorham hated it too. He believed that the 'great stuffed shirt' era dated from the move, 'marked internally by paternalism run riot, bureaucracy of the most heirarchial type, and an administrative system that made productive work harder instead of easier, and a tendency to promote the most negative characters to be found among the staff. Externally it was marked by an aloofness, resentment of criticism and a positive contempt for the listener. . . .'[1] Making due allowances for Gorham's natural irreverence (he teased Reith for seven years by not calling him Sir) he seems to have had a point. When King George V and Queen Mary paid an official visit to Broadcasting House in July nobody was allowed to enter the main hall or the studio tower for half an hour before their arrival. Smoking was banned anywhere in the building between 3 pm and 5 pm. The whole staff, assembled in the concert hall, had rehearsed the national anthem and four cheers (the fourth was supposed to be a spontaneous outburst); and staff who worked in offices along the route the party was to take on its tour of inspection had to stay out of them until the visit was over in case the King and Queen should open a door and actually see them at work. The King was awed by all this, but perked up during the presentation of senior members of the staff. Looking along the line and then up at Reith he asked: 'Where's that fellow Walton O'Donnell?' – a reference to the founder and leader of the famous BBC Military Band, of whose music George V was inordinately fond. The reigning monarchs were and have remained great fans of broadcasting, as the only entertainment they could share with their people without having to dress up as admirals and to inspect anybody before and to compliment them after.

Opinions are in the eye of the beholder. Sieveking dedicated his published

* No name plates were allowed on office doors. It was feared that newspapermen might track down producers and get information out of them.

scripts to Reith in 1934 as to a man who 'has made it possible for an art to flourish by enabling artists and craftsmen to devote their lives to its practice and development in freedom from any limitations save those which have seemed, to an ever modifying degree, inherent in it'. You could not say fairer than that.

The BBC covered the country with a 'national' and a 'regional' service and had the highest proportion of listeners to population than any other country employing a licence system (except Denmark, where the problems of distribution were simpler), and not significantly less than America, where listening was 'free'. It was as strong as rock where, on the whole, the nation thought it should be strong. Its talks department could get pretty well anyone it approached – people of the calibre of Shaw, Wells, Dean Inge, Haldane, Sir Oliver Lodge, Sir Rabindranath Tagore, Archbishops of Canterbury and York, Sir Henry Newbolt. The truth was that the BBC had become the property of the nation, or at any rate the majority of the opinion-forming section of it, and had become almost inevitably an organisation of such size and importance as to awe itself.

Programmes such as the Christmas Day round-the-world link-ups devised by Laurence Gilliam as a warm-up to the King's Christmas Day message were in intention and in fact the high-water mark of Christmas of the thirties. Their titles, 'Absent Friends', 'Empire Exchange', 'This Great Family', set the mood; Gilliam's production flung a marvellous invisible ribbon round the world with the most skilful mingling of technical and dramatic bravura; the style exploited like the Scrapbooks the contrast between pomp and simplicity, as when in 1934 Gilliam found to introduce the king a shepherd, full of years, from Shakespeare's Warwickshire. Stuart Hibberd, the BBC's chief announcer, thought there must have been many people with lumps in their throats as the old man announced the king. Hibberd, as we would say now, did not know the half of it. These programmes lashed listeners into a frenzy of patriotic togetherness. It was not at all uncommon for listeners to rise in their homes as the national anthem saluted the monarch, and those whose emotions had been brought closer to the surface by Christmas drink often found themselves yielding the tribute of a tear. As chance ordered it the BBC was called upon to interpret the nation's love of ceremonial on several royal occasions.

George V had broadcast first when opening the Empire Exhibition at Wembley in 1924, and had become rather good at it, disclosing a paternal but friendly timbre that suited the publicists' image of him as the father of his country. His voice, wrote Harold Nicolson in his biography, was 'strong, emphatic, vibrant, with undertones of sentiment, devoid of condescension, artifice or pose'. He had the gift of endearing naturalness. 'Remember, children, the King is speaking to you,' he once said. The three

Christmas Day programmes made him seem the best-known monarch in Britain's history and touched off an explosion of affection in the 1935 Jubilee that astonished its modest recipient.

On the evening of his death the following November the BBC cancelled all its programmes on receiving the doctors' message that hope must be abandoned. From 9.38 until close-down there was nothing but Hibberd's voice, reading every quarter of an hour the terms of the medical bulletin. 'The king's life is moving peacefully towards its close.' Reith personally read the news of his death, ending with a phrase that could have been held to break the rule forbidding the BBC to express an opinion about anything. 'With our fellow citizens at home and overseas we affirm our loyalty to the crown.' Thereafter it suspended normal programmes until the day after the funeral eight days later. The nation listened to the funeral service and at 2.33 the BBC closed down again except for the shipping forecast and Big Ben as discreet reminders that somewhere life was going on. It is impossible now to communicate to readers too young to have heard it the effect of this solemn leave-taking. A few critics thought the BBC overdid it, but it was sustaining an attitude to royalty that it had done more than any other medium to create. Most of us thought that if the heavens themselves did not blaze forth the death of princes it was as well that the BBC should, and after all George V was the first reigning monarch to die since the birth of broadcasting. And then, ten months later, the BBC's standing as major national communicator was signalled again by Reith's introduction of 'His Royal Highness Prince Edward' to a broadcast that halted conversation all over Britain as the curiously mid-Atlantic voice told us that Prince Charming was no more. That was on 11 December, but by Christmas Day the BBC had still not recovered its spirits. The main programme was 'Music For Christmas' at 9.20 pm, composed of Christmas fireside music from the Regions. Even the loyal Hibberd thought this was a bit heavy for Christmas night and confided to his diary that he could have done with ten minutes of Tommy Handley or Leonard Henry in the middle to liven things up.

However, the view of the BBC held by most opinion-forming folk was summed up by Ivor Thomas, writing in the *Political Quarterly* of autumn 1935. 'When we consider what has happened in other lands we may be eternally thankful that in this country broadcasting was from the start regarded as a public service to be operated by a monopolistic institution independent of direct government control and existing only to serve the public, forbidden to indulge in commercial publicity and directed towards a high ideal.' Reith put it into a single famous paragraph of his autobiography, *Into the Wind*: 'It was in fact the combination of public service motive, sense of moral obligation, assured finance and the brute force of monopoly which enabled the BBC to make of Broadcasting what no other country in the world has made of it.' In 1936 the Ullswater Report recorded its deep sense of gratitude to the wisdom of Crawford in founding the BBC in its established form and to 'the prudence and idealism which have characterised its operations'. The Ullswater Committee took the renewal of the Charter on Crawfordian lines for a further ten years as an act of obvious good sense.

Overhauling my own feelings about the BBC I remember that I liked, admired and enjoyed its sense of occasion. Only the BBC would have thought of broadcasting the song of the nightingale. Only it would have encouraged J. C. Stobart's famous Grand Goodnights that closed the year's broadcasting. Stobart was head of talks, news, education and religion; his invaluable contribution to the BBC was to persuade the eminent to appear on it. His grand goodnight was his own conception, nothing less than a New Year Message to the universe. It included, I remember, good wishes for the new year, addressed in alphabetical order to abbots and academicians to xylophonists and zoologists. (In 1928 he forgot dentists, doubtless a Freudian slip.) The script survives in a recoded fragment rebroadcast in 1932's programme of famous broadcasts from Savoy Hill. 'Here is the London station of the BBC, sending a New Year Message to the universe . . . Hello, all stars and nebulae, greetings to all friendly planets that circle with us on the everlasting tour. . . . Good luck to all the world, to all the brave feet that walk on it. . . .' It was the sort of thing that belonged to broadcasting's ardent boyhood. Another peculiarly vivid glimpse of the BBC's sense of occasion came with the death in 1937 of Marconi. The BBC closed down all its transmitters for two minutes in honour of the man who had started it all.

Although I admired the BBC I was certainly intimidated by it. In the early and mid-thirties I was passing through one of those unhappy phases of youth when you feel that most people are cleverer than you, and the BBC seemed cleverer than anybody, a kind of super Dr Arnold who was always right. It was undeniable that to some its virtues sometimes seemed exasperating. One source of irritation was the honesty with which the BBC, after examining the matter, agreed that it was right and its critics wrong.

It must be admitted that the quality of criticism in the beginning was not high. The newspapers feared the newcomer. 'A subsidised broadcasting service, free from all financial anxiety, had been set up and was about to compete with a business that had been built up by the sweat and toil of generations,' was how Moseley summed it up, and they resented its position as a competitor that had inherited the privileges won by newspapers without risking anything. Some of their attacks were, unfortunately, demonstrably daft; one of the earliest was an attempt to persuade readers that this newfangled invention, as used by the state-protected monopoly, was upsetting the weather and causing thunderstorms by electrifying the clouds.

Luckily this attack was crushed by the coming of an exceptionally good summer. The BBC itself described the newspapers' attitude as fluctuating between definite hostility and mere watchfulness. It ascribed this to jealousy. There was something in this, for some journalists must have watched with longing and irritation and envy the opportunities open to a communications medium that was not subject to the eccentric commands of a megalomaniac proprietor. The press feared the BBC as a rival to its own interests, but had to consider the huge popularity of the wireless. Its attacks were therefore directed against the character and standards of the programmes – again, unfortunately, rather silly ones. Moseley attacked Val Gielgud for broadcasting uncensored Shakespeare, holding that 'certain phrases were distasteful when declaimed before a mixed audience'. He objected to plays which might well reflect the empty and vapid existence of their authors but were totally untrue to the life of the average 'Britisher'. (That peculiar coinage was often used in those days by journalists who were trying to stir the patriotism of the rabble.) He even accused Reith of washing his hands of his responsibility for controlling his staff, an extraordinary charge to bring against a man who forced the resignation of his chief engineer, Captain Eckersley, when he was about to become the guilty party in a divorce action. (Reith told Malcolm Muggeridge in a famous TV interview in 1967 that he had demanded adherence to the Christian ethic only from men who were concerned with the ethical side of broadcasting, a description that scarcely fitted his chief engineer. But whatever the reason, his conscience did for Eckersley's broadcasting career as effectively as if he had preached the sermon every Sunday night.)

Among the mass-circulation dailies there was little serious critical analysis of programmes, the papers preferring to criticise the BBC's programme policies, which they could always attack on one ground or another, rather than the programmes, which they might sometimes have felt constrained to praise. Much newspaper criticism was based on what amounted to stunts which reflected no deeper reflection about the wireless than an editorial guess on which way readers might be expected to react. Sometimes the BBC bowed to the noise. It cancelled a play that dealt with the rescue of survivors from the North Pole by the crew of a Russian ice-ship (it was accused of being pro-Bolshevik) and another about the *Titanic* (it was accused of morbidly exploiting sorrowful memories). These fomentations of public silliness were impossible to respect. It is not puzzling that the BBC's attitudes to press criticism became slightly derisive.

The only other playback the BBC received to its programmes was from the listeners. Reith found very quickly that the letters of approval and complaint regularly offset each other. Many writers failed to acknowledge the existence of any kind of taste other than their own. It came as a very unpleasant surprise to him to find so many anonymous letters of useless vituperation which could not have been increased, he said, if the programme staff had been thorough blackguards. The trouble was, as he saw, that there were thousands who never communicated their views; and he consoled his people with Edmond Burke's reminder that in the same field as half a dozen grasshoppers, filling the air with their importunate chink, a hundred great oxen might be chewing the cud in silence. The *Radio Times* printed some letters from which we see that a large proportion of listeners, then as now, were deeply concerned with the minutiae of broadcasting. 'I would ask you to make a slight correction,' wrote C. E. H. from Stamford Hill in 1925. 'Maas, the finest tenor of his day, was Joseph, not Edward, and he did not die from the effects of damp sheets. He caught a bad cold whilst fishing – a favourite pastime of his – which developed into rheumatic fever and killed him on 15 January 1896.'

There was no scientific measurement of audience opinion until after Reith had left. The BBC held that the steady growth of licences indicated general support of its policy, and the response of its advisory committees and more articulate listeners helped to fill in details. It had no box-office check on its results, nor did it want one, objecting that such a thing might exercise adverse pressure against the wishes of huge minority tastes. The only guide to popularity was supplied by the competitions run by the newspapers, to which the BBC recommended that not too much notice should be paid. In short, although in programme-planning circles they talked about contrasts and alternatives, successes and failures, good programmes and bad (said Maurice Gorham) it was all based on what they themselves thought, plus the unreliable correspondence, unreliable press comment, and remarks overheard among friends, office cleaners, and strangers in trains.

The BBC was undoubtedly right to stick to its policy, but you cannot read its annual reviews of its work without noticing that a honking, hectoring tone had crept into its references to criticism and to the public. It was, for example, positively testy with listeners who did not build their week's listening by choosing from the programmes in *Radio Times*. 'To leave a set switched on in the hope that before the evening is out one will hear something that one wants to hear invites mental indigestion and a chaotic state of mind in which one hears a hundred programmes and understands none.' 'If a man wants to go to a music hall, enters the first building he sees lit up, and finds himself listening to a symphony concert, he does not blame the management of the music hall.' 'The listener must realise that a definite obligation rests on him to choose intelligently from the programmes offered.' It besought listeners to enlarge their capacity to respond to the programmes by turning out the lights so that their birdlike powers of concentration would not be distracted by familiar objects in the room: 'If you only listen with half an ear you have not a quarter of a right to criticise.' It even went to the length of rebuking listeners who were too keen: 'Think of your favourite occupation. Don't you like a change sometimes? Give the wireless a rest now and then.' But the bulk of listeners went on listening with the lights on, complaining when the set played something they did not want to hear, and asking the BBC why such and such a person or thing had never been broadcast. 'Quite the most unsafe question to ask the BBC. In nine cases out of ten the answer is that it has.'

It had an answer to everything. 'There seem to be many more gaps in programmes than there used to be,' wrote a listener.' No,' replied the BBC, 'gaps *between* programmes, yes,' – and explained how there had to be gaps to reduce the unlucky chance that a listener who turned on the news might have to hear the last few minutes of something distasteful to him, such as opera or vaudeville. And if a programme had stirred the listener's feelings, an interval of four or five minutes gave him time to get over it sufficiently to take in the next programme. (This civilised consideration did not long survive.) These intervals were not altogether silent, for they had to consider the situation of listeners who would switch on during one, hear nothing, and presume that the set had broken down or the BBC had ceased to function. They also had to protect listeners like my mother, whose reckless reply to silence from the set was to hit it. After trying and rejecting a metronome, a musical chord, and jingling bells, the engineers came up with the sound of a clock installed with a microphone in a large felt-lined box. It produced a strange, unearthly effect and was quickly called 'the ghost in galoshes'.

Yet the BBC's consideration for its audience was curiously inconsistent. Stuart Hibberd was encouraged to use his famous double good night. He counted a quick four beats to himself thus: 'Goodnight everybody . . . 1, 2, 3, 4 . . . good night', so that listeners could say good night back if they felt like it. This was a pleasant touch; but the identity of him who made it, and of the other announcers, was veiled in the mists of anonymity, as far as could be managed. Anonymity was the rule until 1932, when the names of the so-called Secret Five – Hibberd, T. C. Farrar, John Snagge, Godfrey Adams and Freddy Grisewood – were disclosed to the world by the *Daily Express*. This passion for anonymity spread to include other members of the staff, even when they were producing programmes in which the public took a keen interest. At one time Maurice Gorham was not allowed to print in *Radio Times* the name of the producer, or the conductor of the band, or even the performer, if he were on the staff; he complained that an outside artist who joined the staff simply vanished as far as the public could know. Another time the BBC banned smoking in any studio until Sir Landon Ronald, captured relaxing at rehearsals with an Abdullah, smilingly offered his captor the choice between Ronald with cigarette and concert or no Ronald, no cigarette and no concert. Soon after the ban was lifted, and performers in discussion programmes were positively encouraged to smoke if they wished in order, said Hibberd, to make them feel at home and stimulate the flow of conversation.

One of the talks studios in the new Broadcasting House was designed like a library, with an artificial window and Regency curtains, artificial bookcases and a fireplace without a chimney (the only coal fire in the building was in Reith's office, a grand touch which required a chimney to be run from the third floor to the roof). But two uncompromising articles recalled the speaker to the gravity of his situation. One was the big circular microphone on the table. The other was the portrait of George Washington, staring from the wall as a reminder of the awful responsibility that a speaker must accept if he tampered with the truth. It would be too much to claim that this was not meant as a joke, and a rather good one, but it would be rash to conclude that it was not meant to serve as a little homily as well.

What is certain is that with its income and function assured a great self-confidence and sense of destiny grew within the BBC in the thirties. Already it had achieved so much. It had rescued the Promenade Concerts, by taking over the presentation of them, created one of the world's great symphony orchestras, brought a matchless range of music from ever-growing sources. Broadcasting for schools occupied much of the daytime part of the national programme five days a week and between 1300 and 1400 discussion groups met regularly to hear the programmes broadcast in the adult education service. You get a clear idea of the value attached to the BBC by the nation's chief citizens from looking at the names it was able to recruit to its advisory committees. The one on spoken English had Shaw as its chairman and the Poet Laureate (Robert Bridges), Professor Lascelles Abercrombie, Sir Johnston Forbes Robertson, Professor Daniel Jones, C. T. Onions, Logan Pearsall Smith and Professor Lloyd James, the great expert on phonetics, to help him decide such points as the pronunciation of the 'h' in words beginning with 'wh', and the unstressed 'r' before consonants. (Basically, though, its function was to guide perplexed announcers and to provide them with an authority they could fall back upon when attacked by less well-informed critics.)

Then, in June 1938, to consternation inside the BBC and astonishment outside it, Reith announced that he was resigning his director-generalship to become the chairman of Imperial Airways. It was another kind of abdication, for he was enthroned in fact and legend as one of the half-dozen most important men in the country. His resignation was the biggest mistake of his life, for by leaving the BBC he became a shorn Samson – 'Eyeless in Gaza, at the mill with slaves,' as he bitterly quoted in a letter to Winston Churchill in 1945. Later on he came to believe that his mistake in leaving was in that had he stayed he might have saved the BBC from the backsliding epoch, as he saw it, of the rise of television, and the excesses, as he saw them, of Sir Hugh Greene's regime. But in 1938 he was forty-eight, believed his organisation of the BBC was complete, and longed once more to be fully stretched. On 30 June this strange man took his departure. He forbade any presentation and anything in the way of a farewell. He took the lift down to the entrance hall of Broadcasting House, where his wife shook hands with the senior commissionaire who had been with the BBC ever since it started. For some reason the gesture broke up Reith's fortitude, and he walked through the great bronze doors with the tears running down his cheeks. Then he drove to Droitwich for dinner with two or three of his old colleagues and with his own hands switched off the transmitters and generators at midnight. Before he left they asked him to sign his name in the Visitors' Book and he wrote: 'J. C. W. Reith, ex-BBC.' Ahead of him lay much frustration and disappointment and neglect. Ahead of the BBC lay the tremendous experience of the war. With his departure a great adventure had halted, and with it is a suitable point on which to end this part of the story.

SOUNDS OF WAR

1

PUTTING IT INTO WORDS

The day war broke out I was half-way through the Sunday-morning round of golf on the little nine-hole course which had miraculously survived for more than half a century on a little pocket of common land between Thames Ditton and Esher. Just after eleven o'clock a member who always liked to be the first with bad news drove among the grass and harebells and heather shouting to the players he passed: 'It's started!' And so, to be sure, it had; almost at once the air-raid siren began the first of its disquieting brays. Everyone had secretly expected that within a few minutes of the declaration of war the skies would be dark with Nazi bombers; I searched the sky in the direction of Sandown Park race-course for the fulfilment of the horror but saw nothing. There seemed no point in swelling the crowd of refugees before it became absolutely necessary, so we resumed the game.

Very soon the all clear sounded, but it was apparent from the sharp decline in the standard of play that the Luftwaffe even in absence was getting on our nerves. In the clubhouse the all clear signal had been interpreted as a trap and rumour circulated freely that the Germans were over London, would be there all day, and the roads leading from the capital would shortly be clogged in all directions. It was hard to understand how they could have reached London without anybody seeing or hearing anything. I looked to the north-east for signs of flame, or at least smoke, but nothing disturbed the blueness of the sky, so I went home for lunch.

It was an inauspicious beginning, a microcosm of what the BBC was experiencing. It too had been caught wrong-footed, its careful policy for the emergency having been framed – as, indeed, had Britain's policy toward the Nazis – by dread of the bomber and the certainty of immediate and hideous air raids. Because wireless transmissions could guide the bombers, broadcasting had to shrink to a single home service. Because the expected raids would probably destroy existing communications the single programme would carry mostly news and instructions to the population, backed up by talks from the nation's leaders and requests to the Almighty for his support. No programme was to last longer than half an hour, a decision that would have ruled out symphony concerts, sports matches, and all major drama and features. Variety was to remove to Bristol, drama, music and features to Evesham; gramophone records were stocked by the thousand against the need for filling time. Details had been worked out by a sub-committee as far back as the spring before Munich, and nothing was lacking to emphasise their shrewd farsightedness except the arrival of the air raids. Without them, and with such modifications as were made before 3 September (the rule against programmes lasting longer than thirty minutes was never promulgated), the emergency schedule proved lowering to the spirits. In the legends of the time the air was filled almost to bursting point by theatre organ music from Sandy McPherson, the Canadian who had recently succeeded to the stool of Reginald Foort. Sandy played through long sessions every day except, I believe, Monday and Thursday. The newspapers mounted terrific attacks on the BBC for neglecting its duty to keep the nation cheerful, and the suggestion was raised once more (by Hannen Swaffer) that the whole thing should be handed over to C. B. Cochran. The public attitude was divided as usual between the all too patient, who could easily be persuaded that they were lucky to have any broadcasting at all in such times, and those who were outraged by what they disliked, and in particular by the melancholy manner in which it was presented.

But the BBC was not wholly at fault. It was victim, like the rest of us, of the national instinct which orders us in an emergency to close down as many sources of entertainment as possible, sheepishly reopening them after a few days. The little grey men who always grab control had closed the theatres, cinemas and concert halls, and ordered the largely pointless and uncomfortable black-out. They were also at work in and on the BBC. But the ubiquity of Sandy McPherson was due in large part to the Ministry of Information's order that the names of all broadcasters, including musicians, must be submitted in advance. The BBC could hardly be blamed for cutting through the ritual by making Sandy the only organist on their list.

Where the BBC was free to move it managed extraordinary feats. The shrinking of the home service to a single wavelength was one of them. When a German bomber was near, a transmitter would go off the air, but the listener at home noticed only a drop in volume. He was receiving the same signal from a more distant source. BBC engineers managed to synchronise all domestic transmitters on to a single wavelength without causing a howl. Later they managed to duplicate this system in the Forces programme.* The *Radio Times* containing the normal peacetime programmes had gone to press on Thursday 31 August. It never reached the news stands, for on the Friday the BBC had the message from Whitehall that sent it to its war stations. Maurice Gorham began writing the leader for the emergency issue, telephoning its contents to the printers page by page. Fed up with the official BBC euphemism 'emergency' he decided to use the word 'war', and

* German radio engineers never managed to copy this feat; in Germany when there was a British air raid listeners lost the programme.

sweated out the next thirty-six hours in case Chamberlain should do a second Munich over the weekend. It was on sale on Monday. The second wartime issue went to press the next day, thereby establishing a unique record among weekly publications of having three press days in five days.

However, the machine had marched off in the wrong direction and it took two months to turn it round. The first wartime programmes were built round the fixed points of the Daily Service at 10.15, Children's Hour and the Nine O'Clock News. In the first week a huge tide of music, mostly light and all on records, lapped against these posts, but beneath it a pattern was taking shape. Before the war was little more than forty-eight hours old Mrs L. Russell Muirhead was giving a talk on Making the Most of Dried Fruit, followed on the Thursday by Mrs Arthur Webb on Making the Most of a Wartime Larder and on Saturday by the already famous handyman W. P. Matthew. Mr Middleton was firmly rehoused in his 12.15 slot on Sunday afternoons, but this revered name cannot be passed over with a mere mention. He was a gardening journalist who first talked on radio in 1936, mastering a quiet, casual style that sounded like a man conducting his listeners round a well-stocked and peaceful garden of their own. His talks seemed to enlarge the business of cultivating one's garden into a serene and comforting philosophy, more so than ever in time of war. If Churchill had the luck, as he said, to sound the lion's roar, Mr Middleton's talks appeased a quiet, deeply felt love of the threatened land. He was one of those people with a natural and classless dignity whom everyone instinctively took to; what they felt is well expressed in the fact that throughout his broadcasting career he was never known as anything but 'Mr' Middleton.

Drama and music were back. Richard Dimbleby and David Howarth were already in France with the BEF. The White Coons and 'Songs from the Shows' gave variety the beginnings of a familiar look, but of course the department had had a bad knock. It had taken off for Bristol within half an hour of hearing the six o'clock news on Friday and held its first meeting in the Town Hall on Sunday morning. They listened to Chamberlain's declaration of war and John Watt lifted the ban on jokes about Hitler 'provided they were good ones'. The first fruit of this dispensation was a skit called Adolf in Blunderland, knocked up by Max Kester and James Dyrenforth in which Maurice Denham and Jack Train played Hitler as Alice and Goering as the Duchess. *Bandwagon* returned, prompting a letter from a listener which pointed out that if Hitler had had a 'stinker' (this was a reference to Richard 'Stinker' Murdoch's part in the series) to say to him, 'Oh, you silly little man' whenever he put his foot in it Germany would not be in the state it was. But for some days Tommy Handley and Leonard Henry were the only comedians in Bristol. In spite of Henry's collection of scripts (he travelled down with them stacked in the back of his car) the shortage of material was almost as pressing as that of people. Meanwhile Leonard Henry was on the air, it seemed, as often as Sandy McPherson. Listeners became fed up with the repetition of names; and there was no denying that Sunday, on a national programme with no alternative, was direful. The third Sunday evening of the war put up a religious service at eight o'clock as the BBC's contribution to the first of the wartime national days of prayer. In 1939 these were not held in the widespread dread they attracted later in the war, after it had become noticed that every such appeal seemed to be followed swiftly and inevitably by some disastrous setback to the Allied cause. Still, some of us wondered why the broadcast service could not have been given in the morning.

By November the BBC reckoned its service was back in full stretch. The names of memorable and specifically wartime hits began to appear. *Garrison Theatre* made Jack Warner as famous as his sisters, Elsie and Doris Waters. This show was presented as from a soldiers' entertainments hall and before an audience in uniform. As Private Warner, Jack rode in each week on a bicycle (the catch-phrase 'mind my bike' swiftly passed into general currency) to enact his routine with Joan Winters (as a programme seller) and read a letter from his brother Sid, purporting to come from somewhere in France. *In the Canteen Tonight* replaced *In Town Tonight*. Two important innovations occurred. J. B. Priestley, whose likeness in the full prime of his creative vigour had decorated the cover of the first, stillborn *Radio Times*, began a reading of *Let the People Sing*, the first novel to be commissioned by the BBC for broadcasting. One of the most obdurate obstacles to broadcasting suddenly dissolved when the D'Oyly Carte Opera company signed an agreement at last and on 5 November the BBC was able to broadcast *Trial by Jury*, the first-ever complete broadcast of Gilbert and Sullivan opera.

Radio as campaigner began to hit its stride. Laurence Gilliam and his features department began their superb wartime achievement with *The Shadow of the Swastika*, a documentary series on the rise of the Nazis. Gracie Fields broadcast from 'somewhere in France'. I remember it as the most moving broadcast of the war up to that time. The uniquely clear, true voice soared effortlessly over the full-throated singing of the hundreds of men in the audience; hearing them you shared what Xerxes felt when he saw before him the multitude of his troops and thought how many of them must die. Tonics spiritual (*Lift up your Hearts*) and physical (*Up in the Morning Early*) began on the same day in December, but apart from the battle of the River Plate and the hunt of the U-boats, the war and the weather seemed locked in the same frost. The winter was intensely cold; the ice on the ponds stayed firm for weeks, long enough for me to learn at last how to do an outside edge figure of eight. It was the time of the twilight – the 'phoney' war, well illustrated in Gilliam's 1939 Christmas Day link-up which prefaced the King's talk. It knew it had to say something big about the war; but what? It went to a casualty-clearing station in France where the surgeon said, 'Normally we have plenty of work, I assure you; soldiers in the field catch things just like anyone else.' It went to the RAF fighter station at Duxford and eavesdropped on an exchange between control tower and pilot. 'Hello, Robin! Controller calling. Anything to report, over?' 'Hello controller, Robin answering. Have investigated aircraft, which is friendly; over.' 'Hello, Robin, controller calling. Return to base and land, your relief is now on patrol, over.' Then the pilot said to us: 'Hope you are receiving me clearly. That little job is over. It's chilly up here, but now I'm going to join the Christmas party and wish a very merry Christmas to you all and happy landings.' It went to a farm in Somerset where some evacuee children told how much they enjoyed themselves and how they did not in the least miss London. The general theme was of the British and the Empire as one great family united against a common enemy. 'London calling the Empire. . . . calling across the wild Atlantic, to Newfoundland, to the great cities and white prairies of Canada, across the north and south Pacific and Australia, over the Timor Sea to Singapore and India and across the Indian ocean to South Africa. London calling across the oceans of the world.' The style seems high-flown now, but it didn't then, and Gilliam always knew when to quieten it. His last speaker was the old shepherd from the Cotswolds who had introduced King George V in 1930 and now apostrophised his son. 'I'm getting on a bit now and maybe I shan't be here many years longer. But I've still got my health and there's still summat as I can do. I want to speak in the name of all the other ordinary sort of folks who may be listening at this time . . .' It was an extraordinary time, for in everyone's heart lay the certain knowledge that though nothing much horrible had happened to Britain yet, it lay in wait . . . for whom, and when, none could guess. Some lines from the King's speech put it into words. 'I said to the man who stood at the gate of the year, "Give me a light that I may tread safely into the unknown." And he replied, "Go out into the darkness, and put your head into the hand of God. That shall be to you better than light, and safer than a known way." ' The king had found this sentence in a little book of *pensées* called *God Knows*, written by a middle-aged and hitherto unknown Crowborough poetess named M. Louise Haskins. She was at once immersed in the kind of instant, overwhelming, ephemeral fame that descends on obscure persons who for whatever reason become the target of the communication media. Reporters interviewed her, or tried to, for she was of retiring habit; Hodder and Stoughton speedily got out reprints of her works, and the lines the King quoted sank so deeply into people's memories that after thirty-two years I did not need to look them up in order to write them down.

It was obvious that a second programme, offering with the Home Service a mutually supporting and contrasted alternative, was even more essential in wartime. The question – what kind of alternative should it be? – was answered by the presence in France of large numbers of British troops, the commercial radio station in Fécamp, and the curious popularity of the propaganda talks from Hamburg by Lord Haw-Haw. The troops liked the friendly programmes from Fécamp, and though the station presented no great threat (it could be closed down at any time by the French government, and early in 1940 it was) its popularity set up some sort of challenge which the BBC could and did not wish to ignore. The War Office sent Major Richard Longland, its BBC liaison officer, around the units to find out what sort of stuff the troops liked. They told him they liked news, sport, variety, dance music and crooners, 'because they help us to learn the words of the songs'; and news, sport, variety, dance music and crooners was what the new alternative at first provided. The BBC's Chairman of Governors, Sir Allan Powell, pointed out that though a man did not change his taste when he put on uniform the fact that he listened in groups was bound to affect the kind of programme that was acceptable. 'The BBC is out to give the men the kind of entertainment that they wanted, not what others think is good for them to hear.' As the new programme was to be broadcast throughout Britain as well as to the front, this was a revolutionary statement indeed. The Governors also decided that the BBC's traditional Sunday policy should not be applied to it, thus accepting at last what the BBC's critics had argued for years – that there was no reason why a church service and dance music should not be broadcast on the same day.

The Forces Programme started in February 1940, with the troops in France as its primary audience. In June came Dunkirk, which brought the troops back from France and created an audience no longer separable into troops and civilians; there were only listeners, some of whom listened at home and others in the canteens and messes. The Forces catered for the difference in listening. Planning tried to offer a balanced and contrasted alternative to the Home Service, but started off with the knowledge that when men and women listening in the mess didn't like what the BBC was offering they turned the tuning knob until they got what they wanted, uncaring whether the source was a home or a foreign station and, if foreign, enemy. Mostly they wanted background music. The Germans broadcast a so-called British Forces programme of light music, jazz and news in English; they also presented the BBC with the absurd but curiously formidable competition of Lord Haw-Haw. His appeal was fairly rudimentary, and relied chiefly on the lack of any alternative programme, on the boredom of the phoney war, on the guilty indulgence of the dangerous pleasure of listening to the enemy and a traitor into the bargain, for William Joyce's Irish birth was not publicised until it became a vital part of his defence at his trial. I did not care for his sneering, knowing tone; much stronger arguments would have been needed to shake my belief, based firmly on the facts that had been reaching Britain since 1934 about the cruelties of the régime of bloodthirsty bullies running Germany, that the war was essentially and accurately described as one of liberation. But he won an extraordinarily large following during the period when the BBC was operating one service only. The BBC's Audience Research department* estimated that in December 1939 six million of the sixteen million Britons who heard the BBC's nine o'clock news switched over to Hamburg if the news was followed by a talk. Clearly Haw-Haw called for counter-measures. Luckily the BBC knew its job better than the Government knew its, and resisted suggestions that it should refute him directly on the air. Its answer was to put a popular programme against him whenever possible and, after the Forces Programme was under way, oppose him on the Home with a propaganda talk by some leading Briton. Thus did the enemy plant the seed of the famous *Postscripts* and play some part in emphasising to those in the BBC who may have still doubted it that the interest and attention of the wireless audience in wartime had to be won and kept by considering, as Sir Allen Powell had said, what people wanted.

Maurice Gorham, like many of the men who in 1939 were old BBC hands, believed that by obliging it to consider its box-office returns the coming of war did the BBC a good turn. It obliged it to try different things, which not only attracted new talent to the Corporation but kept the pot boiling too merrily for the administrators (he loathed all administrators) to quench it as they had the ebullience of Savoy Hill. 'The manufacture of frivolity, the construction of laughter, the fabrication of a joke, became matters of high and serious concern',[1] because if the nation did not enjoy its leisure the war effort would suffer. It was pleasant to see how quickly the BBC discovered a tremendous flair for the common or human touch once it had been declared permissible and desirable. The vitally important North American service was one of the early beneficiaries. *Time* magazine in July 1940 praised the new *Britain Speaks* series as 'a vast improvement on the stodgy stuff that BBC used to short wave to North America. With swing bands and torch singers, brisk news and political comments, "Britain Speaks" is at its best when novelist-playwright John Boynton Priestley holds forth'. At home the kind of flexibility indicated in this paragraph was reflected by changes in the news. The readers hung up their dinner jackets and came out of their anonymity. And the most significant fact about this change was that it happened quite casually. John Snagge, who had been transferred to news reading when the war broke up the old outside broadcasting department, said one day in 1940 to S. J. de Lotbinière, then assistant controller of pro-

---

* Audience Research had been started in 1939.

grammes, how farcical it was that the half-dozen news readers, now drawing vast audiences for every bulletin, weren't allowed to put names to such well-known voices. De Lotbinière agreed. Snagge said, 'Well, what do we do, put it up to somebody?' 'No; just do it.' So the following day the nation heard, 'Here is the news, read by Alvar Liddell'. De Lotbinière and Snagge waited for the Board of Management's response. When it came it was only to suggest that the wording was wrong. To say 'read by Alvar Liddell' might lead listeners to suppose that a second voice was going to read it; why not 'here is the news, and this is Alvar Liddell reading it'? Lotbinière, wise in his knowledge of the way things worked within the BBC, warned Snagge that sooner or later it would dawn on somebody that the original change had been made without asking anyone, and that they had better have a reason ready. Snagge instantly thought of the invasion that seemed absolutely inevitable. In Poland the Germans had confused the Poles by imitating Polish broadcasts; what more sensible than that the BBC should make the public thoroughly familiar with the names and voices of Frank Phillips, Alan Howland, Joseph McLeod, Wilfred Allen, Bruce Belfrage, Liddell and Snagge, its most frequent broadcasters? Thus it became official.

In the summer of 1940 Britain was upborne by a surge of protective patriotism which nobody who lived through it can ever forget. A queer thing was that it was neither openly ferocious nor openly patriotic. The nation was possessed by a consciousness of itself as the last defender of freedom, but it saw freedom expressed in idiotic and jocular things which must not be beaten down by the humourless and efficient louts across the Channel. We were certain in our bones that had the Germans succeeded in throwing across an army the people would have defended the island until there was not a stone left to throw; but this emotion was carefully locked away and expressed in self-mocking jokes about war of the kind that stretched back from 1940 to Shakespeare's Falstaff and his recruits. 'Is thy name Mouldy?' 'Yes, an it please you.' ' 'Tis the more time thou wert used.' 'Thomas Wart!' 'Here, sir.' 'Is thy name Wart?' 'Yes, sir.' 'Thou art a very ragged wart.' 'What trade art thou, Feeble?' 'A woman's tailor, sir.' 'Wilt thou make as many holes in an enemy's battle as thou hast done in a woman's petticoat?' 'I will do my good will, sir: you can have no more.' 'Well said, good woman's tailor! Well said, courageous Feeble! Thou wilt be as valiant as the wrathful dove or most magnanimous mouse.'

Between this and Robb Wilton's comic monologues about the Home Guard there was no measurable difference in anything but time. 'The first day I got my uniform I went home and put it on. The Missus looked at me and said, "What are you supposed to be?" I said, "Supposed to be? I'm one of the Home Guards." She said, "One of the Home Guards? What are the others like?" She said, "What are you supposed to do?" I said, "I'm supposed to stop Hitler's Army landing." She said, "What, you?" I said, "No, not just me, there's Bob Edwards, Charlie Evans, Billy Brightside – there's seven or eight of us. We're in a group, we're on guard in a little hut behind the Dog and Pullet." ' A quality in Churchill's famous broadcasts to which not enough attention has been paid is that along with the exalting oratory they often contained some good jokes, usually in the form of a zestful insolence towards the enemy. The imminence of danger bucked most people up; better still, people began to lose their fear of the puritan tyranny that controls so many small but important things in Britain, such as the hours when you can keep open a shop or buy a drink in a pub. When rules were sensible they were scrupulously kept; the queues at the fishmonger's never lost their respect for order. But Londoners defied the bureaucratic clods who barred the entrances to the Underground station platforms; and in pubs on a noisy night of bombs closing time was when the night began to quieten, not when the book said.

We felt exhilarated by the feeling that we were all in the same boat (some compartments, we learned afterwards, were better fitted out than others). Suddenly the wireless began to sound like the nation talking to itself: in the accents of *In Britain Now, The Kitchen Front, Music While You Work, Women in War, Go To It, These You Have Loved, Band Wagon* and *Hi Gang!*, the Churchill speeches and the Priestley postscripts. Memory insists that *ITMA* was there too, but history recalls that the most famous of wartime comedy series was off the air from February 1940 until June 1941.

The Postscripts began in March, following the Nine O'clock News on the Home Service as a counter attraction to Haw-Haw. Their first series, by the barrister and wine buff Maurice Healey, was mildly successful; then, with Dunkirk, J. B. Priestley began to put into words some of the thoughts about their country and the war that his fellow countrymen ardently desired to have said. His theme, too, was that of small, friendly, precious, familiar things endangered by mindless Teutonic louts. He saw what we all saw – for instance, that the extraordinary part of Dunkirk was the brilliant improvisation of a fleet of all the ships, including the little pleasure steamers that until then had never carried anything but passengers on holiday. 'Yes, those "Brighton Belles" and "Brighton Queens" left that innocent foolish world of theirs to sail into the inferno, to defy bombs, shells, magnetic mines, torpedoes, machine-gun fire, to rescue our soldiers. Some of them – alas – will never return.' He talked about one of them, the 'Gracie Fields' that used to ply between the Isle of Wight and the mainland. 'But now – look – this little steamer, like all her brave and battered sisters, is immortal. She'll go sailing proudly down the years in the epic of Dunkirk. And our great grand-children, when they learn how we began this war by snatching glory out of defeat, and then swept on to victory, may also learn how the little holiday steamers made an excursion to hell and came back glorious.'

He talked about his night out with the Local Defence Volunteers – the Home Guard as they were later named – from the point of view of a countryman for whom raids and invasions were only the latest manifestation of the everlasting menace – 'sudden blizzards at lambing time, or floods just before the harvest' – to be met with the resolution of simple but sane men. 'Well, as we talked on our post on the hilltop, we watched the dusk deepen in the valleys below, where our womenfolk listened to the news as they knitted by the hearth, and we remembered that these were our homes and that now at any time they might be blazing ruins and that half-crazy German youths, in whose empty eyes the idea of honour and glory seems to include every form of beastliness, might soon be let loose down there.' He returned to the theme of precious continuity in a talk about a duck who'd managed to ferry her brood to a pond on Hampstead Heath. 'She hadn't asked anybody's advice or permission; nobody had told her to "Go to it" and that "it all depended on her". She had gone to it, a triumphant little servant of that life, mysterious, fruitful, beautiful, which expresses itself as a man writes a poem – now in vast galaxies of flaming suns, now in a tiny brood of ducklings squeaking on a pond in the dusk.'

A Bradford pie-shop had once beguiled the nose of the boy Priestley with its smell of rich and appetising steam, apparently emitted from a huge pie in the window. The pie and the steam survived the blitz on Bradford. 'Every puff and jet of that steam defied Hitler, Goering, and the whole gang of them. It was glorious.' To the literal-minded dullards who might have been puzzled by Priestley's carrying on about pies while the world seemed to be shaking itself to pieces, he replied with a passage that summed up, in a sense, the nation's war aims. 'We must keep burnished the bright little thread of our common humanity that still runs through these iron days and black nights; [and that] we are fighting to preserve and, indeed, I hope to enlarge that private and all important little world of our own reminiscence and humour and homely poetry in which a pie that steamed for forty-five years and successfully defied an air raid to steam again has its own proper place.'

How these passages sound to readers under thirty-five I cannot tell. Those over forty who heard them in 1940 will find it impossible to disconnect the words from their images of that time. Spoken in a voice as rich and unpretentious as a good Christmas pudding, by a writer who had a born dramatist's ear for the spoken word and was instinctively in touch with what most of his hearers felt, their effect was overwhelming. Priestley's audience grew to more than twenty million; he became so popular that he could not enter a shop or a bar without the people thanking him, talking to him – even touching him, as if he were one of the Wesleys a hundred years earlier. As his popularity grew he developed in his broadcasts the vein of social comment and criticism that ran through all his best work. It could be summed up as a refusal to forget, in the middle of all the excitement, that things were wrong with Britain that ought to be put right, and a stubborn insistence that the preservation of Britain against the enemy did not include the preservation of systems that had tolerated slums and unemployment, that a return to peace must bring a fairer share-out.

He had always been a political writer. To those who had read *Good Companions, Angel Pavement, English Journey*, or had seen his fine plays of the mid-thirties such as *Time and the Conways, I have been here before, Johnson over Jordan, Bees on the Boatdeck*, his talks were consistent and to be expected. I, and virtually everybody I knew, felt enormously uplifted by the presence of this powerful voice. He said what most of us knew was right and just: that houses left empty by owners who had gone to America ought to be requisitioned; that it was all very well to cheer the RAF fighter pilots as long as we determined that when the war was won they would not be returned to the economic jungle as their fathers had been; he extended the symbolism of the Bradford pie: it was a national property that should be opened out and shared. The attack on private property assaulted the cornerstone of the capitalist system, and he came under the fire of those who said what a pity he was getting himself mixed up in politics – by which, of course, they meant that they were not going to sit by while a man with a vast audience used his platform on the BBC to put across views they did not agree with. There is nobody the politician fears and resents more, as though he were being taken an unfair advantage of, than the artist who can reach the public with his vision of a better way to run the country.

In January 1941 Priestley began a further series of talks, longer and more sharply pointed than the others but still developing the thesis that the war must be won in order to build a better Britain, not to return to the old one, and still sounding the authentic voice of Us, the people, against Them, the faceless grey men who were always trying to confine the quality of life within a frame that matched their own narrow expectations from it. As the old Britain had been almost wholly the responsibility of Tory governments the talks were inescapably political. The Tory newspapers turned openly hostile and assured their readers that Priestley had talked himself into a fantasy world and nobody was listening to him any more (in fact the figures were as high as ever). It was inevitable that he should be stopped, and stopped he was after six talks. He was never told who gave the order (he had one letter from the Ministry of Information, another from the BBC, each explaining that the other was responsible), but the minutes of a meeting of the BBC's board of management recorded on 21 March: 'Priestley series stopping . . . on instructions of Minister.'[2] He was replaced by among others

A. P. Herbert, who saddened his admirers by taking the side of Priestley's opponents. Silenced at home Priestley continued to be one of the war's most successful presenters of the British cause in the BBC's overseas services. By 1942 his name in the USA had become a household word. But no home speakers ever again captured the hearts and minds of his audience so completely. It was a rotten end to such a bright episode, and explains a certain ambiguity in Priestley's attitude to the Postscripts. He wrote long afterwards that these talks, which usually took him between half an hour and an hour to write, had set out to provide spoken essays designed to have a very broad and classless appeal and had been ridiculously overpraised. He claimed that he'd never been able to see what all the fuss was about. But I believe that he was secretly proud of his success; and why shouldn't he have been? He had always aimed as a writer at expressing complex thought in a style that put him instantly within reach of the crowd, and in the Postscripts he reached it as no popular author had done since Dickens. He referred obliquely to them in an essay called 'Too Simple':[3] 'No matter what the subject in hand might be, I wanted to write something that at a pinch I could read aloud in a bar parlour. And the time came when I was heard and understood in a thousand bar parlours.'

Later that spring the chord of love of country was sharply twanged by an American poetess, Alice Duer Miller, whose 'The White Cliffs of Dover' as read on the air by Constance Cummings was one of the great popular successes of 1941. Reading the poem now you have to imagine, if you can, that period between August 1940 and June 1941, when this small off-shore island really and truly was the only unconquered defender of European civilisation. The thought of Britain finished and dead did not, as far as I recall, ever occur to the British, but it seemed an agonising possibility to friends across the Atlantic. This emotion Alice Duer Miller captured in her poem and the British found it peculiarly gratifying to hear.

> I have loved England dearly and deeply
> Since that first morning, shining and pure,
> The white cliffs of Dover I saw rising steeply,
> Out of the sea that once made her secure.
> I had no thought then of husband or lover
> I was a traveller, the guest of a week,
> Yet when they pointed the white cliffs of Dover
> Startled, I found there were tears on my cheek.
> I have loved England, still as a stranger,
> Here is my home, and I still am alone,
> Now in her hour of toil and danger,
> Only the English are really her own.

It was the winter of the bombs. I had joined the Observer Corps that autumn and had a grandstand view of the blitz from top of Ruxley Towers, Claygate, the wartime seat of NAAFI. Nearly every night brought the pandemonium of throbbing bombers, the ear-splitting crack of anti-aircraft ('ROLL OUT THE BARRAGE', exulted an inspired *Daily Express* banner headline), the always questing and so rarely finding searchlights, the sudden rushing wind of bombs, white sheets of explosion and the red glare of fires – near enough for one to feel dangerously exposed but not so near that one seemed to be the bombers' personal quarry. I watched the sky only a few miles to the north-east, and knew I was lucky to be where I was. The embattled BBC was operating a 24-hour broadcasting service from the huge battleship-shaped, sandbagged and camouflaged building in Portland Place. One night a time bomb crashed through the inner studio tower into the third floor and went off when somebody tried to move it. Bruce Belfrage had just read the headlines of the Nine O'Clock News and announced that the talk after it would be given by Lord Lloyd when the ceiling began to descend on his head. Listeners heard the bang; then silence; then somebody said, 'Are you all right?' Belfrage repeated that the talk would be given by Lord Lloyd. It was his only fluff. He then carried on with the bulletin as calmly as though the interruption had been no more than a heavy cough. This was the first of three bad bomb incidents at Broadcasting House; but the peacetime plans to keep the service going worked superbly. Unlike the German wireless the BBC was never bombed off the air, and never once in the five and a half years of war did the news, for which the people developed a hunger that became a thirst, fail to go out on time. Howard Thomas, travelling to London in December from Bristol in one of those awful long-drawn-out train journeys, was impressed by the solidity of the BBC. 'Steady voices continued to read the news, dance bands kept up their cheerful tunes and the voice of Britain carried hope and encouragement to the Europe which had been engulfed by the Nazi torrent.' Thomas was about to do his bit himself. On Christmas Eve he recorded an experimental session of a programme he had called 'Any Questions?' or, as it came to be known, 'The Brains Trust'.

2

BRAINS OVER BRITAIN

A myth has grown round the success of *The Brains Trust*, to the effect that under the wits-sharpening stimulus of war the nation sat down regularly to hear five men discussing art, philosophy and science. It was true in a way. Begun as a display of knowledge presented in a casual form, it developed into a huge conversation between the members of the Trust and their fellow countrymen. It was framed to meet the demand that the BBC's researchers had noted among the forces for information. (A good lecturer could hold any army mess hall with a straightforward talk on how a thing worked.) Time hung heavily on the young men and women who had been called into the army but in the winter of 1940–1 had nowhere to fight except in North Africa. Management asked for an informative programme that would give the men on the barrage balloon sites (cited because it was about the dullest job of the home defence war) something to talk about. It had the fortunate inspiration of handing the brief to John Watt's Variety Department, with the proviso that the producer he chose must collaborate with a producer from Features. Features picked Douglas Cleverdon, who was to become one of the giants of Third Programme feature and drama production of the fifties. Variety picked Howard Thomas, the future managing director of ABC and Thames TV. The pair went away to shape Watt's instruction that 'it must be serious in intention, light in character' into a programme.

The thought was that Cleverdon's higher-browed approach to broadcasting, and Thomas's experience in the hard world of commercial radio (he had produced programmes from Luxembourg and Normandy before the war) would produce a kind of Chinese metaphysics combination and support and restrain each other. It worked quite well. Thomas thought of the idea of inviting listeners to send in questions to a panel – 'spontaneous answers by interesting people', he said. He thought of the subtitle, *The Brains Trust*, which quickly replaced the official title. Cleverdon's chief contribution was his emphatic insistence on the importance of making it an intelligent programme, in which questions would lead to worthwhile discussion rather than just a straight answer. The choice of the three resident members and the permanent chairman led to some edgy discussion, but proved to be the collaborators' most inspired stroke.

Julian Huxley, a biologist of world reputation, was unanimously picked to uphold science. Cleverdon stuck out for Cyril Joad, a short, brown nut of a man with a high, cackling voice which some thought must prove fatal to the programme's hopes. He was head of philosophy and psychology at London University's Birkbeck College, with a solid if limited reputation as an academician and Left-Wing populariser. He was a good teacher whose most immediately noticeable gift was an unquenchable one of the gab. Thomas stuck out for a Question Master (he thought 'chairman' was pompous and 'compère' imprecise) who would be unabashable, tactful and witty without being a comedian. He brought in Donald McCullough, an advertising man and much-sought after-dinner speaker. A graduate of Edinburgh University, McCullough had filled in time as a Hoover salesman, so successfully that he won a trip on the *Queen Mary* to New York. His gift for telling funny stories endeared him to a fellow-traveller, who engaged him on the spot as advertising manager for Austin Reed. Once launched in the craft McCullough rose like a rocket. (Ancient readers may remember the witty 'Men About Regent Street' campaign he wrote for Austin Reed.) Thomas, then a £6-a-week copywriter in the same firm, was dazzled by this brilliant person, who could dictate in ten minutes a piece of copy that Thomas said would have taken him a day to write. McCullough became known to the wider public as author of a very funny book about motoring, illustrated by Fougasse and called *You have been Warned*.

Thomas's *coup de maître* was his choice of the third resident. He was convinced that the programme had to find common ground between the panel of experts and the vast unknown mass of listeners. To that end he sought a man who was not an expert in anything but knew a bit about everything and could hold his own among experts without selfconsciousness. This role was awarded to a retired sailor, Paymaster Commander A. B. Campbell, who played it with as much glorious distinction as if it had been reserved for him from his cradle. Together the three formed a superbly matched combination of opposing traits. They used to remind me of the animals in Kenneth Grahame's *Wind in the Willows*; Joad was the volatile Mole; Campbell was the resourceful and calm Ratty; and Huxley was Badger, to whose moral eminence the others unconsciously deferred. I do not think it too fanciful to suggest that the programme succeeded because Thomas and Cleverdon reproduced by thinking about it the kind of artistic symmetry that Grahame's genius had led him to. Another of their strokes was to select the residents in terms of human balance, not political. They picked Joad because he was a brilliant talker, not because he was Left; Campbell because he would complement and provoke the others, not because he was to Joad's right. In Thomas's own book[1] the need for political balance is nowhere mentioned. Today it would have to be a producer's second thought.

Behold them, then, on the threshold of fame such as they could never have dreamed of since childhood. It is Wednesday afternoon on the first day of January 1941. The effect of the pre-programme lunch at the Savoy still benevolently lubricates the assembly, which includes J. F. Horrabin, the geographer, and Jean McLachlan, a colleague of McCullough's who is substituting for a guest who has failed to show up. The hands of the clock run up to the 'Go' signal; a little pool of apprehensive silence forms, into which McCullough tosses the first question: 'What are the seven wonders of the world?' Between them the brains manage to remember five; McCullough fills in the other two by consulting the official answer.

It was exactly the type of question calculated to prevent the general conversation Thomas and Cleverdon had hoped for, but later questions produced the characteristic style of contribution. Campbell inserted into a discussion on hypnosis, 'Hypnosis is most beneficial. I knew a man who put his wife to sleep at weekends.' He used to say these things without the slightest intention of being funny; he was merely offering an interesting piece of information. Joad got in a snappy anecdote about Gladstone and Faraday: 'What is the good of this electric machine, Mr Faraday?' 'What is the use of a baby? You can't tell till it grows up.'

In the *Daily Mail* next morning Collie Knox prophesied that the programme would be one of the most popular of radio features. The listening public immediately began to prove him right. By the end of January the producers were receiving thirty questions a day. After three programmes the signs were propitious enough for the BBC to extend the show's run beyond the planned six. It went on to make eighty-four programmes without a break; but the point of take-off was when it was moved from Wednesday afternoons to the perfect hour for it, four o'clock on Sunday. It began to clock up audiences of ten to twelve million. It became part of the nation's life, spilling its influence outside radio as no other programme before or since. The answers the Trust gave afforded texts for sermons, leading articles, letters to the newspapers. The number of letters and cards reached 3000 a week, a figure equalled only by the requests sent to the long-playing organist Sandy McPherson; and the peculiar thing about them was their comparatively small proportion of messages and grumbles from people with grievances and obsessions. The valuable thing, said Thomas, was not so much their questions as the comments they scrawled at the end; the listeners felt closely involved. The format they had devised was copied everywhere; there were Rotary Club brains trusts, church brains trusts, forces brains trusts, village brains trusts at which the speakers were not minor celebrities from outside but the leaders of the community, the doctor, the vicar, the schoolmaster. No programme in the history of broadcasting was so widely publicised until, said Thomas, he reached a moment which as an old advertising man he would have declared impossible – the moment when he flinched when he saw the name of the product in the headlines.

In the first year the star was undoubtedly Joad. He had modelled himself on Shaw, whom he revered, and had Shaw's ability to talk lucidly on almost any subject. We were flummoxed by the breadth of his knowledge, the lightness with which he seemed to carry it, and exhilarated as we had been by Priestley to hear a man who seemed to be clothing in vigorous and colourful language our own thoughts, and able to light up old controversies with argument that seemed to us astonishingly novel and audacious. The answer he gave when the Trust was asked to define civilisation typified what folk enjoyed about Joad. 'I should say that a civilised society was one in which, first, a large proportion of the community cared for and valued for its own sake; secondly, had good taste, that is to say were sensitive to beauty and valued beauty; and thirdly, maintained a high level of moral conduct among themselves and in particular respected the civilised virtues of tolerance, compassion, mercy, justice and understanding. Now if you have a society which in relation to those three values, namely truth, beauty and goodness, does in respect of a large number of its members honour them, pursue them and in its daily life try to practise them, then I should call that a civilised society, even if it was comparatively poor, and even if it had very few mechanical contrivances at its command.' A sub-editor could have cleaned up the passage here and there, but as an off-the-cuff performance it is a virtuosic display. There fell upon him a thunderous popular acclaim. His books sold as fast as they could be reprinted. Mounted police had to shepherd him into lecture halls and out of them afterwards. The phrase he used to give himself time to think – 'It depends what you mean by ...' – was appropriated by comedians and political cartoonists. The suitability of his name for punning inspired the Ministry of Food to call one of its terrible wartime dishes Joad-in-the-hole. The *Sunday Dispatch* signed him up to answer more questions in print. He made a cinema commercial for tea. His clothes – he affected the rustic look – his beard and alert, bright expression made him by far the most photogenic of the four regulars; most of his letters were from women, though his sceptical attitude to religion bought him a good deal of lunatic abuse and many thumping tracts.

Huxley had been brought in to supply a prop of scientific prestige which would give the show standing among its more serious-minded hearers, and at the same time to suffer sparks to be knocked off him by Joad and Campbell. He had in the early programmes a rather chilling manner of putting colleagues down, but his popularity though slower in coming was thereafter never shaken. He never made much money out of his success but enjoyed a very solid correspondence, leavened for some reason by the manuscripts of unpublished writers.

It was of course the interaction of temperament and background that gave the Trust's members the chance to shine. On his own, Campbell had been a modestly successful broadcaster (usually as a teller of tall stories) from the early days. He claimed to have been the first man to break down the rule requiring speakers to use a script, a feat considered so remarkable that when Reith heard of it he asked Campbell if he could bring a party along to the studio and watch him the next time he did it.★ He earned a reputation as a broadcaster who was never at a loss. Among the other Brains, as the representative of common sense and personal observation, he shone from the start. His chief weapon was a calm confidence in himself, the source of which he once explained in a programme; 'I am very far from well-read, in fact I've read very little, but I've travelled extensively, and met lots of interesting people and talked with them, and it seems to me that that's as great an educator as reading omnivorously. People who have read quite a lot are very rarely original – they're second-hand in their ideas. You hear them talking, and you say to yourself, "Well, that's not their idea; it's an idea they've got from some book." ' Thus armed for any encounter Campbell never minded opposing what he'd seen with his own eyes to Huxley's scientific knowledge or Joad's philosophical sallies. He also sounded many of the ordinary listener's prejudices: he thought women teachers were bad for boys, that bright pupils did not do well in later life, that character mattered more than brains, and so on; he believed in ghosts, telepathy and sea-serpents (he claimed to have seen one, adding that it stank horribly), and disapproved of medical interference with natural healing processes. His opening phrase 'When I was in . . .' (usually some extraordinary spot) became a national catchphrase, still not quite obsolete. Joad used to egg him on mischievously. Huxley registered impatience. They had a famous and characteristic clash when a listener wanted to know how it was that when a gale was blowing at eighty or ninety miles an hour and blowing down big trees and fences a little bird was able to fly against it. Huxley pointed out that the bird might be flying against it but relative to the ground it would be going backwards, and that anyway most birds didn't fly in such conditions. But Campbell said, and stuck to it, that he had seen birds flying against an Atlantic gale and making progress relative to the boat Campbell was in. Huxley vainly insisted that tests had shown that no bird could make progress against a gale that was blowing stronger than its maximum speed.

He was totally irrepressible. A notorious teetotaller declined his offer of a pre-programme drink: 'I'm afraid you don't know who I am. I am Lady Astor.' Campbell merely said: 'Glad to meet you. Come on, just one little snifter. Just what you need.' But his unique contribution was his reduction

★ Claims to have been the first man to give an unscripted talk have also been made for Lord Birkenhead (F. E. Smith) and Hugh Walpole. I have to let it go at that.

of discussion to anecdotage. Nobody now remembers what the rest of the panel thought about allergies, but everyone remembers Campbell's story about a friend who was allergic to marmalade; when he had it for breakfast steam rose from the top of his head. He also claimed to be able to sleep with his eyes wide open, to communicate the sight of mirages by touch, to have solved the mystery of the *Marie Celeste*, and to have dreamed accurately the next day's Derby winner. Once the Trust was asked to name the most beautiful words in the English language. After Dr Ernest Barker had chosen 'felicity', Rose Macaulay 'oblivion', and Joad 'over the hills and far away', Campbell came up with 'paraffin', explaining that he liked words that were easy to speak and conveyed the sound of the word rather than its sense.

Thomas loved Campbell because he was always outspoken and unafraid, 'as generous, straight, kind, simple and big-hearted as he sounded'. This was the spell he cast over the unseen and, when the programme was rested and he took off on a music-hall tour, the seen audience. He simply walked on to the stage in blue suit and steel-rimmed glasses, told some stories and held the audience in the palm of his hand. To Thomas, a man steeped in show business who knew how difficult it was, it was uncanny to watch Campbell, without any experience at all of the theatre, doing it so easily.

McCullough's renown rested on his urbane and witty introductions of the panel and the capacity to deal with guests who sought to hog the show, though in this task he was, as we now say, on a black eye to nothing, for however smoothly he silenced someone he was sure to get as many letters protesting against his rudeness as praising his tact. I enjoyed and admired him, for his wit had to be more independent of the questions that fed the others. Huxley took to the showbiz razzmatazz very unwillingly, but became as it were the cornerstone. During the first eighteen months the programme was produced alternately by Thomas and Cleverdon (when Cleverdon was in the driving seat the questions were more serious). Then B. E. Nicholls, the Controller of Programmes, decided that the programme should be responsible directly to him, in London. Thereafter Thomas ran it on his own, bearing the distinction, which his colleagues neither envied nor begrudged, of being the only BBC producer who worked directly under the Controller of Programmes. Every week he submitted to Nicholls the names of the people he proposed to use and the questions he had previously selected. Censorship was of two kinds, based on the need for security and the need to preserve accepted notions of good taste. The latter was concerned almost exclusively with religion and bodily functions. Thomas was once formally rebuked by the Programme Board for failing to control an appearance by Phyllis Dixie, a celebrated striptease artist of the period, in *Shipmates Ashore*, another of his programmes. He was censured for allowing her to use the phrase 'tea and crumpet' – the rebuke went on: 'However, if the word had been used in the plural there would have been no objection.'

When the programme began to gain its huge audience Joad wanted to include more serious questions, preferably about philosophy. Why did Thomas want to go on widening the audience instead of settling down with the audience he had won? But Thomas knew that an audience cannot be held, it can only be increased or lost; he knew that the programme would fade away if it ceased to reflect the larger public; he knew that a balance between the serious and the frivolous had to be kept. An emphatic demonstration of this happened when somebody asked if separation from mother and home (the Government was opening nursery schools for mothers in war work) was good or bad for children. The Trust unanimously commended separation, adding that in its opinion very few parents were fit to bring up children. Even Campbell concurred. The mass public considered itself outraged and it might have gone hard with the programme if Thomas had not restored good humour next week with one of his questions that seemed frivolous but always stirred a national discussion: 'Why do cattle rise from a recumbent posture hind legs first and horses forelegs first?' He had 500 letters about that one.

The war had no softening effect on the prudishness of the public. Joad offended with an aphorism attributed to Confucius: 'What economy is it to go to bed in order to save candlelight if the result be twins?' Objections to this got as far as a question in the Commons by a notorious wowser MP, Mr Mathers; he asked Brendan Bracken, the Minister of Information, what steps he had taken to prevent a repetition of this disgusting occurrence. Thomas rejected questions which he thought too delicate, such as 'How do snakes mate?', 'Why do men have nipples?' and 'What age does *The Brains Trust* think suitable for girls to have boy friends and vice versa?'

His principle for choosing questions was to begin with a broad one which would attract listeners and encourage all the panel to have a go at it. The next two would be chosen to give the guests of the week a chance to dazzle. The fourth would be important and serious but would involve the audience, such as: 'My son is a prisoner of war. I can send him one book, which should it be?' He sat at the table with the Trust in the role of ordinary listener and producer, feeding McCullough little notes: 'Bring in question nine next.' 'Don't let Gould return to the question.' 'Let Huxley sum up.' He studied listeners' letters with the care of an intelligence officer monitoring the enemy's broadcasts, listening for the first hint of boredom. Acting on what his antennae told him, the Trust was taken off in July 1942, after its unprecedented eighteen-month run; and when it was brought back the number of resident brains was increased from three to nine, with a consequent reduction in the appearances of the three pioneer stars. Some newspaper critics predicted that this must inevitably destroy the programme, but Thomas wanted to preserve the popularity of Joad, Campbell and Huxley and had noticed that it had begun to wear a little thin under their prolonged exposure. He further refreshed the format by adding a monthly transatlantic session and introducing 'Second Thoughts' and 'Open Question'. The first was designed to give the brains a chance to correct or develop original answers. The second was a concession to listeners who thought the Brains would do better if they were told a question in advance. (Thomas was always certain that they were wrong, that spontaneity was essential.) 'Second Thoughts' produced a famous contribution from Joad, when he told how he had taken part in a strange experiment in lifting a fat man in a pub. Four persons put two fingers each under each of his armpits and two fingers each under his knees. They tried to lift him and failed. They placed their hands on his head, forming a little pyramid, pressed down for half a minute, then replaced their fingers under his knees and arms; whereon, said Joad, the man went up like a feather. For the next week the pubs within the embattled island were filled with fat men sailing towards the ceiling. 'Open Question' was less successful, but produced Malcolm Sargent's celebrated reply to the question: 'If you were a fairy godmother at the christening of a baby girl, what five qualities or attributes would you bestow upon her in the hope of ensuring her a full and happy life?' As it happened Sargent had not prepared anything, but gained widespread popularity by including faith in Christianity among his gifts. Religion provided Thomas with some ticklish situations, for Huxley argued on behalf of humanism so forcefully that he seemed to floor his opponents. This couldn't be allowed and religion, except in a very broad metaphysical sense, was put outside the show's limits. The BBC's Religious Department produced *The Anvil*, in which they paid Thomas the compliment of reproducing his format but packed the panel entirely with strong Christian believers. In the absence of any representative of the opposition the programme sagged badly, as Thomas had said it would.

Outside sex and religion *The Brains Trust* certainly did not shrink from publicising controversial opinions. It retained its hold because it fed the great hunger we had during the war to hear voices that sounded honest, unbought, trustworthy. A list of the names that appeared in the wartime sessions of the Trust would read like a line-up of the nation's eminent, though of course it did not include eminent folk who for one reason or another were no good at it or did not choose to appear. The significant thing about it was that it maintained the non-political stance; the eminent came from all the professions; indeed the breadth of interests represented was equalled only by that represented by the listeners and those who sent in questions. One day they broadcast two questions in succession from Yorkshire listeners. One was from Jack Haigh, a Bradford coalman, who wanted to know 'Is my horse Ezra pulling or shoving the two-ton load of coal he moves?' The next was from the Earl of Harewood, who asked why some bees worked only on yellow crocuses and others only on purple. Questions of this sort were the means by which the programme kept in touch with its audience. Some of them were gems. A little girl from Gloucestershire sent in one that is still not possible to read without being touched by its innocence and its affection. It was also, please notice, well suited to provoke philosophical–theological–biological discussion. She told of her friend's dog. 'He is kind to smaller dogs, has never fought any dog although he is strong, he does not steal, he is clean and obedient and never chases cats. He hasn't any faults. How is he so good when human beings have to have clergymen and books?' If I had to select one question which illustrated better than any other the relationship *The Brains Trust* established with the people, that would be it.

You have to remember that the public expected to be taken seriously, and resented flippancy as much as lubricity. Thomas and McCullough had to be very stern with guests who mistook the occasion and gave jocular answers to serious questions, or did not obey the rules which assisted good order and manners. In the latter women were the chief offenders. Having been subjugated by the masculocracy within the BBC since its foundation women naturally felt self-conscious and on trial, and tended to emerge (remember that they were always outnumbered) as nervy and bossy. Mary Agnes Hamilton, MP, habitually crashed in unannounced and out of turn.

When they were good they were very good indeed; Jennie Lee and Barbara Ward in particular combined wit, articulacy, knowledge, firm opinions with a delightfully attractive radio presence in which, though you couldn't see them, the male members of the panel seemed to cavort and display. Anna Neagle was another who made a high score by standing up to the critic Hannen Swaffer, whose manner may have been pungent and was certainly boorish. But the Trust remained principally a vehicle for the men, a maker of fresh reputations for some who had already established themselves in their field. Malcolm Sargent and Kenneth Clark were two of these, and Churchill's doctor, later Lord Moran, would have been another had it not been for the rule requiring doctors to remain unidentified. A few listeners caught on, noticing that whenever Churchill was out of the country the doctor disappeared from the programme. The most idiosyncratic, and a rival to Campbell as a much-travelled seafarer, was Lt Commander Rupert Gould. Thomas hired him after hearing some of his talks (a collection of odd little facts) in Children's Hour. Listeners were baffled and awed by his apparent omniscience. He explained to Thomas that he never forgot anything he had read, seeing as it were the actual page of the book. When invited to give a 'Second Thoughts' he declined on the ground that so far he had made no mistakes. Nor had he: no listener had ever written to correct anything Gould had said. He was a curious chap, a genuine English eccentric.

The record for the dullest answers was held by the lawyer, Sir Patrick Hastings. Thomas tried to tempt him with questions calculated to draw him out, but without success. He once gave a terse reply to the question, 'What is the difference between libel and slander?', explaining when Thomas asked him why he had been so reticent, 'You must remember that I am paid very large fees for answering questions like those.'

Omniscience was far from essential equipment, for the listeners liked to hear the Trust stumped particularly on questions that sounded simple. They did not know why a nod for 'Yes' and a shake for 'No' was universally recognised language; on what principle the zip-fastener worked; the origin of handclapping as applause; how red was chosen to warn of danger and green of safety; or how many words were in the average Englishman's vocabulary. On the other hand they did know why a boomerang came back to its thrower.

In 1943 Thomas left the BBC following a row about another type of talk show he had devised called 'Everybody's Mike'. This employed a quiz formula. In the first programme six MPs, three women and three men, answered questions on parliamentary procedure. According to the then Quintin Hogg, one of the six, they had been misled into supposing that they were to appear in a variety of *Brains Trust*; and when it turned out that they weren't he complained to the Governor on the ground that even if Members of Parliament were willing to part with their dignity it was not proper that they should do so on the air, and the BBC should have known better. The Director-General, R. W. Foot, agreed, the recording was scrapped and Thomas ticked off. According to him the request to scrub the programme came from another of the six only after all of them had failed badly in the quiz. He took Foot's decision as unacceptable censorship and resigned, whereupon the BBC removed his name from the credits attached to the *Brains Trust* production. Without him the programme carried on until May 1949, by which time it was aiding the establishment of another famous broadcaster – Gilbert Harding, inheritor of McCullough's role of question master. It was heard no more until 1955, when Thomas, by then a powerful figure within the Associated British Picture Corporation, accepted an invitation from Cecil McGivern, the programme controller of BBC TV, to produce a TV version. The Home Service carried the sound track. But by the mid-fifties the *Brains Trust* had become an entertainment for the minority. As a great popular and serious programme – 'serious in intention, light in character' John Watt had said – its wave had passed.

3

THE MANUFACTURE OF FRIVOLITY

From about 1941 the quality of the small talk in the pubs, the factories, the fish queues and the shops in Britain received some enrichment. Thus a man entering a pub might exclaim: 'Good morning! Nice day!' If the landlord were in a good humour (and he would have been a churl if he weren't, for the pubs did a roaring, shouting trade from 1939 to 1945) he might respond with 'Can I do you now, sir?', to which the reply could be 'I'll have to ask me dad,' or 'After you, Claud.' Possibly these exchanges awaken some faint glow of recognition in the minds of readers under 40; for the older they will be as starshells lighting up a landscape. They were catchphrases from *ITMA*, the most popular variety show in broadcasting history; they and a hundred like them became a kind of instant repartee, understood and enjoyed by the entire population with the possible exception of one or two judges who might have asked, if it had ever been put to them in court, 'What *is* an Itma?'

ITMA began on instruction from John Watt; he wanted another comedy series to back up *Bandwagon*, and he wanted a starring vehicle for Tommy Handley, who in 1938 was firmly established as a radio star but had not yet made the important change from single spot to series. The first idea never got off the ground; it was to put Tommy into an English version of the American Burns and Allen show, with Celia Eddy, a Canadian actress, as the female half. Tommy's instinct for what would suit him preserved him from this one; he asked Ted Kavanagh if he could think of something else. Kavanagh and he had been friends since the early days, when Kavanagh, a hungry scriptwriter, adjusted his headphones one evening to hear Handley broadcasting a sketch Ted had sold to the BBC about a listener who rushed home to hear the Cup Final, dropped off to sleep, and got the commentaries on the Boat Race and the Grand National instead. The pattern hammered out by Kavanagh, Handley and producer Francis Worsley had Tommy as a kind of entertainments officer on a kind of cruise ship, with Celia Eddy as his secretary, Cilly, and Eric Egan as a mad Russian inventor, Vladivostooge. The title was appropriated by Handley from a catchphrase 'It's That Man Again!' created by the *Daily Express* as a headline, intended to reassure by belittling, for some story about Hitler's carryings on. The title, and a certain maniacal play on words, contained the germ of the huge success, but when the first programme went out in July 1939 no great blare of trumpets greeted it or the three that followed it before the war swept schedules off the board and swept Variety to Bristol, where the overworked Handley and Worsley and the underworked Kavanagh were rescued from doubts about the series' future by being summarily instructed to reopen it on 19 September. This time it had Vera Lennox as Dotty, the secretary, Jack Train as Fusspot the civil servant, Maurice Denham as the Russian inventor (renamed Vodkin for some reason), Jack Hylton's Band with a young vocalist, as they called them then, named Sam Costa. The cruise had vanished and Tommy was Minister of Aggravation and Twerps. Because of a temporary rash of public service initials – MOI, WVS, ARP, etc., It's That Man Again was shortened to ITMA.

Whether the script is funny for those who never heard it I cannot say; but it recalls the authentic flavour and for me brings back the very voices and style.

Tommy: Heil folks – it's Mein Kampf again – sorry, I should say hello, folks, it's that man again. That was a Goebbled version – a bit doctored. I usually go all goosey when I can't follow my proper-gander ... (phone rings) Hello – yes – this is ITMA ... no – sorry, the pigeon post is late today, the postman ate the express messenger, feathers and all. I haven't had a word from any of my spies. When I get those spies [those pies] here I won't mince my words, I can tell you. Ring me up again when I'm out. Goodbye or, as they say in Pomerania, 'arf window-screen. Now, where's my new secretary?

Vera: Here I am, Mr Handtorch.

Tommy: Well, puncture me with a portfolio. Are you my new secretary?

Vera: Yes. I'm Dotty.

Tommy: I'm balmy myself. My last secretary was Cilly and you're Dotty.

Vera: Cilly was my sister.

Tommy: Well, splash my spats. Cilly was your sister? I'll have to see a silly-sister – a lawyer – about this.

Jack Train's catch-phrase 'It's most irregular, most irregular' failed to ignite, but Vodkin trailed much of what was to come. Note the ancestry of the following. It goes back to a midsummer night outside Athens.

Tommy: Who are you?

Vodkin: My name is Vodkin.

Tommy: My mother used to use one of your family to pull the cord through the top of my pyjamas.

Vodkin: No, I am plain Vodkin.

Tommy: I must knock you back some time. What's your nationality?

Vodkin: My wife. She was Bavarian.

Tommy: And where is your old Deutsch now?

Vodkin: She is now an interruptor.

Tommy: So's mine. I can't get a word in edgeways.

The spy Fünf turned up in the second programme and Mrs Tickle, the charwoman, in the fourth. I despair of making the young understand why Fünf was funny, since if I describe what he did I have to say only that he (played by Jack Train) used to ring up the Minister of Aggravation and Twerps to say: 'This is Fünf speaking' – and promise some threat. Fünf was the first of the *ITMA* characters to merge into the national life. Otherwise sober and responsible citizens used to telephone each other for the sheer bliss of saying, 'This is Fünf speaking'. Looking at that sentence now I can hardly believe it myself. Well, there was a war on.

Another phrase that caught on in this first series was the word 'Friday'. Any remark ending with the word (or one that sounded like it) brought the response 'Friday?' and the counter-response 'Friday!' People went about Britain all through the winter of the phoney war handing back and forth this one and another – 'I wish I had as many shillings!' – which Tommy borrowed from Jimmy Learmouth, one of the northern comedians of his youth, unknown to fame because he died young. (J. B. Priestley, no amateur judge, thought Learmouth the funniest man he had ever known.)

By Christmas 1939 *ITMA* had become national property inasmuch as no pantomime was complete without a Fünf in it. This success cost the nation dearly, for it inspired Jack Hylton with the notion that a stage version could be made. He hired Ted Kavanagh to write it and Robert Nesbitt to produce, retained Maurice Denham and Jack Train to support Tommy, but the thing never worked. Slowed down to the speed at which characters could move about a stage, its verbal acrobatics lost the key qualities of surprise and pace. The show struggled along through the summer of the Battle of Britain and the winter of the blitz. The BBC's studios at Bristol were badly damaged, and Variety moved to Bangor, where such sights as a couple of decorative males walking affectionately hand in hand struck amazement and fright into citizens whose own brand of nonconformity had an exclusively religious context. A BBC legend which has the ring of probability says that someone telegraphed John Watt: 'FOR GODS SAKE SEND MORE STAGS BANGOR.' Later Bangor accepted the artists and grew to love their free-spending habits. It was from Bangor, in a converted Welsh hall, that in June 1941 *ITMA* was reborn; and here, for the first time, was the format that everyone remembers: the *ITMA* door (the sound of a turning handle indicated a character's arrival, and a slam indicated his departure); the special music spot (these grew into little set-pieces of virtuosic reorchestrations of popular and folk songs); the catchphrases; and the beginning of a host of characters – Lefty the gangster and his pal Sam Scram, Ali Oop the persistent pedlar, the unsquashable Commercial Traveller, the Diver, Claud and Cecil the brokers' men, and Colonel Chinstrap, a military alcoholic whose special line was to mis-hear a word as an invitation: 'Whisky, Sir? I don't mind if I do.'

The *ITMA* door was about two feet high and fitted with every imaginable lock, bolt and bar. It was of all Kavanagh's technical wheezes the most fruitful, since it allowed the characters to spring in and depart with the speed of imagination. The comedy played as fast as it read, thus:

(Door opens)

Cheery commercial: Good morning –

Tommy: Good afternoon –

Cheery commercial: Good evening –

Tommy: Good night

(door shuts)

Tommy: That was a short day.

The great popularity had begun. By the fifth programme of the series it was playing to sixteen million listeners, the biggest audience a variety programme had so far reached. In 1942 the show was moved, door and all, to Windsor Castle for a special and private performance for the King and Queen. They toured the service bases and factories. By 1944, when recorded repeats were being played all over the world, Tommy was reaching more listeners than any other British comedian in history. Its success could hardly be said to fluctuate; the most one could say was that some shows, for various reasons, some of them outside the performances, went down better than others. The crest was the performance given in the Navy's base at Scapa Flow in the January of 1944. Ted Kavanagh remembered how bitterly cold the hall was; the brass instruments could not be tuned properly and the strings of the fiddles snapped. But the warmth of the reception would have melted icebergs. The audience was of sailors and airmen who had all just returned from action, the navy men from one of the murderous Arctic convoys to Russia and back, the airmen from forays with Coastal Command and the Fleet Air Arm. As in the Gracie Fields concerts broadcast from France more than four years earlier the applause had a heart-swelling, moving quality because it came from men whose lives were so precariously held. I find myself gulping a bit nearly thirty years later as I remember the noise of their huge, uproarious delight. There must have been some consistently unusual quality in the *ITMA* audience's laughter, for in occupied Europe the Dutch and the tragic Poles, of whom some did not speak English and none would have understood the puns, listened because they drew comfort from it.

What made it such a very special success? Well, it achieved a unique combination of qualities. Much of its appeal – the catchphrases and the puns and the characters – was that of pure nonsense. At the same time it offered a kind of commentary on the war: the queues for everything, the black-market, the official pep-talks and regulations, the debates in Parliament, the tightening of rationing, the German invasion of Russia, the victories in the desert, the entry of the Americans and Japan, the Bevin Boys, the dam-busting raid, the downfall of Mussolini, the invasion and conquest of Germany, the beer shortage, the flying bombs and V2s – the scripts were pep-pered with jokes born of the day, now incomprehensible to the young, often inserted after the team had broken final rehearsals to listen to Thursday's six o'clock news. Thus on 20 November 1942, as Ted recalled, Sam Scram burst in with the query: 'Boss, boss, have you heard the wonderful news from Libya?' 'Of course I have,' said Tommy. 'What's the Mersa Matruth? Have you heard the news from Algiers? Turned out Eisenhow, hasn't it?' This was the day of the American landings in North Africa.

Its characters were crazy but somehow complete and memorable, like the creatures in Alice. Their impact was derived from the script's constant repetition of boldly drawn characterisation, usually not more than one to a character. Several of them were drawn from life. The diver, whose catch-phrases were 'Don't forget the diver, gents, don't forget the diver' and 'I'm going down now, sir,' was born out of Handley's recollection of a chap who used to dive for pennies – or proposed to do so, though Tommy never saw him do it – at New Brighton. Colonel Chinstrap was an ex-Indian Army officer who loved a drink better than his life. His catchphrase was adapted from a joke in an old *Punch*, sent to Francis Worsley by a listener. It showed a red-nosed gentleman in a railway carriage, above a caption that had the porter shouting 'Virginia Water!' and the old chap replying 'Gin and water? I don't mind if I do!' This part – and that of Fünf, Claud and Lefty, brought fame and fortune to Jack Train, an oldtimer who had scored modestly in radio since the earliest days. (When he told his mother that the variety show he was broadcasting from Plymouth was going to be taken by Birmingham as well she warned him to pack his thick underwear against those damp Midland evenings.)

The man who kept repeating the last words of a sentence – 'I've come to inspect your drains – I said inspect your drains' – was another discovery of Worsley's; he'd met a soldier who talked like that. Mrs Mopp was simply the archetypal office cleaner. Signor So-So was the Italian enemy that nobody took seriously. Some inventions of course were pure fantasy, like Ali Oop the pedlar. His catchphrase with the slightly mispronounced English idiom used as a kind of rhyme, e.g., 'Your hands are grimy.' 'Grimy? Oh, blimey!' This lunatic exchange sank so deeply into the minds of the girl I was to marry and myself that we still use it thirty years later – only between our-selves, I quickly add. Claud and Cecil also penetrated deep. They were sup-posed to be polite bailiff's men and furniture removers, and as well as their 'After you, Claud.' 'No; after you, Cecil' lines they used the rhyming talk – it was called 'clang slang' – that was fashionable about that time. I think it came from American pop music; one phrase – 'See you later, alligator' –

had something to do with jazz, I seem to remember. It spread like a fever to a point where the rhyme was not required to make any sense. 'Don't be beastly, J. B. Priestley,' was one of *ITMA*'s. You'd hear from the bailiff's men serving summonses: 'Is yours for room and board, Claud?' 'No, mine's for dispossessal, Cecil.'

It may sound like pure haphazard jesting, but was really a style of humour carefully and skilfully planned by Worsley, Kavanagh and Handley, three men brought together by a certain amount of chance. Ted was a New Zealand-Irish Catholic disciple of G. K. Chesterton who managed to be pro-Labour and anti-Socialist. Worsley had entered the BBC by way of public school, university and the colonial service. Tommy was born in Liverpool, left school at fifteen, became an office boy, a toy salesman, a chorus boy, a music hall and concert party entertainer, an established radio comedian; like most performers he favoured conservatism. Ted's notion of radio comedy was to exploit sound and speed for all they were worth, using every device of speech and sound effect to create an illusion of inverted reality. He had earlier written scripts for some British attempts at film cartoons and, as Worsley pointed out, *ITMA* was really a sort of cartoon in sound. He also had a journalist's flair for spotting the kind of news *ITMA* could turn to account and was a merciless mocker of cant. Worsley's essential contribution was to be able to spot what Ted was driving at and to help the show to produce it. He also mastered the subtle and difficult trick of keeping a successful show fresh. Many *ITMA* fans resented the two musical breaks because they could see no reason for them; but Worsley knew that without them comic dialogue would start to fail after eight minutes and to bore or exhaust after twelve. This was the hard-earned knowledge of all producers of radio fantasy comedy. Worsley thought that without the musical breaks *ITMA* would have lasted about six weeks. As it turned out the reorchestration of an old favourite became a popular and anticipated spot in the show.

For the *ITMA* style of comedy Tommy Handley was the perfect instrument. Ted said he had the innate sense of the born comedian to an audience's reaction and an uncanny ear for the sound of words. Worsley saw him first as irresistibly likeable – in the same way as Arthur Askey, Jack Benny, Fred Allen – and then as 'creative', with a quick ear and mind ever on the alert for a phrase, a twist, a sound that would translate itself into radio comedy. His style had over the years been converging to meet Kavanagh's love of wordplay. In 1934 he and Ronald Frankau had a flaring radio success with a double act called Mr Murgatroyd and Mr Winterbottom, which certainly was not behind the later *ITMA* in the frenzy of its punning and has some claims, as this extract from a 1939 show suggests, to have been its unconscious forerunner: 'Talking shop – how does your wife get on with the ration book?' 'She knows it all from A to Z – crosses the Ts and dots the eyes of anyone who tried to take her place.' 'Like my wife – she just looks after her vegetables and waits.' 'I don't get it.' 'She minds her Ps and Qs.' 'I like that! Do you know – I dared to tell my butcher off the other day.' 'You must have some guts!' 'No, he had them, and I wanted them.' Etc., etc.

The apparently effortless bubbling of *ITMA* jokes was hammered out week by week at script conferences. Dialogue took up 18.5 minutes of a half-hour show, and Ted aimed at a hundred gags – one every eleven seconds – in that time. It was true that many of the jokes merely repeated catchphrases; the art lay in inventing a fresh way into the catchphrase every week. Mrs Mopp, for instance, had a ready-made laugh with her entrance line, 'Can I do you now, sir?' But she also had to bring Tommy a present ('I've brought this for you, sir'), to propose doing something special for him (with slightly bawdy undertones), and to fade out with initialed adieux. All these ingredients, once they caught on, had to be included each week, and not only for Dorothy Summers' Mrs Mopp. Some way had to be found for Dino Galvani's Signor So-So to say 'Nothing at all – nothing at all!' and Sidney Keith's Sam Scram: 'Somp'n terrible's happened!' and the others. The tendency of popular characters to expand had to be contained. Mrs Mopp used to sign off with 'Ta-ta for now', to which Tommy replied with some rhyming line: 'Aren't you a wow?' She shortened hers to TTFN, and Tommy began to reply in kind. *Mopp:* 'TTFN.' *Handley:* 'NKABTYSIRWU.' 'What's that, sir?' 'Never Kiss A Baby Till You're Sure It's Right Way Up.' At this the listening nation fell helplessly about.

I think the secret was that the show tapped a curiously English (and possibly Welsh and Scottish) delight in playing with something they felt so much at home in and unpuzzled by: the English language. In that sense the show rested on a huge fund of common knowledge. The delight in making puns is a universal human attribute; as for the catchphrases, they did not begin with radio though their power to fix a person in the mind's eye quickly made them an invaluable recognition signal, the aural equivalent of George Robey's eyebrows. My mother used to say 'Meredith; we're in', a phrase which had escaped from some pre-1914 stage comedy. Lupin Pooter used to puzzle his father by exclaiming, 'Then the band played'. I am indebted to Frank Muir for sending me an example of the catchphrase's power and antiquity from the first quarto of *Hamlet*, printed in 1603. 'And then you have some again, that keepes one suit of jests, as a man is known by one suit of apparel, and gentlemen quote his jests down in their tables before they come to the play, as thus: Cannot you stay till I eat my porridge? and, You owe me a quarter's wages; and, Your beer is sour.'

Before the war Arthur Askey's 'I Theang Yow' had caught on so powerfully you couldn't be in any public place for five minutes without hearing it. When Jack Warner omitted 'Mind my bike' from Garrison Theatre he had

300 letters a week asking why. Kenway and Young's 'Very tasty – very sweet' was used by households to spice with humour such wartime dishes as Lord Woolton Pie, a Ministry of Food creation made without meat. But no show ever invented more successful catchphrases than *ITMA*. The pilots of the RAF would shout 'I'm going down now, sir!' and 'After you, Claud!' over their intercoms as they attacked. Ted quoted a boy buried in bomb debris who patiently asked his rescuers, 'Can you do me now?' and doctors told him of patients whose last coherent sentence was a murmured 'TTFN'. It got so that the accidental use of an *ITMA* catchphrase in a political speech or a straight play would break it up, and until they took Tommy's name out of the telephone directory fifty or sixty fans a night would ring him up to tell him that Fünf was after him, offering to do him now, and the like. Enabled by radio to share a pleasure of their people as never before, the royal family joined in. When Tommy explained after their command performance that *ITMA* was finishing its run but would return in the autumn the Queen smilingly replied with the phrase of Ali Oop. 'I see. You go – you come back.'

It sounds daft, but the secret of the catchphrase's appeal was, and remains, simply its easy availability. It put within everyone's reach, on a very simple level, the national vice of using quotations. On another it was almost an exchange of passwords. Indeed British counter-espionage interrogators used to throw *ITMA* catchphrases at suspected enemy spies along with other tests such as questions about Test cricket. The chucking of the phrases to and fro represented a kind of national togetherness, for during the war nearly everybody listened to nearly everything. It was also considered rather witty to be able to apply a phrase from *ITMA* to a situation in your own life. When you said 'I don't mind if I do', you were not just demonstrating a ready wit, you became in a sense part of *ITMA*, the show everyone laughed at. A catchphrase offered a kind of bridge across a situation, a shelter behind which you could conceal feelings too deep for any words you could think of. Stephen Potter told how the landlord of a pub he sometimes stopped at used catchphrases purely as conversational stopgaps without any relevance to the general talk. 'Mind my bike,' he would say. Then a little later: 'Time I gave it the old one-two.' Another customer would enter and with reference to nothing the landlord would say, 'Don't forget the diver'. Potter believed that the implication of the catchphrases was that they established common ground between strangers. Frank Muir suggested that the quick igniters were those that could be used very easily in a number of situations but especially those to do with greetings or farewells. I think he was right, but a list of *ITMA*'s most successful phrases compiled by Worsley reveals no incontestable common denominator. 'This is Fünf speaking!' 'Don't forget the diver!' 'After you, Claud! – after you, Cecil!' 'Missed him!' 'It's me noives!' 'He's a great guy!' 'Boss! Boss! Something terrible's happened!' 'Nothing at all! – nothing at all!' 'Can I do you now, sir?' 'Good morning! Nice day!' 'I go – I come back!' 'Well, for ever more!' 'I don't mind if I do.' 'I'd do anything for the wife.' 'I'll forget me own name in a minute.' 'Smile please – watch the birdie!' 'Taxi!' 'Ah! There you are!' 'TTFN'. I reproduce this list for the nostalgic delight it will give to readers who are old enough, but all it shows is that the mystery is not why catchphrases succeed but why some should fire instantly and others splutter and go out.

The punning was most boisterous when it was inventing names for characters. As well as those I've mentioned there were Hari Kari the Japanese Sandman, Johann Bull the genial spy, Pansy Cowe-Parsley the health-food addict, Walter Wetwhite the impersonator, Sophie Tuckshop the schoolgirl eater, Peter Geekie (he never appeared, but Tommy Handley used the name each week as a symbol for the great anonymous nuisances of war), Miss Hotchkiss, Tommy's formidable secretary. When the war ended many of these were retired in the interests of keeping the show fresh; Ted's invention, bubbling as happily as ever, came up with Major Munday, the Colonel's drinking companion, Curly Kale, a cook, Poppy Poopah, Lady Soneley, Sam Fairfechan, one of the funniest of the line, George Gorge, another eater, Major Munday's daughter Naieve, two Japanese hawkers called Bowing and Scraping, Tattie Mackintosh, Frisby Dyke (another of the great hits), Brigadier Dear, the fittest man in the army, Edward Byegum, a northern industrialist, Professor Preston Pans, a scientist, Luke Slippy, the publicity man. There were others that had no name, such as the cheery commercial and a man who went about filling in long-felt wants.

Tommy's role as a radio character was hard to define. Worsley thought the picture was of a swashbuckling, plausible, quick-witted rogue whose grandiose schemes went crazily wrong, and believed part of the show's popularity was the Elizabethan quality in his reckless attitude to life and refusal to admit defeat and contempt for humbug and bumbledom. Or was he 'the eternal anarchist whose delightfully mad schemes are near enough to man's own plans to have satirical significance?' Or was he – Worsley again – 'a north-country Ariel who likes black puddings and Blackpool rock'? I can't recognise the Handley I remember in any of these descriptions. I think his role was simply to be himself: the comedian, the fixed and solid pivot of reality round which the fantasy swirled, and he remained himself however fantastic the situation the script designed for him. (It was this mixture of a real comedian surrounded by fantastic characters that defeated the scriptwriters when they tried to make a film of *ITMA*).

The Ministry of Aggravation and Twerps faded away after the first *ITMA* series. Tommy became Mayor of Foaming at the Mouth until deposed in 1942. Then he was boss of some vaguely defined factory which became a health spa, a holiday camp, a hotel and a farm called Much Fiddling Manor. After the war Foaming at the Mouth disappeared and Tommy became the governor of Tomtopia. When they thought Tomtopia had lasted long enough they simply brought the Governor home on leave; in 1946 his address was Castle Weehouse, Dire Straights, Loch Tynn, Scotland. Curiously, by an insignificant coincidence, Tommy ended the series in the civil service, as he had begun it: he was made Industrial and Scientific Adviser to His Majesty's Government. The function of the location was always the same, to provide a setting for the show to hold up some distorting and comic reflection of events in the real island.

Ted Kavanagh believed that during *ITMA*'s run Tommy Handley grew into the greatest radio comedian the world had heard, his gift for creative comedy greatly enriched and sharpened by constant exercise. But he never changed from the modest and likeable pro everybody in the business knew. It was still possible for a radio celebrity, known by his voice and photographs, to be able to walk about without knotting up the traffic, and he was spared the insane ballyhoo that accompanies TV success. To himself he was a comedian who had a hit show; he was delighted with success but puzzled and a little daunted by its size; it may have been a wish to make it seem less out of the ordinary that made him insist on answering his fan mail personally. He spent hours in the Savage Club replying to letters from all over the world. He was in the Savage Club on a Saturday night in January 1949, talking about the next *ITMA* script with Kavanagh and Jack Train and others, the day before he had a stroke and died; the fountain of gaiety and fun that had played for ten years was suddenly and totally cut off. 'The BBC regrets to announce the death of Mr Thomas Handley, the comedian,' read Stuart Hibberd in the six o'clock news. The announcement came immediately after the 5.30 repeat, greatly multiplying the shock. I believe it took this sudden death, in what seemed to be the full prime of his art (though he had privately complained of headaches and weariness), to make us realise the full stature and achievement of Tommy and *ITMA*. I was in Brighton then, establishing myself as one of the town's dreaded theatre critics, and remember very clearly how the news was received with the kind of incredulity that masks an unwillingness to believe. I wrote a farewell piece that could only say what every other obituarist said. Because no radio comedian had ever been so popular, because Tommy as a voice had become a friendly and familiar guest in every home, his death was a unique event; never before had so many people felt sharply, with a sense of heavy personal loss, the death of a man they had never seen. (According to Mass Observation the public reaction could only be compared to that to the death of President Roosevelt in the last weeks of the war.) Crowds six deep lined the street along the route of his funeral car; when a memorial service was held in St Paul's Cathedral – the first time a comedian had been so honoured – so many thousands turned up that the doors had to be closed early and the ceremony was relayed to those left outside. It was, said Ted, a heartfelt tribute to a jester but also to the power of the microphone.

The shattered cast faced a professional and personal future suddenly and incredibly emptied, for there was never any question of *ITMA* continuing without Tommy. On the Thursday following his death they broadcast at the *ITMA* hour a programme of some of his favourite music and recalled some of the best moments in the show's ten-year run. John Snagge, called on to pronounce a final toast to 'That Man', found himself closer to breaking up than he'd been in all his career. Somebody thought of the perfect last gesture. The *ITMA* door was gently closed.

4

EVERYTHING INVOLVED EVERYBODY

In the second great war there was very little organised whipping up of hatred of the enemy, certainly nothing at all resembling the sustained hate campaigns of world war one. It wasn't needed. In the first war the civilian population was safe a long way behind the firing, and until after the Somme recruitment was voluntary. To keep up the enlistment figures and the willingness of the women to let their men go it was necessary to build up hate; and such men as Northcliffe and Bottomley, the former from genuine patriotism, the latter to fulfil Johnson's definition of that quality as the last refuge of a scoundrel, kept the pot seething so successfully that when the fiendish enemy was beaten it was impossible to persuade the British electorate that he had not really been all that fiendish and was entitled to a magnanimous peace. In the second war the enemy was in the skies over the kingdom, raining fire and destruction, death, wounds, infinite inconsolable griefs. And there was total conscription. You weren't brainwashed into volunteering; the services came and got you. The people hated the enemy steadily and fairly quietly, and in the beginning still distinguished between the Nazis and the German people and Mussolini and the Italians. In the early days of the Battle of Britain Charles Gardner, reporting from the cliffs of Dover, described a dogfight between Spitfires and Messerschmidts in the slangy, sporty, tally-ho terms of the fighter pilots. To listeners it sounded like a commentary on a sporting event. 'You've got him! Pump it into him! Pop-pop-pop – Oh boy, oh boy, he's going down!' It caused a good deal of offence, no doubt some of it from people who did not want to be reminded that men get killed in wars, but some from others who had not forgotten it but did not think it civilised to gloat over destruction. Duff Cooper's broadcast when Mussolini brought his country into the war, ending with 'He will increase the number of ruins for which Italy has long been famous' was similarly rebuked. (We could never regard the Italians as enemies, thinking of them as allies who had got on the wrong train; when they signed an armistice and came in on our side we felt that the correct alignment had been restored.)

The BBC permitted flippancy in what it felt was the right place. Thus Quentin Reynolds, the American journalist who was in London reporting the blitz, gave great delight with his contemptuous open broadcast to

Hitler, 'Dear Mr Schickelgruber', of which the theme was the absurdity of imagining that anyone with such a ridiculous name could ever subdue a man called Winston Spencer Churchill. But this broadcast, and his earlier one addressed to 'Dear Dr Goebbels', was given in the summer of 1941, after the horrors of the night blitz had begun to fade. The public's attitude to the war hardened as and when the war hardened; by 1943 the BBC's reporters could describe the bombing raids on Germany with unconcealed excitement. But this kind of reporting derived its flavour from the fact that the reporters were physically taking part in the raid, recording what struck them in the presence of danger. You never heard this tone in the news bulletins. They were written to be read as though – but the readers could never quite manage it – good and bad news were the same. The cost in lives was never left out. We learned to wait for one sentence in the news bulletin with a unique mixture of dread and compunction. It often seemed to me that the newsreader was putting himself to it like a rider putting his horse to a bad jump. It was the sentence that ended the account of the previous day's war in the air. 'From all these operations —— of our aircraft are missing.' There was no gloating after that.

Propaganda's theme was that the enemy must be done down, and would be, by a nation absolutely united within itself and with its allies; the great thing was to keep cheerful and keep at it. In this sense everything the BBC did was propaganda. The amount of variety went up by three times. Drama's *Saturday Night Theatre*, the only available theatre for millions of Britons, became a huge draw for the middlebrow audience that wanted good strong plots and clear characterisation. The classic serials emptied the public libraries of any book they chose; the restoration to favour of Trollope, until then fallen into undeserved neglect, dated from H. Oldfield Box's famous adaptations of him.

In 1943 John Dickson Carr sold Val Gielgud the idea, revolutionary by BBC standards and perhaps not very palatable to them, of producing a thriller series in the style of American radio, with shock musical effects, a narrator with a voice like doom itself, and characters presented with the subtlety of a blow between the eyes. This was *Appointment with Fear*. Why we, living through a total war, should have welcomed some fictional frightening on top of all the genuine article, will puzzle younger readers; I suppose it offered the kind of change that was as good as a rest. Its success soon outdid *Saturday Night Theatre* and turned the glare of instant fame upon Valentine Dyall as the storyteller, 'The Man In Black'. Dyall was a thoroughly experienced actor who had been around for years without achieving the notoriety he now received for the trick of using a preternaturally deep voice in a manner that exactly projected the series' aim of giving listeners the shudders, diverting them a little thereby from the vexations of beer and cigarette shortages and mysterious meals in British restaurants concocted without, as far as taste could judge, any familiar ingredient whatever. Val Gielgud was reproached for allowing the standard of radio drama to decline. He thought it had kept its end up pretty well. His difficulty, accentuated by the wartime need to keep the people cheerful, was still the popular preference for the known and the easily fanned prejudice against the novel.

One of his most famous wartime ventures was *The Man Born to be King*, a twelve-part cycle of plays written by Dorothy L. Sayers on the life of Christ. It ran into a storm of objections, some of them contemptible and insulting attempts by a few newspapers to whip up a row, some of them sincere if ridiculous horror at Miss Sayers's insistence on introducing Christ as a character and writing modern contemporary instead of biblical speech. The BBC was accused of irreverence, vulgarity and blasphemy. Mr H. H. Martin, secretary of the Lord's Day Observance Society and a noted trouble-maker, used quite a lot of his society's money to publish an advertisement in which he warned the nation of the danger that might lie in provoking the Almighty's indignation at such a time of national need. The uproar suc-ceeded in forcing the BBC to postpone the broadcast of the second play while its Religious Advisory Committee studied the scripts, but this modest triumph was more than offset by the effect of Mr Martin's publicity as a whetter of public curiosity in a series which was hailed as, and remains, a landmark in radio drama achievement.

To illustrate how wartime pressures were streamlining drama pro-duction, let me add that each episode of *The Man Born to be King* was done inside eight days from first read-through to transmission, compared with the two weeks it would have had in the thirties; and the multi-studio tech-niques perfected by Sieveking and others had given way to productions set up in a single large studio, the actors talking at microphone points linked to the producer's adjoining cubicle. He remained in visual contact throughout. In such conditions the mysterious art of 'playing' the drama control panel died.

Music too shared the quality special to wartime broadcasting of involving everybody because it seemed part of the war. In 1942 a large part of the nation – though probably not the listeners in the messes – sat down to hear the first British performance of Shostakovich's 'Leningrad' Symphony, listening with a good deal of care, not to say anxiety, for sounds that would evoke the heroic siege Leningrad was at that time undergoing. Most of us reckoned that Tchaikovsky did that sort of thing better. Along with the more oblique wartime propaganda came much of the overt kind, pumped out as part of the government's campaign on the home front; but it was difficult to decide where Government- and BBC-originated broadcasts began and ended. The people were exhorted to cut out careless talk, not to pass on rumours, to watch their step in the blackout, to learn first aid, to stay put, to keep their wirelesses low in summer time, above all to cook economically, shop wisely, dig for victory and raise chickens, pigs, rabbits and goats. Nobody took much notice of the warnings about careless or defeatist talk, but the war on waste and the sound advice about food given in 'The Kitchen Front' and 'The Kitchen in Wartime' were important upholders of morale. Everyone could do a bit in this part of the war. Children's Hour salvage competitions produced some extraordinary collections; one winner's amounted to nine tons of scrap, another's included a thousand-gallon water tank and an old car. Outside the houses stood a row of huge bins, one for collecting paper, one for tins, one for bottles, one for kitchen waste. They were known as pigbins, though as far as I know the pigs ate only the waste. It was taken away, boiled up and fed to these omnivorous and unexacting creatures (they would probably have managed the paper, tins and bottles as well) who would return it after some weeks in the form of rashers, legs, loins, chops, feet, knuckles, sausages if you were lucky, and heads for making into brawn. If I enjoyed anything in the war without reservation it was this fulfilment of one of man's deepest instincts, to conserve and to grow. I do not believe it can be flouted, as it has been since by economic systems of growth that depend on planned waste, without some injury to the human spirit. During the war it flowered; and there was a sharp and deep contentment to be had out of raising six hens in the back-yard, digging up the lawn for potatoes, scouring the hedges for the wild fruits, and of the more striking feat, which by practice I mastered completely, of making quite a decent omelette out of dried-egg powder.

BBC attitudes that had seemed deeply ingrained simply withdrew. It was absurd to gear broadcasting to reflect the nation's purpose and to draw the newsreaders from the southern counties only; thus Wilfred Pickles was brought down from the North to boost national solidarity by reading the bulletins in an accent as defiantly Yorkshire as a suit of long underwear. What was more, he finished by wishing his hearers 'good neet, everybody – good neet'. The astonishment his voice caused is a measure of how deep-seated the domination of the South had become. National unity also forced changes in the BBC's sultanesque attitude to women. It was obvious that troops would prefer to hear female continuity announcers, and a handful of them – Joy Worth, Joan Griffiths, Joan Burman, Joan Gilbert – began to appear on the Forces programme. Doris Arnold, Harry S. Pepper's wife, was gazetted variety producer, the first woman in BBC history to make the grade. She was much liked by the public as commère of a record request programme, *These You Have Loved*; and she was joined by other girls with other record programmes: Barabara McFayden, Joy Shelton, Jean Metcalfe, Marjorie Anderson, Lilian Duff. They had in common voices of entrancing and cool upper-class friendliness, with which they introduced the records requested and delivered messages to the troops from their loved ones. Radio became the equivalent of the field postcard of the Great War.

Sandy McPherson started it on the Forces programme soon after it opened, perhaps needing some diversion from the business of playing, and playing, and playing. Peter Haddon, then in Cairo with the BBC's Middle East unit, recalled how his first reaction to the idea – he thought it rather cheap and stuntish – was bowled over by listening to the very first message, recorded by a wife for her husband in which she lovingly talked about the children, how she was coping with the tightening budget, ending: 'But don't worry, Bill dear, they'll be all right and I'll look after them for you and keep the 'ome going till you get back. Goodnight, Bill, I love you.' There was no resisting the truth and depth of feeling in these message programmes and they became a firm favourite which, as we know, endures to this day.

The BBC had to learn to accommodate differing standards of aesthetic judgment. The big song of 1941 was belted out by a young London singer with a big, strong, natural voice, the kind of voice that might emerge from some pub on a Saturday night, a voice born more for the music-hall stage than for the microphone. It belonged to Vera Lynn.

> We'll meet again,
> Don't know where, don't know when,
> But I know we'll meet again some sunny day.
> Keep smiling through,
> Just like you always do,
> Till the blue skies drive the dark clouds far away.
>
> So will you please say Hello
> To the folks that I know,
> Tell them I won't be long.
> They'll be happy to know
> That as you saw me go
> I was singing this song.
> We'll meet again,
> Don't know where, don't know when,
> But I know we'll meet again some sunny day.

The lyric perhaps reflected the decline in popular culture that accompanies a war, but certainly suggested to the multitude something of what they felt when they thought about being separated.

Vera Lynn, easily the most popular female singer of the war years, had begun as a child prodigy, graduated to local bands, and first broadcast with Joe Loss. She became quite well known before the war as what was then called a crooner or vocalist (for some reason, never explained, but which may have had something to do with humility, the word 'singer' was never used in the dance band sphere), first with the band of Charlie Kunz, and then with Ambrose's. Kunz had a remarkably long-lasting vogue as a piano-player, in some part because his strongly rhythmic style, apparently simple and unhurried, sounded easy to imitate.* She began broadcasting on the Forces programme early in the war and was soon dubbed 'The Sweetheart of the Forces'. But it was her message programme, *Sincerely Yours*, produced on the Forces network by Howard Thomas (he was running the *Brains Trust* at the same time), that rocketed her to fame in the third winter of the war. Her approach was what some call homely and others sentimental; some hard cases couldn't listen to her without their toes curling inside their boots. But her audience responded to the quality of natural good nature in her performance. She was, and is, an extraordinarily pleasant woman. She thought she owed her success to the personal touch. She would have nothing to do with facsimile signatures, signed every photograph herself, and used to call on the wives and families of the soldiers who wrote to her, so that her messages across the air had a solid, individual meaning. The listeners, not all of them in uniform, wrote to her by the thousand.

The BBC leadership was a little worried about the popularity among fighting troops of an entertainment that seemed to be handing out a good deal of mush. I think it must be admitted that the Lynn genius responded with special vigour to songs of unabashed sentimentality; far from being conscious of a lyric's banality she articulated every syllable with as much expression as lips, lungs, and throat, teeth and tongue could manage, as though only thus could she do justice to some of the loveliest lyric poems in the language:

> There'll be blue birds over
> The White Cliffs of Dover,
> Tomorrow when the world is free.
> There'll be love and laughter,
> And peace ever after,
> Tomorrow, just you wait and see.

For those familiar with the ornithology of south-eastern England† or

---

* One of the dafter wartime rumours of 1940 was that Kunz – well, the name sounded foreign, didn't it? – was transmitting information to the Germans disguised in his broadcasts.

† This song was written by an American, which accounts for the presence over Dover of birds indigenous to parts of the United States only.

who had a feeling for words it was hard to listen to these without a qualm. Cecil Graves, at this time the BBC's joint Director-General, was also concerned about the effect on morale; he couldn't see how men could fit themselves for battle with these debilitating tunes ringing in their ears.[1] He said as much at a planning committee meeting but was shot down by A. P. Ryan. As BBC liaison officer with the troops Ryan had toured the army camps and found that Vera Lynn was indeed wildly popular, that her photograph certainly did adorn the messes, but that far from lowering the troops' spirits the sentimental songs cheered them up. The truth was, of course, that pushpin was as good as poetry; what seemed unbearable slush to some was to the huge majority as valid and manly as one of Priestley's postscripts. The BBC had run into, and not for the last time, the truth that most people are not aware of grades of quality among what they like.

To keep up unity, resolution and reasonably good spirits was the aim of the bulk of broadcasting. The popularity of the Forces programme with the civilian audience became slightly embarrassing to the BBC, for though the forces liked what they were getting there were plenty of civilians around, in press, Parliament, pulpit, to assure the BBC that the forces didn't really like it, and shouldn't have it if they did. They claimed that a civilian did not change, i.e. lower his tastes, merely by putting on a uniform, and that practically the whole of the services was made up of civilians. But the BBC could reply fairly that under service conditions the civilians' listening tastes undoubtedly tended to change because listening conditions changed from individual to mass listening; and the popularity of the Forces programme among the civilian population refuted the notion that tastes changed. Even so the amount of jazz and similar light material in the forces amounted to not more than one-third of the time. Thus B. E. Nicholls in 1943; and he added an argument that would be used very tellingly against the BBC in the debates ten years in the future about the introduction of ITV. An alternative Home Service, he said, was available all over the country, and any minority with a good receiving set could find good music or other desired programmes by a few seconds of retuning.

All through the war the BBC was not free to pursue a wholly self-chosen path. It was to some extent under orders just as much as the armed services and the civilian community, and its independence would not have lasted six months if it had consistently and carefully given the bulk of the nation the kind of broadcasting the bulk of the nation did not want. It never needed to be told this. But the implication that the art of broadcasting declined in consequence is too absurd to discuss. It was because it had to reach everybody that broadcasting flowered. To explain how it was able to present the nation to itself I must return to the art of the radio feature.

5

THE WIRELESS FINDS THE PEOPLE

Defining creative radio as material that could exist *only* by way of a loud-speaker and a microphone, feature programmes had established themselves before the war as its most promising source. But its most important discovery, vital to the BBC war effort, was that ordinary people were the richest single lump of raw material. This discovery came about through a lucky mischance that had appeared to blast the career of E. A. Harding, one of the great originators of the feature. He had been one of the four members of the Programme Research Section set up by Lance Sieveking in 1928 with himself in charge and Harding, E. J. King-Bull and Mary Hope Allen as his colleagues. They started off with a convinced and fervent faith in radio as a potential art-form on its own; their job was to explore new techniques, to suggest new forms, and to produce frankly experimental programmes. Unluckily the condition that was intended to give them freedom – they were not attached to any particular department – turned out to mean that they could not get departmental backing for their experiments. (A Television Research Section set up for exactly the same purpose in 1953 failed for exactly the same reasons.) However, the section could claim to have discovered the dramatised documentary and the original radio play.

In 1932 Harding had produced with Laurence Gilliam the first, spectacularly successful round-the-Empire Christmas Day broadcast. In 1933 he had been invited to do a similar programme linking the countries of Europe on New Year's Eve. With some help from Claud Cockburn his commentary included some punchy but in the context inappropriate information about the proportion of national income Poland was spending on arms. The Polish government protested and Harding was sent to be Programme Director in the North Region, an appointment considered by some of his colleagues in the South much as the inmates of the Kremlin would have regarded the promotion of a fellow-member to be stationmaster at Omsk. But Harding accepted the job as a challenge to show that Manchester could do whatever London did, and better. He drew on local talent from the *Manchester Guardian*, the law, industry, civil service and the professional and amateur theatre. Geoffrey Bridson, one of his protégés, wrote an exhilarating account of Harding's régime in his *Prospero and Ariel*.[1] Harding met Bridson, then a young poet who was filling in time pretending to be a clerk in insurance, in a pub; he fired him with the revolutionary statement that, since all broadcasting was propaganda, all the people, not just their spokesmen, had the right to use it. Up to then, Bridson claimed, it had stood apart from a vast audience which it merely condescended to address, for which he blamed not just an ingrained BBC attitude but the rule requiring broadcasts to be spoken from scripts. He thought this was why the BBC sounded, until the war blew away the boiled-shirt image for good, the voice of the southern upper-middle class; the script rule required professional people. (Amateurs turned up on *In Town Tonight*, where their stumbling reading of the scripts furnished many a comedian with material for parody.) It was the development of portable recording gear that enabled the BBC to dispense with written scripts and still retain control over what went out. This was used with great effect in 'Children in Billets', done from Manchester in October 1939, in which evacuated children told their stories in their own words.

With Harding's backing Bridson proceeded to put this right. His first success, a dramatic poem-plus-documentary called 'May Day in England', took the opportunity to contrast the pastoral notions of May Day with its modern role as an international labour day. There were three million unemployed in Britain that year (1934), and Bridson's biting verse, 'snarled out in seething anger' by Ewen MacColl, sounded for the first time in British broadcasting the genuine voice of the indignant Left. Laurence Gilliam hailed the play as a creative work of real force, but Bridson's next, advocating Social Credit, was banned by Broadcasting House as seditious. However, he set himself right with a literary feature about Coleridge which impressed London, apart from its merits, with its demonstration that Bridson could write a non-polemical piece when he wanted to.

He was to make a very big contribution to the golden age of radio as one of the fortunate ones whose talent and opportunity and ambition happened to coincide. He wanted to write dramatic poetry, he wanted to reach a wide audience, and divined that in radio he had the medium that would bring the two in touch. He knew as a practising writer that verse written to be spoken could be made exciting – '*charged* in a way that prose could never be', he wrote; and as a young and fertile experimenter his soon became an outstanding voice. Val Gielgud thought his 'March Of The '45', a dramatised reconstruction of the last Stuart rising, was the most distinguished piece of original radio-writing of 1936.

'Steel' (1937) used just about every sound available to radio to convey the drama and excitement he'd absorbed in a Sheffield steel works. Here is a taste of Bridson's power to make you see a scene. 'You can see the lie of a good bit of land from here. How these yards have followed the flat of a shallow valley, up to grimy embankments. On that hillside there is a branch line to Rotherham. But you will notice how those rows and rows of little houses hang down to the very edge of the cutting. Some of the men come from over there; but down here in the valley it all seems very open. Even the sheds appear to be isolated and the standing trucks empty and somehow forgotten. You'll notice the sky, how grey it is. Overhead it is blue, admittedly, but over there behind the houses and all around – it is just the colour of dull metal . . . the horizon forms a sort of milky way for spent and forgotten smoke, which hangs about the city from year's end to year's end. You can see how the black plumes from distant smoke-stacks gradually dissolve in it. Only the white steam of the engines, here, ever melts into the blue of the sky overhead. Or so it seems.'

Here is a glimpse of the early morning, going-to-work scene recalled in popular verse rhythms:

> Wan lights glow in the frosted windows,
> Of dismal shops,
> And doors creak discreetly, as gurgling gutters
> Are choked with morning slops.
> Only the pipes of shivering men are warm,
> Huddling at a hundred tramway stops.

A major talent, then. But his success in putting ordinary people on the air, talking vividly and naturally, was as important as any of his writings – perhaps more, for without such an opening-up of broadcasting the BBC could not have spoken as it did in the war; and though others might have done it had Bridson not, he did it first, in a 1935 piece about the people of the Yorkshire dales, 'Cam Houses to Tam Hill'. He loved the way the dalesfolk talked and longed to put it across to the listeners. But how to do it, remembering the rule about scripts? He thought of inventing a character, to be played by an actor, whom the people would accept and talk to as one of their own. This became Harry Hopeful, created as a jobless glass-blower's assistant who tramped the roads of the North looking for work. He was played by Frank Nicholls, a former amateur who had played parts in other Bridson programmes and was to prove himself, said Bridson, one of the world's great broadcasters. The dalesfolk were completely at their ease with him, and while they talked Bridson listened hard to their tricks of phrasing and dialect usages. Back in Manchester he wrote a script and posted their parts to those who would speak them. But the problem still was how to get them to do their stuff naturally in the studio. Bridson solved it by adapting the animal trainer's technique of patience and repetition. Let him describe it.

'I went back to the Dales a couple of days later with Nicholls and a radio engineer. We took portable gear with us, for I wanted everyone in the show to have seen the microphone first rigged up in his own sitting-room;

after that, it could hold no fears for him. In one home after another we tried the acts out, changing the words here and there and listening to the result on headphones in our car at the front gate. If a speaker sounded unnatural his family was invited to listen over the phones as well – and no critics could be more exacting. After pillow sessions in bed with his wife for the next few days few men were below production pitch when the whole group came down by bus for the final studio rehearsal and transmission.'[2] The technique worked like magic,* and Harry Hopeful became a nationally popular figure. Shepherds, farmers, fishermen, craftsmen, quarrymen, postmen, blacksmiths came from all over the northern countryside to the studio with Nicholls. Bridson's aim of projecting the North was triumphantly realised; Nicholls's untimely death in 1938 robbed radio of one of its best-known and liked personalities.

By then another talent had begun to flower. This belonged to Joan Littlewood, whom Harding had met when he presented the first RADA gold medal for microphone technique to her. She came from the East End of London, had won a scholarship to RADA which, said Bridson, she detested as heartily as the genteel mediocrity of the West End theatre. That sounds like Joan Littlewood all right. Harding asked her to go and see him, and she walked the 180 miles with a rucksack, sleeping out, living on raw potatoes and turnips. As a sharer of Bridson's Leftism, and possessor of a singularly winning radio presence, she was a natural to succeed Nicholls, and they proceeded to do for the industrial North what Harry Hopeful had done for the countryside. Using the same methods of careful writing and home rehearsal to gain their subjects' confidence, they put the millworkers of Oldham and the miners of Durham on the air with an impact that proved 'that everyone was capable of putting his point of view across, often more pungently than those who were paid to do it for him'.[3] 'Cotton' and 'Coal' were in 1938. A year later the war broke out, drama and features shifted from Evesham to Manchester, and the North was invaded by a crowd of broadcasters who now found that the kind of creative radio they believed in had become, like the manufacture of frivolity, part of the war effort. Under Gilliam, in charge of Features since 1936, a famous chapter in the story of dramatised reality began.

Gilliam is one of the great names in BBC history and mythology. It is one of my lasting regrets that I never met him until the mid-fifties, by which time the giant shadow of television was beginning to fall across the face of radio. Maurice Gorham summed him up as a man who combined with wide interests (he had joined the BBC from journalism) a real passion for radio itself, not merely radio as a pipeline for other arts. Rayner Heppenstall, who worked with him for twenty-two years, said he was ill-read, at heart a

* It became a cornerstone of the Scrapbooks.

journalist, his behaviour sometimes appalling, but was still the only creative personality to have emerged in broadcasting in Britain. To Douglas Cleverdon he was a man of inspiring integrity, compassionate and courageous, a bon viveur, unpunctual, extremely good company and a tower of strength to his subordinates. To Bridson he was flamboyant, generous and witty, with a gift for leadership which inspired a group of the most talented writers and producers in radio history. He was a huge eater and drinker and lover of all good things; his nickname was Lorenzo the Magnificent.

Features were of two kinds, the documentary ('The Shadow of the Swastika', 'The Home Front', etc.) and the actuality ('In Britain Now', 'Go to It', etc.). The first was a carefully shaped work of writing, employing actors; the second brought the people to the microphone. Cecil McGivern, recruited to Features from the Newcastle station, made his name with a number of specials of the first type – 'Battle of Britain', 'Bomb Doors Open', 'Coastal Command', 'Bombers over Berlin', 'Women Hitting Back' – in which he displayed a supple dexterity in the difficult business of taking in facts and regurgitating them in dramatic form. He didn't always get them right (he imagined that the Royal Observer Corps could plot enemy aircraft tracks at night; we couldn't, we could only try to get a cross-bearing by estimating the height) but the pictures evoked of the great effort did their job of uplifting morale. (One curious obstacle he had to deal with even here was radio's prudishness; in 'Bomb Doors Open' the trainee bomb-aimer had to talk about lying for hours on his 'tummy'.) Bridson's 'Billy Welcome' and 'We Speak for Ourselves' and Francis Dillon's 'Country Magazine' brought in the actual workers on the factories and farms. This use of broadcasting was so far ahead of anything American radio had reached that when Bridson put Oldham people into his first *Transatlantic Call* (this famous series ran weekly in Britain and America for three years) CBS accused him of using professionals.

Every year the climax of broadcasting was the Christmas Day link-up produced by Gilliam and McGivern. The titles chart the progress of the war: 'Christmas Under Fire', 'Absent Friends', 'The Fourth Christmas', 'We Are Advancing', 'The Journey Home', 'Wherever You May Be'. They were broadcast live at 2 pm on Christmas Day and were sad, sentimental, touching, exciting and emotional. The message was always the same: the nation was resolutely fighting a war of liberation and it was spoken by the people into microphones taken into the homes, factories, messes, shelters. To read the scripts so long after is still to call back yesterday. Even when they sentimentalised slightly they did so only on subjects where the nation had agreed to postpone the look at the thing as it was, such as the increasing strain of separations, the fearfulness of the blitz, and the hideous ordeal inflicted on the country dwellers by some of the evacuees. 'Christmas Under Fire' glanced obliquely at the reign of terror when it put a farmer's wife and her charges on the air. *Mrs Burchall:* 'I've had my little old cottage full and there'll be all of us tonight, but we get some good fun. What was the best time you ever had, Pam?' *Evacuee:* 'Oh, aunty, last winter, when we made a slide and slid down it on your best tea-tray.' *Other evacuees:* 'Oh, blimey, yeah, what fun that was, not 'arf,' etc. *Mr Burchall:* 'And what about the time they stripped the plums, stripped the tree, almost, and they was proper good plums, they was.' *Second evacuee:* 'Oh, yeah, I remember, I 'ad the stomach ache three times.'

Perhaps they were pleasant to each other because they were nervous. It requires a great deal of self-confidence to be nasty in a broadcast. But I prefer to think they were nice because they were nice people; it's the quality that still brings a lump to your throat. The programme went over to the Cotswolds (and remember that this was 'live'; the microphone hung over the table among the remains of the Christmas dinner). 'I don't mind doing without a turkey as long as there's roast beef and Yorkshire pudding after all, and it wasn't too bad.' General response: 'Very good, mother. If you ask me you did us well.' And then they went to a war factory in Wales, where a furnaceman said: 'Christmases have come and gone but never before have we furnacemen worked with greater determination than on this Christmas Day. Aye, we're all in the front line, we carry on air raids or no; and for as long as this war lasts these furnaces shall never grow cold; we'll keep them as warm as the voices of those boys singing and as warm as the greetings from Wales I now send you. . . .' They went to Glasgow, where some sad Poles, their country divided between Germany and Russia, the Katyn massacre by the Russians already a hideous project, recalled Christmas as men recalling something irretrievably lost. 'If any in Poland are hearing us, tell everybody we have not forgotten the holiness of the Polish Christmas, nor our brothers.'

This programme went to the ruins of Coventry Cathedral, the courtyard outside the Church of the Nativity in Bethlehem, to a desert crossroads outside Cairo, and one of the communal shelters where the people were preparing for Christmas night deep in London's Underground. It was no joke, as Howard Marshall's narration said, the shelter life: 'it means great hardship, great strain, no privacy, none of your own things, very little comfort and always the risk of worse trouble.' But the presence of the microphone turned on cries of 'Who cares about the blitz?' 'They haven't got us down.' 'We can take it', and more of the kind of thing that is hard to hear without a twinge of embarrassment now but which stirred your heart then. The broadcasts did not cheat; the voices and the sentiments they brought were those oι the people's war. Most of us, if pressed, would have thought like the woman who introduced the King. 'My children are away, my son is in the air force, my daughter is on a farm, and my two grandchildren are evacuated to the country. We always used to spend Christmas together but we're parted this year for the first time. Sitting here on Christmas Day I remember the last war and its food shortages and how we used to stand for hours hoping to get a few potatoes . . . and now, it's a horrible thing is war but in a way it has its compensations, it's made us realise how good and kind most people are and that's a great comfort in the middle of all this anxiety. In spite of all we've been through I'm thankful for a great deal; when peace returns to us we've all got to see to it that this spirit of neighbourliness and sympathy we've found is carried on and not forgotten.' Spoken by a politician or a churchman it would have meant little. Coming from a citizen it was a kind of proclamation of intent.

In 1941 the link-up was narrated by Lt-Cdr Ralph Richardson, Fleet Air Arm. By then the war had settled into the long slog. The Russians and the Americans and the Japanese were in. Britain had become a kind of unsinkable garrison, taking troops in and sending them out. Richardson's script said, 'I myself can't think of a single home that can look round and say, "They're all here, thank God!"' This was the low point of the war, for while the broadcast was on the air the country was having to take the appalling news from the Far East, where the Hong Kong garrison was that day surrendering. There wasn't much comfort to be had except from fellow feeling and perhaps, as Richardson said, the Empire had been brought closer together.

In 1942 'The Fourth Christmas' went further than ever, to Chungking and Russia. By then thirty-two nations were on the Allied side. Hearing this broadcast you can remember the curious feeling you had that the Germans had become banished from the Christian community; the people of the Allied countries were waging total war on an outlawed race and so could sing the chosen carol – 'Joy to the world, the Lord is come, Let earth receive her King, Let every heart prepare him room And Heaven and nature sing . . .' – without consciously feeling humbugs. In any case, a broadcast of this kind had to bow to diplomatic necessity* as the war became more widespread and new nations, foreseeing the probable outcome, rushed to join the winning side. In 1943, when 'We Are Advancing' went for the first Christmas since 1939 into the newly liberated mainland areas of Europe, they had to give Brazil a piece of it. 'Advance, sentinels of the most noble traditions of the human race! May the undaunted soldiers of the British Empire feel in this Christmas message the yearnings of the people of Brazil for a glorious peace.'

Next year 'The Journey Home' went into a Europe in which the lights

* A 1943 special, 'In Honour of Russia', commemorated the revolution without mentioning Trotsky.

were going on again, but the hopes of peace in 1944, so bright when the Allies were streaming across France after an enemy that seemed totally broken, had faded; and in spite of the excitement of the year the broadcast reflected a note of exhaustion. 'Most families are broken and scattered, for them this Christmas Day is only the memory of a face, the echo of a voice. For a few minutes let radio shatter distance, bring mother to son and husband to wife. . . .' Then it was over and the programme was in the house of the Dyson family in Bethnal Green, together at Christmas for the first time since the war began. The eldest son had been a prisoner of the Japanese since 1941. The twin sons had gone to France together and survived the fighting round Caen in the same tank. The three girls had worked through the raids. The twins had gone home at 11 o'clock on the morning of Christmas Eve. 'We're all here and I thank God for this day. Just like a dream.' Thus Mrs Dyson; as it had done so skilfully in the past six years, the programme echoed with a single family a national mood. There was a lot of peculiarly intense happiness about in 1945. I remember seeing a returned soldier in the *Swan* at Claygate. He had been a prisoner since Crete and now he sat in the bar among the actual sights and sounds of his own village. I've never seen such a blaze of happiness on anyone's face. You could have done with dark glasses to look at him through. It was a level of happiness that only comes when that which was feared lost suddenly turns up safe and well. Lady Violet Bonham Carter in a *Brains Trust* session described how, when the War Office telegraphed to tell her that her missing son had been reported a prisoner, she put off going to bed until she could stay awake no longer, she could not bear to part with such an intensity of joy.

6

THE SOUNDS OF LIBERATION

Under Gilliam the war years saw a huge rise in the output and flexibility of features. Writers and producers learned to fling a programme together at a speed that would have been impossible a couple of years earlier. Topical features such as the weekly war review *Marching On* were often written a day or so before the broadcast and might be partly rewritten during the last rehearsal; the music would be composed and orchestrated a few hours before the broadcast. In May 1943 features' dramatised documentary, 'Victory in Africa', was on the air within forty-eight hours of the German surrender in Tunisia. Then, as reporting techniques improved and the pattern of the war changed into the long, unbroken offensive, the dramatised documentary and the feature came to supplement actuality, the hard news reporting done by taking the microphone to the places where things were happening, and bringing to it the people who were doing them.

The Home Service put out six bulletins a day, at 7 am, 8 am, 1 pm, 6 pm, 9 pm, and midnight. In December 1939 the nine o'clock news claimed between forty-three and fifty per cent of the audiences, and this figure did not substantially alter in any of the other five wartime Decembers. When the wireless was broadcasting something that was not a news report but the thing itself, as when Churchill came to the mike to give one of his exalting speeches, the listening figures were fantastic. One of his broadcasts during the Battle of Britain summer was heard by sixty-four per cent of the adult population, probably better than twenty-two million. Audiences were swollen by a good deal of public listening, and when anxiety was great, as in 1940 and the days before D-Day, a Churchill speech or a news bulletin would hold the bars of the pubs in silence. Always the news began with the bulletins, read impersonally and formally, composed to sound a solid, authoritative and trustworthy report of all the latest news that could be broadcast without risk to the war effort. Increasingly it was backed up by reports from the home and fighting fronts. These were personal and informal, designed to illustrate the news in voice and sound; and from them emerged the names that were to become better known than those of any of the oldtimers who had followed the fighting with notebooks and typewriters in earlier wars.

In the early war years the studio recording machines were still about the size of a fairly large kitchen mangle, but the mobile units no longer needed the laundry van. The smaller model could be carried in the back of a saloon car, or set up in an aircraft. It could work off a 12-volt accumulator and was compact enough to be carried by hand to places where a car could not go. It still could not make a continuous recording lasting longer than four minutes (the duration of a single disc) but it was fast and mobile and its output could be fed back to the BBC from any telephone line or, less reliably, short-wave transmitter. This was the equipment Richard Dimbleby took to France as observer with the BEF and Gardner took down to Dover for his account of the dog-fights. But in 1939 the war in the air and on the western front was lying quiet. It fell to Edward Ward, hastily sent out to cover the 1939-40 Soviet-Finnish war, to carve a little piece of broadcasting history by taking a microphone and recording gear into a front line. What happened to Ward and Dimbleby subsequently showed how much a career depends on luck.

Bernard Stubbs was sent to replace Dimbleby, who went to Egypt. Hardly was he below the horizon when Hitler struck at the Low Countries and France. It fell to Stubbs and Ward (who gave a striking account of his escape from Bordeaux) to describe the débâcle. After that Ward replaced Dimbleby in Egypt and was captured outside Tobruk by the Italians. (He spent the next three years in prison camps, until the Allied advance into Germany liberated him in 1945, whereon he picked up a microphone and resumed duty as though he'd never been away.) In Greece and the desert Dimbleby was having his own bad luck as the bringer of hopes followed by defeats. He was accused of over-optimism and brought back to London. It fell to Godfrey Talbot, Frank Gillard and Denis Johnston to report the unbroken success story of the Eighth Army from El Alamein to Tripoli and on into Italy. Dimbleby was returned to the correspondents' pool for normal duties. On his first day back the best assignment they could find for him was a visit to a demonstration of army cookery in Salisbury Plain, a chore he accepted, said Gillard, cheerfully, without question or comment. But the cards were about to be shuffled for him. He gave an outstanding account of flying with a bomber crew to Berlin, beating his old idol Ed Murrow to it by a few months. (The Lancaster was nearly overturned, and Dimbleby was airsick. He kept talking, and somehow the engineer with him kept the needle in the recording groove. When the bomber reached home safely Dimbleby had to shove his way into the night express for London to broadcast his eyewitness account; a woman, seeing a young man in civilian clothing, rebuked him for not giving up his seat to a soldier.) More important, he had begun to help the planning of *War Report*, the supreme achievement of news in the field in the BBC's war.

The embryo of *War Report* had existed since 1940, when the chances were that Britain itself would be invaded. The BBC appointed war correspondents and recording engineers in all its regions, equipped with cars, recording gear, and secret lists of transmitters and telephone lines. If the Germans had succeeded in landing and occupying a part of the country there would have been at least some chance of the BBC receiving and broadcasting truth. In 1943, when the invasion of Europe across the Channel was a project accepted as certain by the captors and captives as well as the liberators, and the only unanswered questions were when and where it would strike, S. J. de Lotbinière began to build a news-gathering operation to accompany the fighting.

Newspapers were restricted to one correspondent each in any theatre of war, and Lotbinière had first to persuade the Services that this wouldn't do for the BBC's handling of the invasion. In March he was allowed to prove his case by sending two teams to cover a big second-front exercise named Spartan. As the most experienced correspondent there, Dimbleby was in his element. He wrote a valued confidential report full of good advice. Reporters must have jeeps. They must drive them themselves and not depend on an Army driver. They must have dispatch riders with them to take their stuff back. They must – 'this,' he wrote, 'is a delicate point' – train recording engineers to behave like the officers whose status they assumed by putting on the uniform. Always a stickler for doing things right, his sense of occasion, which was to make him such a good describer of royal events, was revolted by the young engineer they gave him in Spartan, who wore his cap too rakishly, smoked all the time, called private soldiers, military policemen and sentries 'Old boy', and attracted a senior general's attention by calling 'I say' with the cigarette still drooping from his lips.

So many people were involved in the organisation of *War Report* that I could have written this section using different illustrations and names without any cost in accuracy. It became a huge undertaking, involving thirty-two British and Empire reporters and as many engineers and transmitting staff, and calling at need on the resources of the American radio networks and the new services programme established jointly by British, American and Canadian radio for the Allied Expeditionary Force. (It was run by the BBC's Maurice Gorham. Its signature tune, an arrangement of 'Oranges and Lemons', will bring back that summer to readers now nearing and passing their fifties who were then soldiers and airmen; they heard it coming out of radios in ships and trucks, said Gorham, all the way from Normandy to the Rhine.) Every source that could bring to the people at home the sounds of their men's war was used. Edited by Laurence Gilliam and Donald Boyd it used the best of all available dispatches from all the active fronts, cut into a fast-moving commentary on modern warfare such as the world had not yet heard.[1] Its special quality was that it never faked its sound effects. The voice, or the background sound, always came from where it said it did. (One of the major propaganda errors of German radio was to mix the true and the false, in a way which undermined its listeners' confidence.) The reporters now had the piece of equipment the engineers had promised them; a truly portable recorder. Tested in action at Anzio it could be carried easily by anyone who could carry 40 lbs easily. It was not much bigger than a portable gramophone, carried twelve double-sided discs which could take more than an hour's recordings, a clip-on microphone and a detachable dry battery. It was so simple to operate that the reporter could manage by himself; and it was these machines that brought the first accounts of those happenings on 6 June 1944, which engaged the hearts, minds and spirits of more people than had ever been moved by a single event in the world's history, for until broadcasting no communication of news had been so universal and instant.

I tried to get in on the invasion as a member of the sea-borne Observer Corps which had been formed to send trained spotters with the ships to discourage them from shooting at the RAF, which they did with appalling frequency; but they turned me down. From the post in Claygate I would have had a matchless sight of the vast fleets of gliders moving south, but I wasn't at Claygate either; I had been sent on a course to the RAF's Aircraft Recognition Centre in Southport, and it was in the mess there that I heard the unforgettable reading by John Snagge of the first D-Day communiqué and, later that day, the first of the *War Reports* from the beaches. The news that the huge enterprise was finally committed, the possibility of defeat, the chance that perhaps it was the beginning of the end, the certainty that all must be paid for with the lives of husbands, fathers, sons, were concentrated into a fierce, unremitting hope and anxiety. How can I describe it now? I can only say that I sought refuge in Shakespeare. I found myself repeating over and over again in my mind, as though it was something to hang on to, 'O God of battles, steel our soldiers' hearts!'

The hunger for news brought to triumphant fulfilment the long hopes of broadcasting men that one day they would be allowed to show what radio could do. In *War Report* spontaneity, daring, flexibility, enterprise and improvisation got the better of precedents, protocol and caution. The whole operation was based on speed and professionalism. Earliest messages were rushed back across Channel by ship or plane and car to a transmitting point at Fareham. In Broadcasting House they were re-recorded and typed out for censorship and then the master disc made containing the edited and censored dispatch. By 17 June the first mobile transmitter (codenamed Mike Charlie Oboe) had landed at Arromanches in the tail end of the gale that might have wrecked the invasion, and thereafter censorship could be done before a message was sent to London. Larger transmitters followed MCO but were left behind when the great breakout began and it was MCO, in its three-ton truck, that had to pursue the pursuers, staying as close as it could to the

Channel coast so that its signal would still reach England. After Arnhem *War Report* used high-powered transmitters, Mike Charlie Nan for the British and Mike Charlie Peter with the Americans, and on these the reporters could transmit direct to London and out to every corner of the world. The objective was to get the news back fast, and to meet it they did things that before the war could never have been imagined.

Frank Gillard borrowed the Brussels Home Service in September 1944 to get news to the BBC of the Second Army's attempt to join up with the airborne troops near Eindhoven. When Chester Wilmot reached Brussels five days later with his account of the desperate fighting for the bridge at Nijmegen, Mike Charlie Nan was out of service and nobody in London was listening for it. Wilmot broadcast on a medium waveband that he knew listeners in Britain might hear, and asked any who heard him to tell the BBC he was trying to get through. Only one attempt was ever made to rehearse *War Report*. Allowed at last full play for its advantage of speed it scored some notable scoops, bursting in on scheduled programmes with the first news of Himmler's suicide and the first full account of the German surrender to the British at Luneberg Heath. But it was the sustained picture in sound of the war that made them such absorbing radio for the listeners at home, as the excitement and suspense of the invasion were followed by the hard fighting for Caen, the American breakthrough at St Lo, the days of pursuit when the Americans were running off their maps, the exultation when the Falaise gap seemed to be closing on the whole German army, the sunburst of the liberation of Paris and Brussels when the British covered the last seventy-five miles in thirteen hours, the shock of Arnhem and the German counter-offensive, the Rhine crossings, the foul revelations of Belsen and Buchenwald, the link-up with the Russians at Torgau, and so to the evening of 5 May 1945, when the campaign on the western front and *War Report* ended together.

I offer some extracts from the reporters' dispatches as an echo, to be caught by those who can hear it, of the last great feat of arms Europe will undergo.

'We're over the coast now and the run in has started – one minute, thirty seconds. Red light – green and out – get on, out, out, out fast into the cool night air, out, out, out over France – and we know that the dropping zone is obstructed, we're jumping into fields covered with poles. And then the ground comes up to meet me. And I find myself in the middle of a cornfield – and overhead hundreds of parachutes and containers are coming down.' That was Guy Byam* landing with the parachutists before H-Hour.

'We dived into the cloud. We could see nothing. The glider pilot could see nothing, all he could do was hang on to his controls and follow us about

* Byam was one of the unlucky ones, his plane was shot down over Berlin in a daylight raid in February 1945. Wilmot survived the war to become one of its most successful historians; he was killed in the early Comet airliner disaster in January 1954.

in the murk. The rear-gunner yelled suddenly: "The glider's hit." The skipper said, "Glider pilot, glider pilot, are you all right?" There was a short pause, then the voice came again: "All right, we're with you." The navigator ... was shouting to the skipper, and when we came out of the cloud and away from the flak, why there was the landing zone just as we had been studying it on maps for days and days. "Casting off," said the little gruff voice, and ... the tug lunged forward free of the glider's weight. I looked down as we went into a turn to come home. There was nothing but blankness now. But there were a lot of gliders swooshing down in that blankness.' That was John Macadam, an RAF pilot with the glider tugs.

'The scene on the beach until one had sorted it out was at first rather depressing because we did see a great many barges in difficulties with these anti-tank screens and we noticed that a number of them had struck mines as ours had struck mines. But then we began to see that in fact the proportion that got through was very much greater, and that troops were moving along all the roads, and that tanks were out already and going up the hills, that in fact we dominated the situation.' That was Howard Marshall, landing at dawn with the British Second Army.

'Long stretches of empty roads shining with rain, deserted, dripping woods, and damp fields – static, quiet – but here and there a movement catches the eye as our aircraft on reconnaissance roars over a wood – three German soldiers running like mad across the main road to fling themselves into cover. And, much nearer the battle area than they, a solitary peasant harrowing the field, up and down behind the horses, looking nowhere but before him and at the soil.' That was Richard Dimbleby, over the German lines.

'Almost as though on conveyor belts, the regular stream of ducks [DUKW, amphibious landing craft] was moving. Hundreds of them, they went out empty from the shore, changed from wheel-drive to propeller a few yards out and made tracks, or rather wakes, for the merchantmen lying out to sea. Two thousand tons they brought in on this small sector yesterday and it will be nearer three thousand tons today.... As you come in towards the beaches it's rather like driving in on the roads towards an industrial town. It's like a great, enormous industrial area.' That was Michael Standing and Howard Marshall on the build-up.

'In the last couple of days, when things have been quieter, he's found time to make life a little more comfortable. He's winkled the snipers out of the ruined houses and he's probably now living in the comparative luxury of a cellar or an outhouse. ... A few shops have opened up rather cautiously in the less shattered villages and the Tommies are getting along fine with the language, the inhabitants, and la bière – which, I imagine, consists of ninety-nine per cent water.' That was Alan Melville's account of life returning to the liberated villages.

'Just round a bend we came across the beginnings of the destruction. Rubble and masonry were being shovelled into a great bomb crater which completely blocked the whole road. Beyond that the scene was one of total and absolute devastation, every building a total wreck, trees and poles and petrol pumps lying askew across the road, wires trailing everywhere. We picked our way ahead, thankful for the fierce fire of our guns which were pouring concentrations into Colombelles factory at that moment and keeping the enemy up there quiet.' That was Frank Gillard, entering Caen. Then – 'The road from Falaise to Argentan runs straight across rolling country. Driving down it this morning we came over the brow of a hill and there, reaching right back out of sight, was an enormous column of prisoners, such a sight as I haven't seen since the last days in North Africa. They were trudging three abreast, packed tightly together, the weary, tattered remnants of the German Seventh Army.' Gillard again, north of the Falaise gap which the Allied armies never quite closed.

'It's a city of violent contrasts – a city celebrating the entry of the Allies with wild enthusiasm and gaiety – and yet a city still at war, with all its gaiety broken by gun flashes and the rattle of machine guns at street corners. You can walk down the boulevards in the sunshine and imagine for a moment that you are in a peaceful prewar Paris – when suddenly from the rooftops comes the crack of a rifle, and you see a Maquis lad answering back from the cover of a doorway.' Howard Marshall, three days after Paris had been freed. And in Brussels – 'There had been Germans in the streets only an hour before, and not a flag had been in sight; but by the time we arrived every building was plastered with flags and streamers. The streets were decked with banners – "Welcome to our liberators," "Welcome to our Allies," "Through Belgium to Berlin". Thousands of women and children have made themselves special dresses in the Belgian colours – red skirts, yellow blouses and black scarves or bandannas. And these all appeared as if by magic just as the Germans left.' That was Chester Wilmot.

'The crew chief is on his knees back in the rear talking into his intercom with the pilots. The rest of the men have folded up their yellow Mae Wests, as there is no possibility of our ditching in the water on this trip. They're looking out of the window rather curiously, almost as though they were passengers on a peacetime airliner. You occasionally see a man rub the palm of his hand against his trouser leg. There seems to be just that – oh – sort of a film over some of their faces, as though they were on the verge of perspiring but they aren't. Every man the whole length of this ship is now looking down at this Dutch countryside.' That was Ed Murrow with the First Allied Airborne Army at the beginning of the Arnhem battle which signalled, as one of the Americans put it, that the picnic was over.

Of all the war reports, two of the best remembered were the accounts given by Guy Byam and Stanley Maxted, the Canadian, of the British withdrawal from Arnhem back across the Rhine. They were flown back to Britain and, dirty and exhausted, with the shock of battle and great danger still on them, talked from a few notes of the defeat that in the autumn of 1944, when final victory had seemed as near as if the Allied hand had only to close its fingers, was one of the bitterest of the war. 'We lay down flat in the mud and rain and stayed that way for two hours till the sentry beyond the hedge on the bank of the river told us to move up over the dike and be taken across. Mortaring started now and I was fearful for those that were already on the bank. I guessed it was pretty bad for them. After what seemed a nightmare of an age we got our turn and slithered up and over on to some mud flats. There was a shadow of a little assault craft with an outboard motor on it. Several of these had been rushed up by a field company of engineers. We waded out into the Rhine and a voice that was sheer music spoke from the stern of the boat saying: "Ye'll have to step lively, boys, 'taint healthy here." . . . We slid down the other side on our backsides, and sloshed through mud for four miles and a half, me thinking, "Gosh, I'm alive, how did it happen?" ' That was Maxted. 'The weeks to come will tell how valuable has been the stand of these men . . . who put out nineteen fires in the building they were fighting in, men who fought when tanks cruised up and down the streets thirty yards away blasting the walls that were their protection into rubble, and other men who fought on silently in groups in the woods, who died round their gliders, who died in the skies; and amongst these . . . the men of the RAF who took them there and who so gallantly tried to re-supply them.' That was Byam. 'Your men are no foreigners to us. Maybe they never saw Holland before they floated down over it, to liberate her people and the world. Some of these brave young men will stay behind in our country for ever. They shall not rest in cold foreign soil. The soil of Holland will proudly guard your dead as if they were the deeply mourned sons of our own people.' That was the Dutch writer Johann Fabricias, giving his postscript to Arnhem.

Normally the continual reaching out of death wasn't harped on; the reporters had been describing victory, not yet the cost; and after the Rhine crossings in March the reports picked up again the accelerating advance. 'The great sensation these days is exhilaration. How often we've dreamed of this. In the long dark nights of the London blitz, in the shelling on the road to Damascus, in the dreary sandstorms or blinding heat of the desert, in the white dust of Sicily and then in Normandy when it seemed that the SS divisions would never crack, I've looked forward to this day, and now here we go through the ruins of Germany. . . . In the areas we've already overrun we've liberated over two million of slaves, chiefly Russian and Polish but also French, Czechs, Yugoslavs and others. We've seen them in bands of several hundred at a time. They're not always emaciated, starving, ragged. Sometimes you wouldn't know they were slaves, except for their language and the fact that they're laughing and chattering, waving and singing. . . . I've seen women on their knees, tears running down their cheeks as British tanks rolled past and they knew they were free. What a story that told, millions of Ruths sick for home, who stood in tears amid the alien corn and even now many of them will go back and find their homes destroyed and their families dead or gone. Is there any measure for the rivers and tides of sorrows and tears that the Nazis have set flowing in Europe?'

That was Matthew Halton of the Canadian Broadcasting Corporation, summing up the feelings of the Allies as they moved farther into Germany and to the appalling discoveries that awaited them. But let the last word be from Robert Dunnett, for his account in May of a dance got up by Polish women for the Canadians who had rescued them. 'The dance has just broken up in laughter and in happy conversation. Now we're going to have a waltz. Some of them are dressed in the white and red and black – very pretty costumes that they bring from Silesia and from Cracow and they're going round with their skirts swinging in the light of the candles – there's no electric light here – just candlelight, soft, soft candlelight going up to the wooden roof and casting shadows on the floor and on to those pretty dresses.' For the moment, at least, the graces and kindlinesses of humanity had won.

The Observer Corps post I had been on closed down on the evening before VE Day in Europe. Another man and I entered the closure in the log book and ceremonially fired the Verey pistol we had been given five years earlier to signal the invasion, should we have happened to see it. Next day I went back to clear out my belongings and took them home, aware in some queasy corner of my mind that I was now out of work. Thames Ditton was going crazy, but my girl, released the same day from her job on the farm, and I were shy of crowd celebrations. I cycled to the pub and managed to get some quart bottles filled up with draught beer; we stayed indoors that night listening to the war reporters, now victory reporters, describing the scenes from the London streets, and cried a little into our beer. The spring grew into summer. A scratch Australian XI resumed a kind of Test series against an English XI; through open windows there came once again the sounds of cricket over the wireless, the 'tock' of a bat, pattering applause that would unexpectedly swell into a huge shout, the lazy hum of commentary. Howard Marshall was back. It seemed the essence of summer radio. Then the coalition government was dissolved, and as the campaigning began for the first general election for ten years Winston Churchill's 'Socialism means Gestapo in Britain' broadcast told the British that the national unity of wartime, of which the BBC had become such a stirring sounding-board, was over too.

BLASTS OF CHANGE

1

HOW TO BE A TV CRITIC

One Sunday morning in the spring of 1952 Guy Schofield, then editor of the *Daily Mail*, invited me to join him in the Feathers. We were exchanging the low-keyed chat proper on such occasions when he suddenly asked me what I thought about television. My intuition told me at once that the question was not idly put. I suppressed the frivolous answer that rose to my lips. As yet, I replied, I had had few opportunities of watching it, but it was clear that an instrument capable of taking a picture into so many homes must be one of, etc., etc. He thereupon confided that the present TV critic, J. Stubbs Walker, was to be made science correspondent (his reviews had been notable for their authoritative comments on how the picture got into the set and out again) and asked me if I would like to try it. I said I would, provided I could receive a signal, for I lived in Brighton, well beyond the farthest limits of fringe reception.

The *Daily Mail* was the first popular national to take TV seriously enough to provide a review of the previous evening's programmes. To explain why Schofield invited me to write it I must explain how I qualified for it. When the war ended I had one of those life-changing strokes of luck. The managing editor of the *Sussex Daily News* group had rejected my earlier request for a job, explaining that he had to find room for his own returning staff. But in September 1945 he wrote to say there might be something for me if I cared to go down to Brighton to see him. At the interview I sold him my so far untested qualifications as a drama critic and golf reporter as hard as I could, and accepted a job as sports sub on the *Evening Argus*. As such I made no overwhelming impression but wrote one or two articles for the features page about golf and the cinema, so when the golf season reopened in the spring I seemed the most proper person to cover it. It happened shortly after that the sharp and acid wit that had got the young film and theatre critic his job (he was Leon Sinden, brother of Donald) took him across the line separating what the editor and the local cinema and theatre managers agreed was the permissible and non-permissible. I was asked to take on his job too. I had also become music critic because somebody had to do it. I had no objection, for my aim was to pick up as many specialised jobs as I could and get off the 'diary', the daily list of engagements for which reporters were marked.

By 1946 I was film and theatre critic for the evening paper and a book reviewer and golf correspondent for the morning paper. On top of attending concerts, film showings and first nights and the Sussex golf tournaments I wrote a Monday column of polemics, a Thursday column of showbiz chat, a Saturday essay, and a column about golf – about 5000 words a week for not really enough money to live on. But I got my golf, theatre, cinema, music and books for nothing. True, I had to write about them, but I was in the middle of that joyful phase most writers go through once of being able to knock the stuff off easily and confidently. I was newly married, living by the sea in the only town in England that seems to have escaped the blight of the puritans and philistines. In that period immediately after the war every day seemed to restore some lost amenity. One didn't need much money because there wasn't much to buy. My wife came home one day with a pound of beef sausages that looked, smelled and tasted something like beef sausages; we exulted over her find as though she'd discovered a cache of whisky. Such were the extravagances of 1946/7. I never had a better time in my life.

As the *Argus* drama critic I sharpened my wits on all the plays – about thirty a year – that opened in Brighton before going to London, most of them at the beautiful little Theatre Royal. Some came to the Dolphin Theatre, which also housed for a year or two the repertory company founded for its nurslings by H. M. Tennent. I once saw the young Richard Baker (later a TV newsreader) play Sebastian in a very fetching purple and silver costume. The critic on the morning *Sussex Daily News* was Derek Granger, who later became literary consultant to the National Theatre. Together we relished the sensation of being large fish in a little pool, and began to meet an expanding circle of theatrical folk. Although some of the visiting companies doubted the authority and responsibility of our notices, those whose plays we praised spread the word in London theatre circles that in Brighton were two young critics of amazing perception, lucidity and wit. I was enjoying myself so much that in 1949 I blew myself out of the *Argus* by writing some pieces for the London *Evening Standard* and was fired for collaborating with the enemy. I sold the *Brighton Herald* a weekly theatre piece and freelanced in the ailing magazine market until the *Daily Mail* telephoned me one day in 1950 when I was feeling poor and unlucky. For fifteen guineas a week I became the oldest novice in Fleet Street on 'Who? Why? Where?' – a column of gossip so-called because every item had to start with one of those words. I believe the idea was suggested as a joke to the then Lady Rothermere by Noël Coward. I felt the shame of this base employment keenly. It seemed the more ridiculous because nobody could understand what a man of thirty-five with no Fleet Street experience was doing in a gossip column of a silliness that could only be endured by young sparks fresh from the universities who thought it all the greatest lark in the world. However, the title changed, the column became comparatively sedate. I even came to accept it for a brief period when it was run by a journalist who was as big a misfit as a gossip as I was. We developed the practice of rarely originating stories ourselves, so were spared the indignity of questioning strangers about their personal affairs. The column was written in a genial haze of pipe smoke from contributions sent in by freelances mostly, for some reason, working from the National Liberal Club. We promoted friendly little competitions, the most successful of which invited readers to supply a name for a bench installed in a park for the use of old folk with money collected by Girl Guides.

I did not know that behind the scenes strings were being pulled on my behalf by theatre folk who liked my stuff in the *Brighton Herald* and thought it a pity I hadn't a Fleet Street outlet. (Derek Granger had already gone to the *Financial Times*, where he soon became easily the best of the overnight theatre critics.) When Stubbs Walker switched to science he uncovered a hole into which I might fit. But first there was the question of getting a signal. The Brighton dealer to whom I confided my problem sold me a set which he said would pull in signals from outer space, and installed for it a tremendous aerial on a mast so high that it had to be braced by stays fixed to the house. On rough nights the wind howled and sobbed through the rigging and there was some question whether the mast was a hazard to aircraft and should have a lamp hung on it. Like the old films in one of the What the Butler Saw machines on the Palace Pier, the picture I got flickered and faded and sometimes disappeared altogether, but I would have put up with a lot worse to escape from the gossip column. I reported myself equipped for duty.

In 1952 radio was by far the dominating half of the BBC. The centre of the BBC's organisation was still in Broadcasting House, and it was in the pubs round Portland Place that contact with producers and performers was to be made. Stubbs Walker explained to me that meeting them would be an essential part of my work, and he took a morning off from covering science to take me round the pubs. We went to the Stag's Head, the Windsor Castle, Shirreff's Wine Bar, the George, and the Bolivar. In any one of these (sometimes in all of them) one met the élite of radio and most of the other newspaper correspondents. In each place Stubbs introduced me as his successor. I was, and am, a poor hand at beer drinking. I detest the barbarous custom of drinking in 'rounds'. I would much rather have stood a round of pork pies when I was, as the primitive phrase has it, 'in the chair', but I felt to some extent on probation. The George was then the most fashionable pub (it was called the Glue Pot on account of the difficulty one had in getting out once in) and we drank there until closing time. I was still hoping to eat something more than a bar sausage, so Stubbs took me to a club called the M.L. There I was introduced to Gilbert Harding, then climbing towards his zenith as a radio and television personality. He was declaiming in his rich, fluent tones Wolsey's speech on his downfall –

> Like little wanton boys that swim on bladders,
> This many summers in a sea of glory.
> But far beyond my depth . . .

When Gilbert got on to Wolsey it indicated that his celebrations were about to enter a downward curve, and shortly afterwards I was swept out of the M.L. in his wake and left alone on the pavement, my eyes watering in the strong light of a rainy afternoon. Thereafter I promised myself, and stuck to it, to drink no more beer (I switched to white wine) and in no circumstances to miss my lunch or enter a drinking club; and by carefully timing my arrival at a pub to within about twenty minutes of closing time I was able to keep myself in fairly good shape.

Much of the drinking was social, but some was a deliberate unwinding. Most broadcasts were still originated live; elaborate productions were, as Rayner Heppenstall put it,[1] a fruitful source of nightmares; the drinking took on something of a feverish quality, as of aircrew giving thanks for a safe return or trying to stun the memory of a bad trip.

2

TELEVISION THE HARD WAY

When I became attached to broadcasting television was making most of the news. In the summer of 1952 nearly two million houses grouped round London, Birmingham, Manchester, Glasgow and Cardiff had television. The popular newspapers were beginning to taper off their reviews of radio programmes. George Campey, writing a weekly column about broadcasting in the London *Evening Standard*, by 1951 was usually leading his column with a piece about television. Like the columns of all Beaverbrook writers, it was heavily influenced by Beaverbrook's well-known preference for short sentences – 'There are no long sentences in the Bible' – an aphorism that was fatal to the prose style of most of his contributors. But Campey's column vividly evokes those days when everything television did was interesting. 'Is TV breaking family life?' he asked. 'Will TV change drinking habits?' 'Is this the end for Gilbert Harding?' 'What kind of people does Sir William Haley think we are?'

The BBC had begun the world's first high-definition service in 1936. Gerald Cock, the first director of television, believed that by 1939 it had reached the take-off point. There were only 20,000 viewers, but the range of sets available had widened (twenty-two firms showed models at the 1938 Radiolympia) and the price was coming down. You could buy a table model with a $4 \times 3\frac{3}{8}$-in. screen (it certainly brought the family together) for £21 and a cabinet model with a huge (22 by 18) screen for £200. The ordinary man was beginning to realise that he could have it in his home for a few shillings a week. It is certainly true that in a little under three years television created, or foreshadowed, the nucleus of the vast thing it became. By 1939 it had done a Coronation, Wimbledon, the Derby, Test cricket (it showed part of Len Hutton's record-breaking innings of 364 not out), big fights (Jock McAvoy *v*. Len Harvey), the Cup Final, Varnishing Day at the Royal Academy, and a quaint tribal custom of the times called the Theatrical Garden Party. It had achieved the most dramatic outside broadcast of Chamberlain's return from Munich. It had done the Boat Race and the Promenade concerts. In the three years it presented 326 plays, including a Laurence Olivier *Macbeth* and a Redgrave/Ashcroft *Twelfth Night* done completely from the Phoenix Theatre. The Canadian actress Joan Miller had become, one might say, the world's first television personality as the Switchboard Girl of Cecil Madden's weekly magazine, *Picture Page*. As Programme Organiser, Madden was a tireless and fertile innovator. Everything done later was attempted in however experimental a form. John Piper talked about art. Marcel Boulestin cooked. Mr Middleton gardened. David Seth Smith (the Zoo man) introduced animals. Bernard Shaw turned up again and stayed to tea. The television talk, studio drama, comedy, opera, ballet had established a secure foothold. All was swept into the dark at 12.10 on the afternoon of 1 September 1939. Without dramatics, without even an announcement, the sound and picture disappeared.

This was the service that reopened at Alexandra Palace in 1946, in an atmosphere of excitement, enthusiasm and adventurous improvisation that appealed greatly to Maurice Gorham, TV's newly appointed head. He had been sold on TV since before the war, when he used to console himself for the stuffiness he thought he found in Broadcasting House by driving over to the Palace where Cock's service was being run on a shoestring by people who, said Gorham, worked too hard, grumbled continuously, and loved their jobs. He relished his evenings in the crowded studios among the lights and colours, the glimpses of clowns and professors and performing dogs, and the general air of slap-happiness that television had brought back to the BBC.[1] Like Captain Lewis twenty-five years earlier he earnestly longed to retain and expand this pleasant atmosphere and believed there was no limit to what viewers could hope to see (the word 'viewers' was unsatisfactory but no other ever stuck). As it turned out, television's development proceeded on lines almost exactly parallel to early radio's, reproducing most of the frustrations as well as the excitements and adding a few of each.

The first programme was an outside broadcast of the June Victory Parade. That night at Alexandra Palace Margot Fonteyn danced, David Low drew a cartoon, Leslie Mitchell compèred a variety show and George More O'Ferrall produced Shaw's *Dark Lady of the Sonnets*. About 100,000 viewers in the Greater London area, watching on receivers little different (some were the very same) from those of 1939, saw the programme reopen with the Mickey Mouse cartoon film that the closure had silenced. They also gazed for the first time on Macdonald Hobley, a young actor recently demobbed from SEAC, and the enchanting Sylvia Peters, who were making their début in the new and promising career of TV announcer. Everything went well, said Gorham, except that the chairman of the BBC governors (Sir Allan Powell) 'dried'. Gorham had already noticed that television's machinery, the blazing lights and the advancing cameras, tended to make people who were not performers forget what they intended to say next, even what they had just said, not to mention who and where they were.

As in radio's early days there were plenty of stirring forecasts of the waves of enlightenment and art that TV would pour across the country; and they were brought up sharp, just as radio's had been, against the Luddites of the news, sporting and entertainment industries. The Stoll theatre would not let Ivy Benson and her all-girls band appear on TV. The Amateur Athletic Association refused permission to televise athletics from the White City, the theatre managers wouldn't let TV take relays, the cinema withheld old films and newsreels, the big variety agencies threatened to blacklist artists who appeared on TV. Gorham could not show the Derby, league football, the Cup Final or professional boxing. Luckily Wimbledon and Test cricket remained. Like Reith twenty-five years before him Gorham spent a lot of his time trying to persuade the Luddites that far from ruining their enterprises television would give them the biggest boost they ever had.

TV did as radio had done. It used what stage and music-hall talent it could get and created entertainment of its own. A frustration unknown to radio was the state of the nation. Exhausted and close to ruin, it could give television a low priority in the national plan for revival. In the fuel crisis of the appalling winter of 1946-7 the Government closed down TV altogether for a month. Equipment was old-fashioned. The outside broadcast unit, still the size of a small military convoy, had no shelter and was maintained in the open-air car park at the Palace. However, TV had inherited from radio the general understanding of what broadcasting was about. It did not have to fight the battle for series all over again – indeed, though hardly anybody spotted it at the time, the likeness of television's programme pattern to radio's meant that it must inevitably compete against radio and extinguish it.

By 1949 TV had found Philip Harben, second of a long and glorious line of TV cooks, and Muffin the Mule, first of an army of puppets that would squeak and jerk across the screen. *Picture Page* returned with Joan Gilbert. Fred Streeter illustrated talks on gardening. Eric Robinson conducted. There was a vogue for cabaret, supplied by continental artists who could be flown over in defiance of the British variety managers' threats. The Sunday play had arrived. Jack Hulbert had a huge success in *Hulbert's Follies*, one of the first light entertainment series to have the stamp of a thoroughgoing experienced old theatre pro as producer, designer and chief performer. Robert Barr had written the first TV documentary series, 'It's Your Money They're After' and 'I Made News'. Sport, outside broadcasts of almost anything, throve. The most significant kind of programme to emerge from those early years was exactly the kind that had emerged first from early radio. It was factual, but fitted into no special category, though later it would proliferate and harden into departments such as documentary, current affairs, news magazines, arts features, travel, natural history, further education, etc. In those days it was only interesting. It was naturally broadcast at peak time. 'Should one of the main events on Monday night have been the cooking of whitebait?' Campey asked in June 1951. 'Should the longest item on Wednesday be a film about the dairy industry?' The BBC had no doubt about it. The wide-ranging programme schedules were as natural to TV as they had been to radio. I need not elaborate on the policy, readers will find it word for word in Part I of this book. Television took you round a glass-blowing works at 8 pm and alternated Pouishnoff and Terry-Thomas because it believed it was its duty to bring to the audience the best of everything that could be brought. The public's preferences too were as they had been in the twenties. It liked plays best (provided they told a good story), outside broadcasts of ceremonial and sport, and a good laugh. But because television in the early fifties was as fascinating and new as the wireless had been, the public was susceptible to appeals to its curiosity by the type of programme it might not have expected to enjoy.

The full-length musical work made the bulk of the audience very discontented, but *Music For You*, Eric Robinson's pot-pourri of classical works, was extremely popular. A ninety-minute version of *Swan Lake* caused more frowns than smiles but *Ballet for Beginners*, a series explaining how ballet was taught, drilled, created and performed, had a wide following, probably among the families where there were little girls for whom ballet was the ultimate magic. Concerts and recitals went down quite well when personalised as in *The Conductor Speaks*. People liked to watch some special knowledge or talent in action. The business of presenting people was being learned. The audience (and some people in sound) thought that all that was necessary was to let them see, as well as hear, *The Brains Trust* and *Twenty Questions*, etc. But TV had learned very quickly that the production methods it required had to be broken away from sound and structured anew. The essential difference was that viewers couldn't look at the same picture for more than a few minutes without becoming aware of frightful strain. Even when the speaker was Algernon Blackwood narrating one of his stories, the picture of his marvellously grained old face had to change to relieve the viewer's eye. With talkers who demonstrated, like Philip Harben, there was no problem. The camera showed what he did. When the speaker only talked the illustration had to be devised by the producer. It was perhaps the most special of television's arts. Grace Wyndham Goldie, a great creator and shaper of the form, explained how it was done.

'He can choose still pictures, photographs, or prints and get them specially enlarged. He can get film specially shot, or use such little existing film as is available, and get it specially cut. He can write, or get someone else to write, short scenes and get actors and actresses to take part in them. He can use animated maps and diagrams if he designs them and can persuade someone to make them. He must plan all these illustrations so that they fit logically into the speaker's arguments; visually into a pattern acceptable to the eye; practically into the possibilities of camera movement, lighting, and scene changing.

And when all that is done, the real difficulties of the talks producer begin; difficulties involved in persuading distinguished people who have never faced lights or studios or cameras, who are not accustomed to giving any kind of performance or repeating any sort of "effect", to look natural in un-natural surroundings, to talk naturally and yet to time, to remember the thread of their argument without a script, to give "cues" and take them.'[2] It took four weeks to prepare one of these programmes. She spotted that the result was something nearer the sound feature programme or the film documentary than the sound talk; yet it was neither, because it had to satisfy the eye and be performed 'live'.

This kind of television was an early success, and when you think about the frightful ordeal indicated by Grace Wyndham Goldie's description of a TV performance you can only marvel. She could have added that television was not only live, but hot and glaring. The dazzle and heat of arc-lights were in-tense enough to shrivel Muffin's hair off his ears and cook Harben's omelette before he could slide it from bowl to pan. (The lighting required for indoor TV gave the authorities a reasonable excuse – though their real one was that they were not used to the idea of television – for banning cameras from the wedding of Princess Elizabeth and Prince Philip in 1948. Gorham's men had the mortification of having to relay the proceedings inside the Abbey on sound only.) Soon cameras became more sensitive and the studios cooler, though the light still shrank your pupils to pin-points. Gorham thought too that the business of making up had become a very harmless matter, but it lasted long enough for nervous non-performers to work themselves into a state and contributed greatly to the feelings of inadequacy and horror that seized so many before a broadcast.

I made my own début about this time in a discussion about newspapers with Malcolm Muggeridge. I accepted the invitation because I would not have liked myself had I funked it, and spent the next three days in steadily tightening dread of what I had committed myself to. Muggeridge took us out to dinner (he was at that time the all-smoking, all-drinking boon com-panion). I had not then made the important discovery that drink before a TV appearance had the effect of relaxing some people, of whom I was evidently one, to the point of torpor, and was disconcerted to notice that I could not remember any of the points I had put with dazzling brilliance in the pro-ducer's office when he asked me what I proposed to say. Back in the studio the floor manager's face tensed when he saw my suit, a black and white hound's-tooth check. He explained that it would strobe and wanted me to change suits with him. I managed to fend him off, but the effect on my self-confidence can be imagined. I would gladly have paid a studio hand £10 to break my leg. When the programme came on the friends my wife had in-vited in to watch thought I was going to faint. The relief of not fainting, of discovering that I could think of a sentence, the realisation that it was all over, intoxicated me with the euphoria I used to enjoy after a safe flight. I felt that my life had been handed back to me. This degree of stage-fright inevitably wore off, but though I became accustomed to going on TV I never crossed the line that marked the good from the bad. It was exasperating to estimate the difference in earning power between a journalist like myself who could do it with a typewriter and one like Robert Robinson, who could do it with his face as well; but I received so many sharp hints from Providence that it did not intend me to be good at TV that I decided it would be dangerous to aggravate it by continuing the attempt.

The wonderful thing was that some people, mostly MPs and lecturers who were used to thinking fast on their feet, and one or two natural performers like Muggeridge (though he had once been a teacher), took to it like birds to the wing. Leslie Hardern, a public relations officer with the Gas Board, was one of the earliest and best of these. He presented *Inventors' Club*, in which inventors came to the studio to explain and demonstrate their ideas; in terms of human interest it was one of the richest and most rewarding programmes of its or any other time. Another was *Painter's Progress*, devised and presented by the painter-teacher Mervyn Levy. This series encouraged viewers by simple demonstration and instruction to try painting for themselves and rewarded the best efforts by showing them on the programme. Like so much TV of those days it was enjoyed with peculiar intensity; you watched it with the absorption that the optimistic forecasters had always insisted that television would demand (how could they foresee 130 hours of it a week?).

It was the accidental discovery that pictures came over particularly well on TV - the camera could move in on a portion of a canvas and strangely energise some special feature of it - that led to these art series. *Picture Page* made a number of discoveries of this sort, purely by wondering what to show next. One day S. E. Reynolds, an early producer of the show, brought in an escapologist who was prepared to do his piece hanging by a chain in a straitjacket from the top of the Alexandra Palace tower. The only way Reynolds could show him was by shoving a camera out of the window and pointing it upward, securing pictures so stimulating that everyone wished they could write a play for TV of which such a shot might be the climax. Another time someone discovered accidentally that a TV camera could see better than the human eye in some conditions. They pointed a camera out of a window on to the broad expanse of northern London, almost hidden in the haze. But when they looked at the monitor they saw the Flying Scot steaming through Watford. They discovered that a TV camera very effectively showed jewellery and other precious objects in large close-up without the smallest distortion; out of this a vast section of TV would grow.

The side of television that had to be written, cast, learned, rehearsed and performed was much harder to come by. The audience took the talks, the outside broadcast trips to the London Docks, the Zoo, Northolt Airport, in their stride because they did not know what they liked in those areas of TV; it was all new. From drama and variety they had the expectations they remembered from the theatre and the cinema, and expected those standards to be met. But there was little money about, and the equipment of the early days taxed everybody on both sides of the camera to the limit.

I must here remind the reader that the standard vision unit of a TV production consisted of four cameras connected to a producer's gallery above the studio floor. The picture each camera took came up on a monitor screen in the gallery. To the right of them was the picture that was being transmitted. The producer planned his pictures at rehearsals and chose the one he wanted by barking the camera number at an assistant who then punched the appropriate button. It was not so far removed from the principle of the old radio drama control panel. When the equipment became flexible and reliable and everything was going well, riding this control panel in the gallery was as exciting as making a successful trip across Niagara Falls on a tightrope in a high wind. In the early days it was like trying to do the same thing weaving the rope as you went.

Before 1950 none of the cameras had turret lenses. Two of them could be pushed back and forward – 'tracking', as it is called – on wheeled camera supports known as dollies. The other two were mounted on iron men, so called because of their amazing intractability. A producer could only move an iron man in between shots. The dollies were pushed about by studio hands in plimsolls, but when they had moved in for their close-up there was only one possible shot to follow. They would slowly move out again. If the producer had cut to a second camera his picture would have included the first. This problem of keeping the cameras out of each other's vision called for much ingenuity in the visual scripting of a TV programme. Another intrusive factor was the virtual certainty that a producer would not get through a show without at least one camera 'going down' on him, i.e. flickering out, thus converting what had begun as a coolly plotted four-camera sequence into a scene of wild and despairing improvisation. Robert Barr told me once how his camera Three went down after ten minutes of a 60-minute documentary. He quickly moved camera Two to cover some of Three's shots. Meanwhile Three had been repaired but Two was flickering ominously. He could not put Three in to cover Two so brought in One. In the excitement nobody noticed that the cables connecting the cameras to the gallery had begun to tangle like a piece of knitting, and before anyone could prevent it two of the cameras were stuck together back to back – like a pair of mating dogs, Barr said. There was no way to move one forwards without pulling the other backwards except by unplugging the cables and untwisting them. After this it was natural enough that the engineers in their haste should have stuck the plugs back into the wrong cameras, so that in the gallery the producer was getting the picture of Three on his monitor for Two. Producers got into a state in which if they had been told that their houses had burned down with their wives and children in them they would have replied absently, 'Is that so?'

All the while the actors were going on with the play, but even if things were going right in the gallery a producer never knew when one of the cast was going to 'dry'. As Gorham had said, television tended to have this effect on performers. In films the director could cut out the scene and retake it; in the theatre an actor could walk over to the prompt corner; in radio he read his part. Only in television was there no possibility of covering up a dry; and of course this fearful knowledge greatly increased the actors' chance of having one. It seemed to take them different ways. Old repertory players who learned their parts by visualising the printed page sometimes mentally turned over two at a time, going straight from the bottom of page 19 to the top of page 22. It was confusing to the producer, who could not understand why he was going to finish five minutes short, and to the audience at home who suddenly found they had lost their grasp on what was happening. Some actors simply lost the power of speech. Once a murder play was supposed to end with the inspector bursting in, whereupon the murderer's nerve would crack and he would confess. 'All right, Inspector, since you know everything I may as well tell you the rest,' etc. Well, the inspector recognised immediately that his partner had dried, so resourcefully begun to feed him the lines. 'I understand you have something to tell me, Mr Carruthers.' Goggle. 'Do you want to say that it was you who did the killings?' Goggle. 'With that dagger on the mantelpiece?' Goggle. A stagehand thought some improvised action might shock the actor back to normal, so he pressed the button that rang the telephone on the set. As though kicked from behind Carruthers stumbled forward, picked up the receiver and said to the Inspector: 'It's for you.' Just as in early radio, early TV plays faithfully copied the presentation style of the theatre, including the raising and lowering of a curtain and a bell to signal the beginning of the next act. Another play, set in the Far East, was about a secret affair between a planter and another's wife. He was supposed to break the news that he was leaving for England; and her realisation that she was being discarded was to be the curtain shot. But one look at his face told all. The dry was on him. An old actor whose nerves were still cool fed him his line. 'I hear you're going to England, old man.' Looking him fully in the face he replied, 'No I'm not.' There was nothing to be done but lower the curtain. Sometimes, though, improvisation worked brilliantly, as when an actor who was playing the Prince of Morocco in *The Merchant of Venice* dried after discussing the lead and silver caskets and fainted. The camera lost him as he was about to topple and picked up Portia's perfectly apt closing line:

> A gentle riddance. Draw the curtains, go,
> Let all of his complexion choose me so.

A lot of good actors would not appear on television because of the disaster stories that went round, and playwrights were heard to say that while they did not object to TV doing that sort of thing to Shakespeare it was not going to do it to them. But under Val Gielgud and then Michael Barry drama found an astonishing number of star actors willing to appear in the classical repertory; and a loyal pool of lesser known players was ready and willing to appear in anything whatever.

The terror of the dry was conquered with the invention of a prompter's cut out. He could wipe out the sound before giving the cue. The audience could tell by the sudden deadness of their sets and the look of pain on the actors' faces; and sometimes the prompter's voice was a shade quicker than his finger on the button. But it was an important step forward, and what with one improvement and another the rise in viewing figures and its accompanying rise in artists' fees and equipment standards, the Sunday play and its Tuesday repeat became an institution and drama was establishing names to watch for. With better cameras the directors mastered the grammar of cuts, mixes, fades, tracks, wipes and so on inherited from the cinema and which the audience had always taken for granted it should see, and learned to handle them on the run. On live TV many things remained impossible. It could not fade out an actor in jodhpurs in Berkshire and fade him in immediately in a dinner jacket in New York; the writer had to insert a little scene between these locations so that the actor would have time to change gear and bound across to the appropriate part of the set. The writers soon learned to write scripts that did not require these athletic feats. But nobody could make a TV play a comfortable thing to do.

The first star to be created by television, defining a star as a name that draws audiences to a play merely by its presence among the cast, was Peter Cushing. He had been acting for twenty years, mostly in costume drama (Olivier took him to Australia on his 1948 tour with the Old Vic company). He had his first TV part in January 1951 and eighteen months later owned one of the best-known faces in the land. He found it gratifying to be recognised in the shops, to have the greengrocer compliment him 'on a nice bit of acting' the night before. He played sixteen TV productions at the rate of one a month, from French drama to Aldwych farce. He brought a sharp intelligence to everything he did and a haunting gentle strength to his serious parts. But he never conquered his dread of television. He described to me once the very real sense of fear and loneliness that descended on the set, as though he was acting on a deserted island. He missed the audience even more at the end, when instead of offering the soothing unction of applause the play just stopped; the cast took off their make-up and left with technicians hurrying to catch late trains, with nobody to say goodnight to but the nightwatchmen who jangled their keys and waited to lock up.

Another name one learned to watch for was that of Rudolph Cartier, a producer who came to Lime Grove trailing clouds of glory from his association in Germany with Max Reinhardt, Erich Pommer and the famous UFA film company. He liked television because the small screen enabled him to force the audience to see what he wanted it to see. 'In the theatre,' he said, 'it is impossible, the audience can be distracted by the hang of a curtain. In the cinema the audience looks at the landscape.' He was fond of quoting Pommer's axiom 'Always remember the poetry is on the left'. This referred to the way a film or TV script is set out, the dialogue on the right and the instructions to cameras on the left. Nobody was within a mile of Cartier in the trick of making a picture on a TV screen seem as wide and deep as Cinemascope; and it was done on equipment that was still more of a clumsy and unwilling conscript than an eagerly co-operative servant. As he said to me once, 'One only discovers the possibilities of TV by attempting the impossible.'

You can see how difficult it was and how dependent drama was on the central pillar of a good script. Yet it had to be a new kind of script, something between the theatre and the movies. Whereas the theatre dramatised words, using colours and blocks of movement to present them, television needed much more of the kind of movement that was as important as the words; instead of the words indicating the movement they ideally came out of the action. The trick is the source of the movies' art and the rock on which the industry is built. Television as a visual medium inherited the obligation to give the camera something to look at while the actors were talking; but because of the limitations of the studio it had to be something that decorated the plot rather than drove it along. This is why plays brought in from the stage were so popular. The public enjoyed the quality of the talk and acting. Between them and the new play written for television there lay a huge gulf; we were painfully aware that swans were revealing themselves as geese; Barry had to take much harsh criticism for giving a hearing to writers who were not ready for it. When the words were not compensating for the want of visual appeal, and the actors were not recognised stars, these plays when they were bad seemed bad indeed. Still, Barry could see his path plainly enough. He knew that TV would have to create its own drama to back up the arithmetically dwindling stock of stage plays, and that this would come from new plays, serials, drama series, and adaptations of books. (The last was an expedient frequently recommended by critics, who did not know that in those days of a thriving film industry the pictorial rights of almost any book capable of being dramatised were bought almost automatically by the movies.)

Barry and his team set their teeth and toiled along the route they had to take, being refreshed just about often enough with the huge success that they knew TV could have if only it could get the money, the writers and the actors. When they did *Two Gentlemen of Verona* as an outside broadcast from the Old Vic Theatre, it was exciting to know that the national audience was seeing the national theatre presenting the national dramatist for the first time in many of their lives. (How they hated it!) One enjoyed the same delightful sensation of cultural experience spreading across the land like sunlight spilling across a dark plain when one watched Joan Greenwood's superb Nora in *A Doll's House*. And in 1952 Barry had the satisfaction of watching a new play become not only a smash hit on television but instantly make its way into the theatre and cinema. This was Frederic Knott's classic puzzle, *Dial M for Murder*.

In the field of new plays for television, however, writers remained as scarce as mushrooms in December. There was not the money to entice writers who could do it. And those who were willing could not quite do it. But progress inched along. They started a drama script unit of young writers who set themselves to master the business of telling stories in a non-stagy way. Donald Wilson arrived from films as drama script supervisor, bringing with him a very strong professional talent for spotting quality and demonstrating it. Barry's own 'Shout aloud Salvation', a play about the Salvation Army, was one of the first successful pieces specially written for TV. They began a fruitful exploration of novels. *The Pickwick Papers, Kidnapped, The Three Hostages* were done as serials. Margaret Lockwood starred in a fine adaptation of Wells's *Ann Veronica*. The young Barbara Jefford turned up as Hardy's Tess. But the most consistent early new writing came from people who were learning to use the machinery and, though it used drama techniques, belonged more to the field of the radio feature. It imaginatively re-created fact, using built sets, rehearsed actors and written dialogue. The first original postwar script for TV, Robert Barr's 'Mock Auction', was adapted from his radio series, *It's your Money they're after*. He wrote another called 'I want to be an Actor' which Barry produced, much enjoying, said Barr, the freedom to talk about the script with its writer and discuss ways to improve it. Barry wrote one of his own, 'I want to be a Doctor'.

The most famous and influential writer in this field was Duncan Ross, a film documentary maker from the school of John Grierson and Paul Rotha. He joined the BBC's TV service in 1947 as the first holder of the unofficial title of Documentary Writer and Script Supervisor. He wrote a number of feature-length documentary dramas of which the best remembered was *The Course of Justice* series, a dramatisation of various court procedures all the way from the local magistrate's to the High. Ross inspired a lot of similar work about doctors, police, and social difficulties such as abandoned children, marriage, old age, alcoholism, habitual crime, etc. In one of these, Caryl Doncaster's 'Pattern of Marriage', the cameras gazed lovingly for the first time on the beautiful face of Billie Whitelaw as the child bride entangled with marriage difficulties. It was, as I recall, a terrible script, but the advantage a bad documentary had over a bad play was that it dealt in truth. When they were good – and they usually made new plays seem very second-rate – they had a terrific impact. Colin Morris's 'Rock Bottom' changed the course of his career for the young actor who played the hopeless drunk. He was Philip Latham, whose identity subsequently became inextricably merged with that of Willy Izzard in *Mogul* and *The Trouble Shooters*. The seed of the BBC's best drama series was planted in the struggling early fifties; *Z Cars*, *Maigret*, *The Trouble Shooters*, *Dr Finlay's Casebook* all grew from and owed their success to the quality of vivid authenticity, of respect for the integrity of the subject, that the early documentarians looked for and set out to reproduce.

As an independent form the dramatised documentary did not last because the techniques available suddenly went past it, making possible something much more special to television – actuality on film. Duncan Ross invented *London Town*, an intricate magazine format for its day (1951), in which Richard Dimbleby and producer Stephen McCormack learned the business of running a show from the studio and switching smoothly from film to matching studio sets and back to film. As the television network spread programmes could drop live outside broadcasts as well as film into a studio-based magazine. In 1952 Cecil McGivern launched *Special Enquiry*, the most ambitious current affairs series yet attempted, with a hard-hitting programme filmed in the slums of Glasgow with Robert Reid in the studio calling in Jameson Clark as reporter in Glasgow. This kind of thing established a basic technique of television reporting which proliferated into a score of later programmes.

Light entertainment under Ronnie Waldman struggled against the same economic bonds as Barry. The rewards he could offer were not attractive to the top talent. He had to rely on the occasional bonus appearance of star talent that foresaw how big TV would become and was willing to invest some time in learning how to do it. The pleasant young Canadians, Bernard Braden and Barbara Kelly, were a couple of these; they started *Evening at Home* in 1952, a vestigial domestic comedy series which went down well enough for them to want to try again. In the same year Donald Peers, the singer, and the radio star Frankie Howerd moved over. Frankie had seen that TV comedy required its own style, and had a large success in 'The Howerd Crowd' by mastering the hitherto untried trick of playing to the television audience while in front of a studio audience. But the visits of such big guns were fleeting; and when Waldman managed to create his own he could not keep them. Television made stars of Terry-Thomas and Norman Wisdom, and priced them out of its market. The most idiotic opposition Waldman had to fight came from sound radio, which held Bernard Braden to a clause in his contract limiting him to sound broadcasting only and prevented his return to TV in a fresh series written for him by Frank Muir and Dennis Norden. Like Barry, Waldman had to accept a lot of stuff he would as soon have done without. I remember watching with growing consternation the first variety show I saw as a paid observer. I was wondering how I could truthfully avoid lacerating the feelings of everybody concerned when the little dog the principal singer was carrying in her arms performed a kind of rough justice – I suppose the poor brute was exasperated beyond endurance – by nipping her on the nose.

There was no such thing as a pilot show for light entertainment or a dummy run before an audience over closed circuit. Everything was tried out on the air in full view of the public and presented with the assumption of smiling self-assurance that show business cannot do without. To some of the newspaper critics this apparent insistence that a dud show was not a dud show was the last straw; they set about Waldman with a violence much sharper than anything impresarios or performers in the theatre would have taken. But Waldman was a very tough and resilient person, and far from resenting such attacks welcomed them as reinforcements in his fight for more money and better equipment. He knew there was no future in finding variety acts. He was looking for performers who could be funny. He had the consolation of knowing that though variety and comedy contained most of his flops they represented only two strands of light entertainment. He knew too that the light entertainment pattern would resemble radio's, much of it lying outside show business in the fertile territory of relays from ice shows, dance halls, etc., panel games, quizzes and entertaining features. Here he had some noted successes. His own 'Kaleidoscope' was one. Michael Mills, one of Waldman's little group of energetic and irrepressible producers, put on spectacular musical biographies of C. B. Cochran and Marie Lloyd (with young Pat Kirkwood as Marie) in the teeth of technical obstacles that would have crushed him had he known they made his job impossible. The Christmas party, an innocent saturnalia in which announcers became actors and departmental heads appeared as conjurors and story-tellers, used to pull in the biggest variety audience of the year. I much enjoyed – it was for some time my favourite programme – *Come Dancing*, a relay of ball-room dancing competitions from some large hall. This was television bringing one half of the audience a glimpse of the other half's pleasures, and presented for me a picture altogether delightful and mysterious. I was fascinated by the carefully moderated abandon of the dancers, by the billowing and sequinned skirts of the women that made them look like telephone cozys, by the matter-of-fact acceptance by the tail-coated men of the disfigurement of huge cardboard numbers on their backs, by all the signs that here was a world with conventions and an aristocracy all its own. The very names were enchantingly at odds with the swirling and clacking rhythms, yet somehow perfect. What else could you call Sid Perkin and Edna Duffield, the champions of many a crowded floor in 1952?

But Waldman's great success, the first smash hit of the dawning television era, was the panel game, *What's My Line?* This was an American format sold to the BBC for twenty-five guineas a performance by Maurice Winnick, the shrewd impresario who had been the first man this side of the Atlantic to spot that the panel game would be big business. *What's My Line?* required a panel of four to guess the job of challengers selected from public volunteers, and a questionmaster who could steer the bashful towards answering clearly and restrain the forward from being pert. It opened in July 1951 and thanks to some inspired casting soon became a favourite. Jerry Desmonde, Sid Field's straight man, represented good old showbiz. Marghanita Laski, the novelist, was the elegant blue-stocking. Elizabeth Allen, the very beautiful actress, was the sweet-tempered heroine. Gilbert Harding was the crusty and unpredictable intellectual. The thing was steered by young Eamonn Andrews, whose contribution was as vital as anyone's, for he was a person of singular charm and firmness, able to control the game with the light and assured authority it needed. But the undoubted star was Gilbert Harding, hoisted by this game to a dizzying pinnacle as the first super-star of the telly. He was an odd, sad character who would probably have been more content as a schoolmaster or lawyer but was cursed with some perverse streak that made him throw away anything that looked like becoming a solid achievement. In 1939, having sailed through his bar examinations and within sight of his finals, he closed his law books for ever for no better reason than that the war broke out. In some strange fashion that he only half acknowledged to himself he was also stage-struck. After wandering rather aimlessly from one thing to another (at one time he was a policeman in Bradford, of all things in all places) he joined the BBC's monitoring service when the war began and did well as one of four sub-editors who prepared the daily digest of foreign broadcasts for the War Cabinet. He frequently relayed his report to Churchill, who pleased him once by asking after he had been off duty for two weeks, 'Where is that man with the succinct mind?'

Gilbert was a very literate and cultivated person, and his deep, fruity voice was a fine communicator for him, but the quality that set him on the road to fortune was a certain humour of crotchetiness for which he repeatedly – and publicly – wrung his hands. Little things worried him dreadfully. He would not endure the totally pointless, time-wasting process of having his ticket clipped in the Underground, and went to absurdly troublesome lengths to avoid it. He began on the entertainment side of radio as an outside broadcaster, having something to do with the Midlands farming programmes organised by Godfrey Baseley. When Baseley's wife asked him to tea and poured the milk in first he went into a fearful tantrum. Mrs Baseley gave as good as she got and the occasion perished miserably. Next morning he was full of remorse and telephoned to apologise. Like the dog who bit people in James Thurber's story, he was always sorry afterwards.

He got his real break in radio as questionmaster of *Round Britain Quiz* and *The Brains Trust*. He liked these erudite affairs and was always benign in them. His reputation as a cantankerous and opinionated party soared when *We Beg to Differ* became a hit. He became newsworthy, finding to his amazement that the editors of newspapers were anxious to canvas, for ready money, his views on such undyingly interesting topics as pre-marital sex, the cooking in British hotels, women, divorce, education and the treatment of crime. He was thus a natural choice for the grumpy intellectual's chair in *What's My Line?* The formula might have been invented to plague him into excesses. He detested circumlocutions, bastardised English, genteelism and any other form of middle-class coyness. (He never accepted Eamonn Andrews's coinage 'the blindfolds' for the 'masks' that the panel had to wear when the celebrity whose identity they had to guess appeared.) He could not bear it when challengers deliberately or innocently returned evasive answers. It was embarrassing to watch him bullying some chap whose only offence was that, like most of his countrymen, he could not speak his own language properly. But he could also display a sensitive and gentle tact. Casting about in his mind for some explanation of his success he thought it was that most people had lost the courage and the ability to speak up for themselves; they liked to watch him do it for them. To himself he seemed the phoniest of celebrities and his achievement the flimsiest. He was haunted by a sense of impending doom. He seemed to me, watching him in the programme, a bear tied to a stake to be baited by the populace. When he had become the most popular figure in television he was saddened by the clownish behaviour of total strangers who were gratuitously offensive; and then he seemed like the weary old gunfighter in the westerns, goaded by louts with more drink in them than sense.

His fellow panellist Marghanita Laski described very well the hectic glare which beat about a successful panellist. 'What I gave was minimal – the ability to play a parlour game far easier than any I should choose to play at home. The right reward for what I was giving would have been congratulations from neighbours after the British Legion fête, rather less effusive congratulations than went to those who have sung or danced or organised. Here the scale of the reward was distorted by the size of the audience. But the public was clearly prepared to give disproportionate rewards for the pleasure of having TV personalities to recognise.' This was what worried her most, to know that she was a private, uneasy, fallible human being, and to be treated as a contact with magic, a godling. Frightened that she might come to believe in and need the crowd's measurement of her existence and value she got out of television, lucky in that she had her true vocation as a novelist beside her all the time. Poor Gilbert, lacking any such resource, felt more and more trapped by his fame. He punished his ailing body hard until, one day in November 1960, he collapsed and died with a certain grim aptness in the front hall of a BBC building near Broadcasting House.

Thus, from 1946 to 1952, the television side of the BBC slogged on, learning how to use the slowly increasing supply of tools, hampered by bans and shortages and the ridiculous and damaging hostility between the sound and the vision halves of the BBC. When Robert Barr, who had left sound in 1946 to join television, returned for a visit to Broadcasting House, a senior sound producer ran into him at the door. 'Good Lord, I thought you were dead.' 'No I'm not,' said Barr. 'No? Ah, yes; gone to television; same thing, old chap.' Then one day everything changed. The television people walked in, the morning after the Coronation, aware that for the first time television had had a bigger audience than radio. It never again had a smaller one.

3

THE DAY THAT MADE TV

The national spread of TV had been held up by delays outside the BBC's control. The five main transmitters were not finished until the autumn of 1952. The next stage should have been five medium power stations to fill in the secondary areas, but the Government withheld permission to build them until July 1953. This would have meant that the north of Scotland, Northern Ireland, Newcastle and almost the whole length of the south coast would not see the Coronation. Under this spur the Government let the BBC set up temporary stations to serve the most crowded parts. These were really booster stations, which took the strong signal from the main transmitter and rebroadcast it into areas cut off by some natural obstacle, such as the South Downs. Brighton was one of the lucky areas. The BBC put a station on Truleigh Hill and one never-to-be-forgotten day the local engineer came to adjust my set to receive its signal. I saw for the first time in my house the same quality of picture, as clear and solid as if carved on glass, that I used to envy in the BBC's studios at Lime Grove. It was not before time, either, for though I had not taken the editor of the *Daily Mail* into my confidence I had the devil's own job writing about programmes I had only fitfully seen. I once reviewed a whole play – it was the Quintero brothers' 'One Hundred Years Old' – from what I could hear on the sound track. The summer was the worst. It was as though, in the winter, the signal nipped briskly along to keep warm, and still had a good glow on when it reached Brighton, whereas in summertime it tended to become languid and disconnected, like a group of hikers straggling on a hot day. However, the hard times were over for the BBC as well as for me. With these boosters the BBC was able to raise its national TV coverage to about eighty-four per cent of the population, a much higher figure than any other country in the world had then achieved. Though frustrating and even dangerous politically (the BBC was accused of laggardness and excessive caution) the delay had its advantages. The big one was that producers were able to learn, practise and experiment with the equipment on fairly small audiences. The adventures described by Robert Barr and others took place, as he put it, in the dark. By the year of the Coronation they knew how to do it; the question was, how to get hold of what to do? To this the Coronation provided the most stunning and spectacular answer in broadcasting's short life, once the powers organising the event had consented to let TV do it.

Early in 1952 the BBC made its formal request to the Earl Marshal's office for permission to televise the service inside Westminster Abbey. The Earl Marshal's reply, issued as part of his Coronation committee's announcement about the day's arrangements, was a flat no. Officially the Corporation accepted this frightful blow with the obedient reluctance proper to one public body in dealing with another. Unofficially it began a tireless campaign to persuade the Duke of Norfolk and the Archbishop of Canterbury, regarded as the two most hostile members of the committee, to reconsider. For once the BBC had Fleet Street on its side. To the newspapers it seemed outrageous that a medium which could enable the people to see, and to some extent participate in, such an important and moving event as the crowning of its young Queen, should not be allowed to do it. The first chink of hope appeared when the committee agreed to hear the BBC's case, for once they had described their objections it was fairly easy for the BBC to answer them. They were anxious about the amount of lighting the cameras would need; they were told that the lighting suitable for the film cameras would suffice. They were anxious about the risk of live television broadcasting some unseemly or provocative incident (the Americans had introduced the so-called 'Peeping Tom' cameras into their coverage of the 1952 presidential conventions): they were shown how, should anything untoward pop up on the screen, the producer could cut to another camera with the speed of thought; and they were reminded that the BBC's reputation would not let it pursue sensationalism. Their real objection was based on the undoubted fact that there never had been a televised service of a Coronation from Westminster Abbey. The propriety of introducing such a novelty agitated them greatly. Peter Dimmock, who would be in charge of the BBC's Abbey coverage for TV, spent weeks battering away at this prejudice; what finally won them over was a demonstration he gave inside the Abbey which showed that the lighting was nothing special, the cameras were not, as the committee had supposed, the size of birdwatchers' hides, and could be concealed. It was the concealment that swung the trick, for like humanity in general the Duke and the Primate unconsciously felt that an intruder you could not see was not as objectionable as one you could.* One day they told Dimmock, 'Well, all right.' He had already chosen where his cameras ought to go; now he had to work out how to place them so that no matter where one stood not a camera could be seen. The pictures that everyone remembers were those shot from high in the triforium behind the altar, looking down upon

* An apocryphal story says it was the old Queen Mary who decisively tipped the scales, when her doctors forbade her to attend the Coronation. She was determined to see it and intervened on television's behalf, but she died before the great day arrived.

the whole length of the nave, and the closer shots of the Queen taken during the service. The first presented no great problem, the second called for a coup de maître; Dimmock dug a hole in the choir where the orchestra was to play and put in it his smallest camaraman, 'Bud' Flanagan, to shoot from between the legs of the musicians.

Once the Earl Marshal had withdrawn his opposition he became astonishingly co-operative, even to the extent of changing the music to which the Queen and all the nobles and commoners and ambassadors would make their procession out of the Abbey. Someone had written a special march. Dimmock urged that it did not sound very well suited to the mood of the occasion and got Norfolk to change it to Elgar. So as the glittering throng passed back under the choir screen and along the nave the orchestra went into 'Land of Hope and Glory'; it is doubtful whether at that moment there was a dry eye in Britain.

Preparations for televising the Coronation had begun a year before the day. It was to be television's longest sustained broadcast, and to mount it the BBC brought into London almost every item of television gear it could lay its hands on. In and out of television excitement began to rise, for this was the time when the leader-writers were talking about the New Elizabethan age and the great days for Britain that had accompanied the presence of a woman on the throne since the reign of the first Elizabeth. That year, what with Hillary and Tensing climbing Everest, England regaining the Ashes and Gordon Richards winning the Derby it really did seem for a time that some benevolent force was trying to cheer us up. Of these hopes Coronation Day was the perfect expression and television upheld it superbly, from the moment just after ten o'clock in the morning when the adorable Sylvia Peters, her eyes as big as saucers, introduced the commentator Berkeley Smith outside Buckingham Palace, to the inspired and unplanned epilogue at 11.30 when the cameras returned Richard Dimbleby to the now empty and still Abbey.

Rehearsals of the service had been so thorough that the predicted moment of crowning, estimated for the benefit of overseas broadcasting organisations, was less than two minutes out. No television broadcast had ever been so carefully prepared and polished. And though the biggest personal triumph belonged to the young Queen, whose solemn and unaffected sense of dedication was so extraordinarily touching to watch (never before had the onlooker been made to feel so aware of the *weight* of the duties heaped on her), the BBC basked in an unaccustomed radiance of reflected glory. It owed a tremendous amount to S. J. de Lotbinière, head of outside broadcasts, and to Peter Dimmock as the man in charge in the Abbey; for Dimmock had an intuitive eye for the difference between what was seemly and what was only stuffy, and though nothing could have exceeded his tact in punching up the pictures he was determined not to miss punching up those he felt the public would want to see. His own favourite was his perfectly timed cut to the boy prince Charles in the Royal box as he watched his mother being crowned. My own most vivid recollection is of the long, long procession of breeched and robed bigwigs marching from the top of the TV screen to the bottom, while Richard Dimbleby from his perch behind the triforium rolled the evocative names round his tongue. For others it was the shot of the Queen's handbag on the seat of the coach; people liked best of all the casual glimpses that identified the sovereign with the woman. But whether TV was showing the ritual or the quick glance all was success. The Americans said that only the British could mount such a superb pageant. *The Times* reported from Paris that the French could not find enough words to describe their envy and delight. (The French, with some Dutch, Belgians and Germans, had been able to watch it on the infant Eurovision network, a fantastic engineering improvisation lashed up for the occasion.) Over twenty million Britons watched it (compared with slightly under twelve million who listened to it on wireless) and ninety-eight per cent of them enjoyed it very much indeed, according to figures released afterwards at a joyful press conference. The *Daily Express* man asked, as was his bounden duty, 'May we know what it was that the two per cent did not like?' Huw Wheldon, then TV press officer, rose to the occasion by quoting a well-known showbiz gag: 'Well Bob, you must remember that if our Lord came back to earth two per cent of the people would complain, "There he goes again, always walking on the water." ' I was delighted with the aptness of this reply, which increased the strength of my conviction that Wheldon must become the next Director-General but two.

For Dimbleby it was a great personal triumph, earned by seven years of hard self-training for this kind of work. He had left the BBC staff in 1945 to become a freelance performer and promptly set himself to learn the differences between reporting for the audience's ears and their eyes. His first job was as second-string TV commentator to Freddie Grisewood at the Victory Parade; thereafter he was associated more and more with such important national occasions – the Festival of Britain, the early TV broadcasts from France, the deaths of King George VI and Queen Mary. He earnestly desired to be the best and became so good at it as to make everyone else in the BBC seem not only inferior but intolerably so. He was good because he combined the most thorough professionalism with the natural gifts that his profession needed. There never was anyone like him for doing his pre-broadcast home-work. He would put in hours of work compiling details of everything that he might need if everything went right, and about ten times more detail for use in case something went wrong and he had to fill in. All this material was noted on cards, cross-indexed and carried with him. He became an absolute master at splitting his brain into separately functioning compartments, one of them registering what he was seeing, the other describing it in smoothly flowing prose. But what set him unchallengeably above the others as a describer of events was his feeling for the occasion he was describing. He dearly loved a lord, not in any flunkeyish manner but because he loved the idea of continuity for which the holders of hereditary titles stood. In the same way he loved very old buildings and ceremonial; they were evidence that things went on. Ritual was one of the comforts of life because it accompanied events that came round regularly like the seasons. To him the state opening of Parliament was as delightful as hearing the first cuckoo. Royalty symbolised for him the apex of these things. He held them in genuine romantic awe, and their funerals, weddings and crownings were events of mystical and national importance. It was because most of the public shared this feeling, or believed they ought to, that he became such a matchless interpreter of the big scene.

For the Coronation he was in his box in the triforium without a break from 5.30 in the morning until 2.30 in the afternoon, but for him the nine hours passed as though two or three. He said afterwards that he had never been so tired as when he finally left the Abbey at half-past midnight, seventeen hours after he entered it, and never felt so acutely the strain of describing a great public occasion, or so proud and glad that he was able to contribute to it. His performance, and the less acknowledged performance of de Lotbinière and Dimmock in the background, ended for ever the doubts about television's place at these functions. It had shown that not only did it take nothing from them, it added much to have them interpreted as it were by such a sympathetic commentator.

The most obvious effect of the Coronation for television was on the demand for sets. In the next year the number of licenced sets rose by fifty per cent, and though the BBC still regarded sound as the senior service (*Radio Times* continued to print the TV programmes at the back) the sound audience never again exceeded television's except when it was carrying some sporting event such as a prize fight that television had not been able to secure. The other, more important consequence was among the large number of the opinion-leading class who had not hitherto bothered with television. They were astonished to see how good it was. Television became, and stayed, the nation's most popular mass medium and, in the minds of the politicians and other social leaders, the most influential. Whereas before the Coronation the BBC had some difficulty in persuading the eminent to appear on it, afterwards it had some difficulty in keeping them off.

4

RADIO FLARES AND FALLS

In terms of popular appeal radio as a separate arm of broadcasting had begun to decline slightly from a 1950 peak, when the number of sound-only licences reached 11,819,190. By 1952 it was down to 11,244,141. Significantly the figures for sound and TV licences combined increased from 343,882 in 1950 to 1,449,260 in 1952. The BBC's Director-General, Sir William Haley, hoped and believed that those who bought TV sets would continue to listen to radio, and for a short time it seemed that they might. In fact radio, thanks to the drastic reorganisation of its services in 1945 – an effort that half killed war-weary staff hoping for some easement of the strain – entered a new period of blossom time.

On 29 July 1945 the BBC resumed its peacetime Home and Regional services. One the same day the Forces programme became the regular and permanent alternative, called the Light. Haley also promised the Third Programme. The reorganisation thus preserved the wartime division of listeners into categories to be served by whole stations, and appeared to some to be a killing blow at the old National-Regional set-up which had been carefully planned to offer listeners the full range of radio on one channel or other. The balance between them tried to offer a choice of casual or more concentrated listening, but they were mixed; there was never a time when you could say that the National was more popular or serious in intention than the Regional, though its title of National laid certain additional responsibilities on it.

Haley presided over an important revolution, by no means to everyone's liking. The virtue of the old scheme was that listeners who preferred light entertainment would suddenly come up against something more solid. Because it was too much fag to get up and switch over, they might stay tuned, like what they heard, and thus would the beneficent advance of culture be spread. Now those listeners would stay tuned to the Light, confident that they would not be upset by any highbrow type of experience. But this objection was unsound since although it cut both ways, it was applied only to the Light. Few objected that listeners to the Third might lose touch with the world of easy laughs and sensational thrills and light music that the great majority favoured; it was assumed that the minority was intelligent enough to switch, but that the majority was not. But Haley's notion that listeners should be offered three choices of listening to suit their mood took account of the probably irrevocable change in listening habits inculcated by the Forces programme, and of which the Third Programme was an extension of huge importance; in a way it helped producers, who now found themselves catering for different audiences in much the same way as *The Times*, the *Daily Telegraph* and the *Daily Express* catered for three different kinds of readership. They could fashion their styles more confidently, not needing to coax.

The job of the Home was to reflect as much as radio could of the life of the whole community. The Light's was to entertain, and to interest without failing to entertain. The Third's was to broadcast only those things that had artistic value and serious purpose, ignoring their length or difficulty. In the event there was a good deal of adventurous overlapping: the Home took much of the Third's music; the Light took the whole two-hour rebroadcast of the Third's 'Hiroshima', an adaptation of John Hersey's terrible account of the first atom bomb attack on Japan. The Third's *How* series with Stephen Potter and Joyce Grenfell launched a style of wit that spread right across broadcasting. Soon most of the critics who believed that the Third was a contradiction of broadcasting principles had to admit that producers and writers had never been offered such opportunities. The BBC, said Louis MacNeice, was one of the least interfering patrons writers had ever had, and Geoffrey Bridson admitted that without the Third much of the finer radio would never have reached the air. It also served other media; when the Lord Chamberlain banned Jean-Paul Sartre's *Huis Clos* to protect theatregoers from its supposed blasphemies the Third put it out without cutting or changing a word. It broadcast over five hours the full version of *Hamlet*, the entire *Man and Superman*, the whole of Shakespeare's history play cycle on consecutive nights, embarked on a three-year history of European music, inaugurated hour-long lectures. Giles Cooper, John Mortimer, Robert Bolt, Harold Pinter, Alun Owen, N. F. Simpson, and John Arden were a few of the dramatists who got their first hearing on the Third; others aided and comforted included Stan Barstow and the Leeds combination of Keith Waterhouse and Willis Hall.

Features had been made a separate department in 1945 and with Gilliam at its head continued to be the great originator of radio. 'No programme service can live a healthy life on a diet of classics. Radio must initiate or die,' he said. Supplying programmes to Home, Light and Third, he found a host of writers to radio – John Betjeman, Elizabeth Bowen, George Orwell, John and Rosamond Lehmann, Viola Meynell, Geoffrey Grigson, Laurie Lee, C. V. Wedgwood, Herbert Read, Rose Macaulay, V. S. Pritchett – the list could become a catalogue. Drama at that time still relied mainly on the stage. In 1946 only three plays were written for radio, one in 1947, two in

1948. Gielgud said that sound drama tended to rest on its laurels with a certain amount of self-satisfaction and noted the continuing dearth of outstanding new plays. His difficulty was as it had been in 1930; plays were hugely popular, but the audience wanted what they knew and liked. Within this convention drama flourished – the audience for *Saturday Night Theatre* was a steady round ten million – and created its own company of masters of aural acting, bearing names as distinguished as any in the theatre. For listeners the names of Gladys Young, James McKechnie, Stephen Murray, Belle Chrystall, Norman Shelley, Mary Wimbush, Laidman Browne, Marjorie Westbury, Carleton Hobbs, Vivienne Chatterton, Valentine Dyall will sound a deep chord of grateful recognition; one sat down to hear Gladys Young, to whom must be accorded the crown of crowns, with an ear that had learned to appreciate the subtleties conveyed by her voice much as one sat in the theatre to watch the technique of Peggy Ashcroft.

As a national repertory theatre, then, radio drama thrived. As a centre of new writing for radio it flourished in the mid-forties and fifties on the popular level of original and classic serials and thrillers – creating, indeed, for millions of listeners to the serials a kind of secondary fictional national life running alongside the real one in such hits as *The Robinson Family*, *Mrs Dale's Diary*, *The Archers*, and that everyday story of a special agent, *Dick Barton*. *The Robinson Family* was the first of this doom-stretching line, having been started by Alan Melville as a propaganda vehicle in the Overseas Service during the war. It was aimed to bring home the realities of rationing, the black-out and the call-up to overseas listeners, who enjoyed it so much that in 1945 Maurice Gorham brought it into the new Light Programme under its new name of *The Robinson Family*. It soon confirmed that the daily serial as established in the USA and Australia would build similarly vast audiences of habitual followers in Britain. Where the Robinsons trod the others duly followed. *Dick Barton* was started in 1946 by Norman Collins, who had succeeded Gorham as head of the Light, as an early-evening audience hooker with Noel Johnson as the intrepid agent, though because of the BBC's fondness for anonymity on behalf of actors it took some months for his name to leak out. Dick was in the line of action-packed heroes, intellectually far behind even the beefiest of them. Bulldog Drummond was an Einstein to Dick, who had been carefully constructed as a chaser, not a thinker. At first his writers' imagination dwelt upon death rays, plague-carrying rats, acid baths, man-eating orchids, ghosts, Nazi werewolves, and a hundred other extravagances, but when the BBC discovered that the juvenile audience was larger than the adult the stories became less abstract; for, as Geoffrey Webb, one of the writers, observed,[1] it meant little to the child listener that the villain planned to enslave a nation, whereas a hulking brute swinging a cosh was recognisably villainous. The characters were suitably adjusted to the needs of the children. Dick had to renounce smoking, drinking, and the love of women (his girl friend Jean Hunter, introduced originally to provide someone for the villains to kidnap, was phased out). Even his housekeeper had to go (she later became Mrs Dale's mother). A code of conduct drawn for Dick bound him never to break the law, tell lies, talk politics, kick, knife, gouge or swear. Swear-words even in foreign languages were out, and Dick relieved his feelings in such expletives as 'Good grief!' Soon eight millions followed him every evening, and the discipline imposed on him did not prevent anti-Barton sermons from those people who always suspect, and want to stop, anything a lot of other people enjoy. He was blamed for childish delinquencies. The *Daily Worker* said he was a Fascist lackey.

There was not enough depth in Dick to last. It says much for the qualities of production and story-telling that he stayed four years. By then Mrs Dale, a very different cup of tea, had insinuated herself into the nation's heart. She opened her diary every weekday at 4 pm in scripts first written by Jonquil Anthony and the future Lord (Ted) Willis. The names of those taking part were once again concealed and Fleet Street had to ferret them out. This time there were more to ferret, for the writers had grasped the secret that the potential interest and length of life in a serial is multiplied by the number of characters in it. The purpose of *Mrs Dale's Diary* was to mirror provincial life from the point of view of the middle class; when it began the lower orders were brought in exactly as Shakespeare had brought them in, as comedy relief in the characters of servants, charwomen, gardeners, etc. But as the social climate altered outside the serial, so changed the reflection in the mirror. There was, for example, a sensational upheaval in 1962, when the Dales left the comfortable suburb of Parkwood Hill to live in Exton new town, where Dr Dale helped to form a group practice within the National Health Service and Mrs Dale was invigorated by the change to the point of standing successfully for the local council. Through twenty-one years the stories spun on and on and on, skilfully rearranging the crude and disorderly stuff of life as their listeners knew it into a shape more to their comfort.

The Archers differed from Barton and the Dales by being born out of a genuine passion for its subject. Its creator was Godfrey Baseley, a Midland Region broadcaster who loved the world of farming and longed to impart it to radio. The seed of *The Archers* was a monthly series called 'Down on the Farm', in which Baseley and other commentators visited a real farm to hear and tell about the work. It succeeded in transmitting a whiff of the farmyard to the urban millions but did not satisfy his aim to provide some sort of service to farmers. The BBC gave him a new magazine programme aimed at farmers and their families, but that did not work. Then, at a meeting organised to ask farmers what kind of programme they really wanted, one Henry Burtt of Lincolnshire rose and pronounced the sentence that was to

Baseley the falling of Newton's apple. 'What is really wanted is a farming Dick Barton.' Later on he captured Baseley's imagination by explaining the risks and cliff-hanging situations inseparable from the farming business. Baseley saw the dramatic possibilities, but though he thought of projecting them through some universal farmer type he lacked the knack of creating dialogue. He asked Geoffrey Webb and Edward J. Mason, writers of Dick Barton, to try a sample script; and on the Monday of Whit week 1949, Midland listeners heard Dan Archer and his cowhand exchange the first words of the serial. 'Well, Simon. What do you think?' 'Ah well – 'er might and 'er might not.' They were assisting the birth of a calf. In those two lines, Baseley complacently reflected, they had 'laid the foundations of thousands of scenes where anxiety, doubt and suspense have all played their part'.[2] The Light Programme took thirteen more; and when *Dick Barton* was pensioned off *The Archers* took its place as the early-evening audience hooker. It has stayed there ever since, though its hooking powers have long lost out to television.

My imagination did not seem to require *Dick Barton*, *The Archers* or *The Dales*. In so far as I was ever hooked by these entertainments it was by Charles Chilton's science fiction *Journey into Space*. But the peculiar quality of broadcasting is that you cannot avoid becoming aware of what is widely heard even if you do not yourself hear it. Everyone knew whom the comedians meant when they got an easy laugh with a single line of supposed parody of the Dale style, 'I'm worried about Jim'. I was aware of Jock and Snowy, Dick's companions. I could not but know that the diarist's husband was a doctor called James, that she had a mother named Mrs Freeman, a cat called Captain, a gardener named Monument and a char named Mrs Maggs. I was aware that Dan Archer was a farmer of standing in a village called Ambridge, numbering among his neighbours an eccentric named Walter Gabriel who always sounded as though he was speaking while breathing in.

The realism of the serials troubled some listeners whose reason was less firmly seated than their loved ones would have wished. When Gwen Dale married in 1951 the writers invented some anxiety as to whether her wedding dress would be ready in time. In several dozen letters and phone calls listeners offered to lend her their own. In 1955 Baseley caused national pandemonium by killing off Grace Archer in a stable fire. Telephone lines to the BBC were blocked for hours, and the death completely upstaged the opening of ITV in the newspapers next morning. Baseley always denied that this was a deliberate publicity stroke, pointing out that the decision to kill Grace was taken more than three months ahead. Nobody believed him. The Salvation Army praised the serial for reminding listeners that in the midst of life they were in danger of death, but the most emphatic statement made by the incident was to illustrate the power of a serial's devisors. Over their shadowy but strangely real world their hands held life and death, and there was no appeal. Once Baseley considered that the time had come to replace Dan's herd of Shorthorns with Friesians, which were becoming popular in the real world because of their high milk yield. As a matter of courtesy he confided his intention to the secretary of the Shorthorn Society's Council. The latter was confounded by the possibility of so many farmers obeying Dan's lead as to jeopardise the livelihood of Shorthorn breeders, and persuaded the BBC's legal department that the Charter did not contain a licence to ruin people. But the discomfited Baseley had the last word. He killed off Dan's Shorthorns by giving them foot and mouth and then, in due time, replaced them with Friesians.

The value of employment in the serials was its steadiness rather than its spectacular financial rewards. The BBC made a big occasion out of the Archers' 1000th performance in 1954, but when I met Harry Oakes (Dan Archer) at the party in Birmingham he was only on about £25 a week. Noel Johnson, the creator of the part of Dick Barton, managed to screw his employer up to £20, at a time when Dick was a household name. The BBC used to argue that the format of the serial, not the actors, was what counted most; it was proved right rather brutally when in 1963 it had to let Ellis Powell out of *Mrs Dale's Diary*. Although she had played the title role since the beginning the audience accepted Jessie Matthews, the star of the musical stage between the wars, as her replacement without protest. The BBC used to tell the stars that their big money would come from the fringe benefits, the personal appearances. This was certainly true for Harry Oakes; as 'Dan' he could have opened a fête probably every day of his life. But poor Johnson could hardly go about in the person of Dick Barton, entering fêtes by vaulting over gates or burrowing tunnels. His most lucrative offer was from a firm of breakfast-food manufacturers, who believed that Dick's signature on every packet would help their campaign to corrupt the appetites of the young; this he had to decline because copyright in the character belonged to the BBC.

I never heard anyone discuss *Mrs Dale's Diary* or *The Archers*. Devotion to them was very much a private pleasure, perhaps something the fans felt a bit sheepish about acknowledging; it would have been like talking about their dreams. But loyalty to them was lasting; of all radio's dramatic fictions the serials yielded ground to television the most stubbornly. In its last year (it was killed in 1969) the Dales still had two and a quarter million listeners to its 11 am broadcast and 1,700,000 to the other at 4.15. In 1972 *The Archers'* lunchtime audience was playing to 1,600,000.

Who needs a Script?

In Haley's reconstruction the Light and Home were supposed to compete against each other as if the opponent were an outside organisation, though each had clearly differentiated aims. The Light's target was sixty per cent of the audience against the Home's thirty and the Third's ten per cent. As we know the Light soon took more than its share, but it hardly mattered; there was so much audience to be shared. For ten years, the listening figures for the big variety successes were vast. *ITMA, Have a Go, Merry-Go-Round, Twenty Questions, Much Binding in the Marsh, Variety Bandbox, Ignorance is Bliss, Forces Favourites*, and later on *Take it from Here, Educating Archie, Ray's a Laugh, Life with the Lyons* and later still *Hancock's Half-Hour*, pulled in fifteen to twenty million. *The Archers* had its daily twelve million. *Any Questions*, a fairly serious discussion programme, had nine million a week. The Light Programme's letters feature, *Dear Sir*, had eleven million. Twenty-five million heard the Queen's 1953 Christmas broadcast. The 1952 Cup Final was heard by a third of the population and the Derby by a quarter.

A new ingredient in variety programmes was the rise of the series that needed no script. They were quizzes, record request shows and panel games. They sprang from the economic laws of radio. If a format could be found that involved the public in some way it could last for years because the public itself refreshed it every week and often supplied the words for it. Another way to keep it going was to 'dramatise' the cast of the panel: you picked a hero, a heavy, an intellectual and a charming lightweight. This was the formula invented, I believe, by Mark Goodson and Bill Todman, a pair of former newspapermen who became the undisputed stars of the American panel game business and were to leave their imprint on the age in *What's My Line?, Twenty Questions, The Name's the Same* and a score more. An appeal of these guessing games was that the audience was offered the answer and could then wonder at the panel's wit or folly as it stumbled towards it. It sounds a frail base, but by 1972 *Twenty Questions* had run for half the lifetime of the BBC on nothing but the innocent fun of listening to four pleasant people trying to guess the name of an object. Sometimes the panel, still chosen for its dramatic potential, handed out opinions on questions sent in by the audience; in 1950 *We Beg to Differ* raced to success on the slender device of airing the more popular and banal of the standing disputes between men and women, such as women as motorists, men as cooks, etc., etc. The appeal here was in the spontaneity and wit with which the players displayed their personalities. It was no bad shop window for the gifted talker, for a certain Doctor Hill, endowed superabundantly with the gift of the gab, rose from a seat on *We Beg to Differ* to become chairman of the BBC – admittedly not at a single leap. Personality, the ability to shine on one's own without benefit of gag-writers or authors, became better than money in the bank if the lucky owner could turn his gift to advantage on the radio. Even the comparatively humdrum turn of playing gramophone records could turn a person into a personality and a personality into a star.

The record show had been with radio almost from its birth, having spread from an experimental 'Gramophone Hour' begun in 1924. The first disc jockey, though this pungent title had not yet reached Britain, was Christopher Stone, the London editor of *The Gramophone*. To him goes the honour of the discoveries that a programme of snippets is extremely popular and that no sound is more gratifying to a listener than that of his own name. Stone's success was based on a marvellously friendly microphone manner and a good catholic taste. He played foxtrots, Stravinsky, Bing Crosby, a cathedral or a cinema organ with equal enjoyment, though when it came to the rising 'hot' dance records he had to segregate them into a special programme, such was the shock and fury they excited among his regular listeners.

The programme that combined record requests and messages was born during the war and flourished hugely after it, but now the emphasis was as much on the performance of the jockeys as much as on their choices. Some of them – Jack Jackson, Sam Costa, David Jacobs, Richard Attenborough, George Elrick – became powerful arbiters of popular taste, courted assiduously by the music industry as the bandleaders of earlier years had been. Jack Jackson, once a trumpeter with those bands, was the most original of the jockeys, using the new tools of tape recordings with such skill that he not only presented a gramophone show that was as entertaining as a variety bill but did it all from his home in the Canary Islands. But though the public welcomed such elaborate gimmickry it did not disdain meeker efforts. Elrick became a favourite by endearing himself to the housewives as 'Mrs Elrick's wee son George' and humming the signature tune as though in an irresistible surge of high spirits. This was in *Housewives' Choice*, a favourite shop-window for records and jockeys from 1946 to 1967. The money was not much – Peter Brough was paid £30 for his week's work in 1952 – but to be invited to do the show was a mark of distinction that few of those invited cared to decline. It was a kind of honorary decoration, like being chosen as Roy Plomley's castaway on that other record programme, *Desert Island Discs*. Apart from this there was useful publicity value in talking to millions of women five mornings a week. The jockeys had to flatter their audience's tastes and not indulge their own. Indeed the predictability of the class of record acted as an unofficial time check. If you heard a burst of classical music from *Housewives' Choice* you knew that the time must be running up to ten o'clock.

Thus the record shows proliferated, reflecting at the end of the BBC's first half-century a spectrum of taste as wide as the whole of radio, from *Record Review* on Radio Three to the distressingly idiotic exchanges between the jockeys and their listeners on Radios One and Two.

At their best the non-scripted shows made an important contribution to the art of radio. *Have a Go* was one of the best ideas anyone ever had, though nothing could have been simpler. Its begetter was John Salt, programmes director of the North region, but its essential ingredient – it travelled about, visiting a different place each week – puts its origin among the features with the people begun by Geoffrey Bridson before the war. Although devised as a quiz the questions were only the means of getting people to talk. The show succeeded from the start, in 1947 reached its peak audience of twenty million (overtaking *ITMA* as the most popular programme) and toured the land in triumph for years. Its compère was the actor Wilfred Pickles, who had been brought to the nation's attention during the war when Brendan Bracken, Minister of Information, conceived the desperate device of asking the BBC to hire a northcountryman to read the news as a demonstration of national unity. Pickles and his producer (first Philip Robinson, then Barney Colehan) agreed about what they wanted: to capture through the quiz the simplicity, the sentimentality, the variety and vitality of ordinary people. But the key figure was Wilfred. He developed a gift for persuading people who had never seen a microphone to talk to him at their complete ease; the programme soon became a parade of local persons interviewed by him, the questions and the money often thrown away.

Its appeal lay somewhere in the pleasure we all take in hearing someone talk unselfconsciously, as a human being, in a show business context. Often the interviews amounted to the brief story of a life, presented in as it were a vivid flash to the listener's imagination. It was sad, funny, compelling admiration and respect and laughter of a size no radio programme had ever equalled. Wilfred's approach dug deeply into his public's emotions. He set great store by stoicism, on the level of 'there's lots worse off than us'. He had a particularly soft spot for the afflicted, taking his programme regularly among the sick, injured, aged and orphaned. He said he thought it helped people to get their values right when they heard stories of human decency, sacrifice, suffering, courage and humour and saw no reason why persons in hospitals should be cut off from participating in a show whose object was to travel among the people.[3] Barney Colehan recalled that these programmes, including the visits to St Dunstan's and Roehampton, were the most popular of the series, but one has to admit that they did not appeal to everyone. Some listeners did not want their radio to remind them of other people's suffering in a light entertainment show. To some it seemed that Wilfred was making commercial use of the afflicted – and so, albeit inevitably, he was inasmuch as he was paid for his work. This objection did not amount to much. In so far as the complainers had a case, it was that Wilfred's attitude to suffering was sentimental. He presented only its bright face, the cheerful courage of its victims. You never heard anyone in *Have a Go* who was resentful or embittered. In the generally upbeat context of the show it would not have done. Its object, as Pickles said in his opening remarks every week, was 'to bring the people to the people'; but he prefaced this by calling his show a half-hour 'of homely fun'. I think he must be acquitted of the charge of exploiting suffering, but it dogged him to the end of *Have a Go*'s run and followed him into *Ask Pickles*, a hugely popular television show which specialised in bringing about the fulfilment of such daydreams as the majority of the audience might consider simple, homely and upbeat. Possibly the worst that could be said of Pickles was that he turned on his audience's emotions in a direct and unsophisticated way which gratified the many and embarrassed the opinion-leading few.

The Forced Retreat

The BBC hierarchy which had grown up with sound radio believed or hoped that sound and television would exist as equal partners in the art of broadcasting, from which the discriminating public would choose sound only, or sound plus pictures, according to which fitted the subject best. It was an attractive vision which I could not but want to share, and not such a wild one either, for as we have seen radio developed the pattern of all broadcasting entertainment. It was built of music, talks, plays, religion, features, documentaries, sport, variety and comedy, quizzes, serials, series, panel games, news bulletins and weather forecasts. Television added one thing: pictures. But they were the lure that captivated the mass audience. If television offered radio with pictures, that was what we wanted. And although radio contributed as much to the art of broadcasting in the ten years following the Coronation as in the decade preceding it, the sheer loss of audience for much of its best specialised work forced the BBC to retreat from its frequently repeated insistence that radio would 'continue to provide a full, rounded, creative service'. Frank Gillard, the director of Sound Broadcasting, was still saying it in March 1964, the year two of radio's once most precious assets were written off – the Features Department and Children's Hour.

Radio's plight had begun to show in the late fifties, when even the more serious weekly journals were dropping their radio criticism and covering television only. There was no help for this in the popular dailies and Sundays. In the *Daily Mail* I wrote only about TV programmes, of which more than a few did not really reach the standard at which criticism would be applied, and had to ignore work on radio which represented a craft at its peak. All attempts to draw up lists are ridiculous, but I think of the cool and fastidiously witty features of Nesta Pain and Jenifer Wayne; of Kay Cicellis's documentary, 'Death of A Town', on the Greek earthquake of 1953; of the funny and elegant literary and musical satires by Henry Reed and Donald Swann about Hilda Tablet, the composeress; of *Under Milk Wood*, possibly the best-known serious radio work of all the BBC's first five decades, yet only one of a brilliant stream of productions by Features in its golden decade after the war.

Dylan Thomas was one of sound's most prized protégés, as a writer of poetry and as a reader of it, though to my ear his poetry voice sounded like a man parodying the art and could not be compared with his magnificent reading of his own autobiographical prose. It was one of these, his 1947 *Return to Swansea*, that led to the commission to write *Under Milk Wood*, which thereupon entered seven years of curious adventures. Douglas Cleverdon said Thomas wrote the first half quite quickly but then got stuck with other work and other calls on his time, notably the social obligation of drinking pints and pints of beer and stuff in the Gluepot and other places. Cleverdon persuaded the BBC to take the unprecedented step of paying Thomas so much per thousand words on delivery, but the work was not completed until the eve of his disastrous lecture tour of America. There American bourbon settled his affairs, as it will those of anyone who drinks it in sufficient quantities; but it is arguable that the assassin was the British tax system, which fines writers so heavily for success. Thomas had made a fair sum out of writing for films and got into a frightful tax muddle from which only a lucrative American lecture tour could rescue him. He brought the completed manuscript to Cleverdon, who had it typed and returned. He took it on a pub crawl and lost it, giving birth to the legend that the only copy of the work had been rescued from some Soho dustbin. He told Cleverdon next morning what had happened, adding that if he found it he could keep it. He then sailed for America. Cleverdon searched Thomas's drinking route and found the manuscript in the Helvetia. A few years later, after Thomas's death and the tremendous success of *Under Milk Wood* had combined to lend his name something of the romantic aura attached to any poet who dies young, Cleverdon sold it. It fetched £2000.

Between 1949 and 1955 all the radio works submitted for the Italia Prize were productions of Gilliam's Features Department. It continued to dominate these international scenes until its death. Louis MacNeice said that for liveliness of mind and enterprise Features were unlike any other group of writers he had ever met. It had extraordinary range. To explain to visitors what Features did Gilliam wrote a memorandum declaring that the aim was to have about twenty people ranging from the poets like MacNeice, through the middle range like Cleverdon (said Cleverdon), to tough Fleet Street journalists like the Robert Barrs, so that whatever the subject might be somebody in Features could handle it. Perhaps its extreme versatility in the end harmed it. Its work was arguably overlapping with that of other departments; whereas Features could, and did, produce features that sounded like plays (from 1947 to 1955 *all* the Italia prize awards for drama were won by

Features), features that sounded like original musical creations, and features that sounded like documentaries and current affairs productions, other departments never made the radio feature. The art of pure radio as defined by Sieveking* remained with Gilliam's department; but the techniques it had developed began to spread, noticeably in Drama with the arrival in 1953 of Donald McWhinnie as assistant head. One can see how he altered Drama by looking at the BBC's Italia Prize entries for 1956–62. Five of them were from his department; they included two Samuel Becketts, a Harold Pinter and a Giles Cooper.

The decline of Features began in 1959 when Gilliam was asked to reduce the number of his producers. He did this not by firing anyone but by not recruiting, relying on retirement and resignation to decrease his staff. Strategically this was a mistake for too many of the survivors were middle-aged and the department was not being refreshed, as Drama was, by the arrival of young blood more alert to the need to continue the exploration of radio. Some younger ones, including Barr, Norman Swallow and Denis Mitchell, had already gone to television. The output of some of the older hands had begun to flag. And apart from drawing away contributors television was taking huge bites out of the evening audience for radio, forcing a heavier concentration of resources upon daytime radio to which the traditional kind of feature, expensive in money and time, was inappropriate. Geoffrey Bridson believed that Gilliam's principal error had been a failure to realise that economy had become a major factor and one in which a number of cheaply effective competitors had long been underselling him.[4] Gilliam's tightly knit band had always believed themselves to be unpopular with the administration branch, and rather relished the fact that they were mostly out of their offices, mixing with writers and other eccentrics in pubs, when the admin. men telephoned. Gilliam continued not to spare himself in his habitual enjoyment of life and was sometimes a bother at afternoon meetings when he would drop asleep because he had had a good, entertaining lunch with some congenial spirit. Even producers close to him seem not to have known that he had already begun to die of cancer, and the awareness that his department's existence had become imperilled came on them quite suddenly.

Following weeks of rumour in the newspapers, leaked by producers who must have hoped that if the threat to Features became known the public would insist on rescuing it, the news was broken to the department on a bad day in February 1964. Its separate existence was no longer convenient or necessary. Producers were invited to share themselves between Drama, Talks and Current Affairs, and Light Entertainment. They were guaranteed freedom to produce in any form they liked provided the appropriate department agreed. The intention was in part to introduce their skills to less experienced colleagues

* See p. 43.

but rather more a device for keeping their jobs. An end had been reached of nearly twenty years of achievement, to which Gilliam's death in November supplied a tragic full stop.

Those directly affected looked on the ending of Features as one of the two most damaging misjudgments made by sound radio in the face of television's assault. Others saw it as an inevitable writing off of a diminishing asset. Whatever the cause, there can be little argument about the effect. Douglas Cleverdon summed it up by saying that there had been a noticeable decline in features of imaginative or poetic creation; and there were now no young poets working in radio as writer-producers injecting new vitality into the art and maintaining the standards set by Bridson, MacNeice and others.[5]

The decision to end Children's Hour was a good deal more arguable, because it seemed to be throwing away what most of the public would have said was the brightest jewel in the crown and what the BBC might have been expected to designate an area of special historical and cultural importance which ought to be preserved from rational considerations of money and audience. It had been given an extra fifteen minutes a day in the postwar reorganisation of 1946 and went on as splendidly as ever with its traditional job of providing 'a children's BBC' which would do almost everything the parent service did but at a level suitable for children. The *Toytown* stories were repeated annually. Commander Stephen King Hall continued his talks on world affairs. They discovered Anthony C. Wilson's Norman and Henry Bones, the boy detectives, Barbara Euphan Todd's *Worzel Gummidge*, Anthony Buckeridge's *Jennings at School*, they developed more programmes about the countryside in *Nature Parliament* and *Cowleaze Farm*. The writer Noel Streatfeild, in an article on Children's Hour in 1951,[6] thought its success almost unmitigated as an instrument of the policy of offering listeners the best. It paid the children the compliment, she said, of considering them intelligent human beings, never played for the large audience by pandering to possible lower tastes, and had its reward when the selections came in for the Request Weeks, for the children showed an instinctive preference for quality, and would go for things such as *Nature Parliament* and leave out a serial that the producer had had secret worries about. It took the children's classics (*Little Women*, *Rebecca of Sunnybrook Farm*, the Arthur Ransome *Swallows and Amazons* stories) into homes where there may not have been books. It taught children the art of listening.

The beginning of the end can now be seen to have been the decision to show Children's TV at five o'clock, thereby forcing children in TV homes to choose between the sound and the pictures. As was already known from the American example their choice would be for the pictures. Noel Streatfeild urged the planners to think before it was too late about the danger 'of squandering the old magic to show children the new one'; but if ever her counsel found attentive ears their owners lacked the power to end a competition which, however idiotic, was also unavoidable. Five o'clock had been the time for children's hour because it was the best time; it had to be so for television as well. The audience figures held steady until the year after the Coronation; then what had once been radio's audience alone had to be split two ways with the rise of television and three ways with the coming of ITV. It could be said that numerically Children's Hour was no longer a significant part of the nation's life, and as the audience continued to decline and the costs of television to swell there was at any rate a sound enough financial motive for saying, as in 1964 the BBC said, that there was not enough audience left to justify the expense of employing the people to provide a daily programme.

It may well be that the audience had declined to the point at which it was failing to attract young writers and performers, who do not like playing to empty houses; the service would have been maintained by the dwindling group of old hands from the great days. It may be that the imaginative responses of children are not blunted just because television adds pictures; perhaps television's adaptation of *The Railway Children* stimulated them as much as radio's; but when I think of *Dr Who* I wonder if the stimulation is of equal quality. (Dr Who was a magician/scientist whose role, assisted by a boy and girl, was to defeat attempts by other scientists, often from outer space, to subjugate the earth. Sometimes these enemies were humanoids; but the most popular ones were definitely metallic. They were called Daleks. They were the shape of caster sugar pots, were armed with ray guns that annihilated by vaporisation anything they hit, and spoke in dry, metallic, mournful and monotonous tones, like those of the unseen speakers who announce train arrivals at London's terminals. Whether it was because of their destructive powers or because their voices were easy to imitate these robots became as popular to their audience's generation as Bonzo dogs and Pip, Squeak and Wilfred had been to mine.)

Television is obviously more effective than radio in programmes like *Blue Peter*, in which the object is to demonstrate some nimble art or craft and instil the desire to do likewise. When I watch the skill with which Valerie Singleton, John Noakes and Peter Purves, the story-readers of *Jackanory*, or the puppet-masters of *Watch With Mother* reach surely and sensitively for their audience, I would find it very difficult to make out a case that television had not restored much of what appeared lost. Three things, however, are unarguable. The radio Children's Hour was as much a part as music of the complete service the BBC had declared it would maintain for listeners. Children had been deprived of the best chance they would ever have to learn the art of listening to radio, a very different thing from watching television; the connection between the ending of Children's Hour and the arrival of the kind of half-conscious hearing of Radio One is plain to see. It was a sad and sharp demonstration of the kind of false progress according to which 'instead of' is held to be as good as 'in addition to'. Perhaps the loss fell heaviest on the parents. They could no longer have the deep pleasure of sharing with their children a delight they had enjoyed when they were young.

5

HOW MERRY-GO-ROUND BEGAT
ALF GARNETT

I suggested earlier that radio lost its audience not because it was so different from television but because it was so much like it. You can see by retracing the growth of comedy how talent moved over into television from radio almost without breaking step. Until the wave of the satire shows represented by *That Was The Week That Was* began to roll in 1962 and let in the journalists, there was hardly a good comedy series on TV that had not been written by reliable professionals who had learned their business in radio. When you look at broadcast comedy you see a tree with several branches stemming from a single trunk.

In 1948 the big comedy successes were still hangovers from the war years. *ITMA*'s chief rivals, Eric Barker's *Merry-Go-Round* and Kenneth Horne's and Richard Murdoch's *Much Binding*, were carved out of wartime service shows, much as the York civil plane was carved out of the Lancaster bomber. Horne and Murdoch converted the RAF station at Much Binding into a country club. Barker turned the naval base of 'HMS Waterlogged' into a pleasure and health centre called 'Waterlogged Spa', and in 1948 had the gratification of beating *ITMA* out of top place with a show that challenged it on its own ground (it had already been passed occasionally by lesser material, such as *Twenty Questions*, *Ignorance is Bliss*, Carroll Levis's *Discoveries* and Michael Miles's *Radio Forfeits*). A thoughtful and clever writer and actor, Barker's importance as an innovator has been undervalued; perhaps he wrote his best stuff for other performers. He created funny and solid characters whose names are still good for a reminiscent chuckle. The most popular character in HMS Waterlogged was the First Lord of the Admiralty (pronounced Admirality), a loud-voiced and unabashed Cockney who had worked his way up from dustman and whose appointment was supposed to have been one of the first acts of the new Socialist Government. Barker took him out of the Admiralty and promoted him to the House of Lords as the first Baron Waterlogged. He had a daughter named Phoebe, pronounced Pheeb, who was never heard. Barker played the managing director of the spa, with his wife Pearl Hackney as his loving secretary, and Jon Pertwee as a variety of comic characters; older readers need only hear the words 'As long as you tear them up' to remember his Devonshire postman who had once been a bugler in Plymouth barracks. Another of the show's famous creations was Flying Officer Kyte (Humphrey Lestocq), a comic extension of the demobbed RAF man who, as Barker put it, 're-solved all the troubles of humanity down to the basic elements of RAF slang'.[1] The catchphrase that gave a kind of seal of public approval to a comedy series was 'Steady, Barker', used as a reminder to himself by the managing director. Barker had grateful testimonials from listeners for whom the phrase proved a helpful alternative to cursing and a clearer of the air between couples whose bickering had reached flash point. After they'd said 'Steady, Barker', they could not, it seemed, help smiling.

Much Binding was powered by the sunny charm of Horne as station commander turned managing director and Murdoch as adjutant turned assistant. It greatly pleased those who liked their comedy to be kindly and middle-brow; it was the favourite show of King George VI and brought Sam Costa to eminence as a kind of batman who entered each week bearing the catch-phrase, 'Good morning, sir. Was there something?' I wish I could remember more about it, and about Jewell and Warris's *Up the Pole*, Charlie Chester's *Stand Easy* and Bonar Colleano's *It's a Great Life*, of which all recollections whatever have utterly gone if, indeed, they were ever there.

The long success of *ITMA* had succeeded in persuading the public that comedy shows were written by somebody and not, as they had supposed, made up by the comedians as they went along; the profession of script writing became respectable, and Ted Kavanagh found himself the revered doyen of the craft. From his eminence he did much to help young strugglers; and it was in his office one day after the war that there occurred the meeting of Frank Muir and Denis Norden, no less worthy to be chronicled than the first meeting of Gilbert and Sullivan. Neither of them remembered what was said in Ted's office, and perhaps the real meeting of minds was the chance encounter the same day in a Regent Street cinema where they had each gone separately for want of anything better to do. The second feature was a romantic drama set in period France. The hero was drinking in a café, sad because his girl had left him. His friend, an older man, said something like: 'Don't worry. She will come back.' The hero replied, 'No. Women are different than men.' The older man said, 'Ah, monsieur is a philosopher.' At this two laughs rang out, one from Frank and the other from Denis. They each looked to see who the other laugher was; and thus was begun a partnership that lasted seventeen years and greatly enriched the nation's stock of laughter.

They began to labour separately for various comedians on the Kavanagh list and were brought into collaboration by Charles Maxwell, the producer who devised the *Take It from Here* series as a vehicle for Jimmy Edwards, Dick Bentley and Joy Nichols. Edwards was a former RAF pilot and graduate from the Windmill and *Navy Mixture*. Bentley, a venerable figure of forty, was an actor and singer from Australia. Joy Nichols had been a child prodigy on the abominable Australian commercial radio and thus, though only twenty-one, was the most experienced in radio of the three. The format was the standard one of the day; sketches alternated with songs and band numbers. The novelty, once Muir and Norden had got their eye in, was an exuberant delight in fooling about with words and a comic view that was bookish rather than music hall. Like every comic writer of their time they had grown up on Stephen Leacock, P. G. Wodehouse, S. J. Perelman, and the Marx Brothers, but they also heard about Boccaccio, Chaucer, the *Thousand and One Nights* and others too humorous to mention, as Frank put it in a celebrated lecture on comedy delivered in, of all places, the Concert Hall in Broadcasting House. They shared the national fondness for puns, and invented some that still cannot be read without the eyes watering. *Joy:* 'What'll you have for supper? I've saved you a soda scone.' *Jim:* 'Nay, lass, I cannot eat a soda scone so late. It makes me feel so disconsolate.' That one came from 'Trouble At T'Mill, or Loom 504', one of the skits on current films that most of us remember best about the early *TIFH* shows. Curiously enough, no writers had satirised them before, so Frank and Denis were working at a lucrative vein. Loom 504 parodied all the clichés of the northern industrial novel in which characters named Seth Oakroyd and Jess Hardcastle held lanterns at each others' faces, called each other by their full names, and outfaced the starving mill workers when they stormed up the drive. It is still very funny after twenty-four years. *Dick:* 'Wait! I demand to be heard. I am Reuben Bentley, the editor of your two local papers, the Drooling Sun and the Drooling Star. I've got the Sun in the morning and the Star at night.' *Jim:* 'Upstart! What dost thee know of Drooling? Thar't an outsider – tha doesn't even talk like us.' *Dick:* 'I can't do a Midland accent. Seth Oakroyd, I must speak!' *Jim:* 'I'm a hard man, Reuben Bentley, but I'm a just man. Speak thy mind.' *Dick:* 'Right. Four score years ago, this town –' *Jim:* 'Thank you, Bentley. That's enough.' *Dick:* 'No. I won't rest till I get better conditions. My dream is to found a brotherhood of all workers at the mills. I've even found a name for it – the Mills Brothers.' *Jim:* 'Enough! Get out, or I'll have you thrown out by my yardman. And if he isn't here I'll use three footmen.' And so, unflaggingly on.

The film and book parodies ended each show for years until superseded by a more successful creation, the Glums. Here the central figure was the unlucky Eth, who had been processed by the fictions in her women's magazines and the commercials on ITV into a dim awareness that somewhere a better world was possible, in which she would ride in open cars with her hair streaming in the wind and her kitchen table would have a formica top. The hideous essence of Eth's plight was that all her strivings were doomed.

Her fiancé, Ron, was of an intractable imbecility unimagined by the writers of the advisory columns in the magazines and his father, the dreaded Mr Glum, was always devising schemes to defraud her of the savings that would set her up in marriage. Muir and Norden invented the Glums as a kind of parody of the genteelisms of *Mrs Dale's Diary* and denied passionately any intention of making any serious observation about the human condition. But they gave the Glums a core of true pathos. Eth never had a funny line and remained from first to last in the wistful character of someone who wanted a better bread than could be made from the only wheat she could get. June Whitfield's performance was up to all the demands the writers put upon it, and altogether the Glums must be taken as refuting Muir's and Norden's claim to be pure fun pedlars and as representing a development of true character comedy on radio. I could never listen to the introductory music which led to Eth's opening, usually despairing wail of 'Oh, Ron!' without a pang. *June:* 'Oh, Ron ... If only we could get married without all this fuss and palaver. But I'm only the bride. I've got no say. Whose day is it? That's what I want to know! Whose day is it?' *Dick:* 'Saint Swithins?' *June:* 'Honestly, Ron, they've got me so worked up. I didn't sleep a wink last night.' *Dick:* 'Neither did I, Eth. I didn't even get into bed. Just stood in my dressing-gown and thought.' *June:* 'You were worried, too?' *Dick:* 'No, Eth. My dressing-gown tassel was caught in the wardrobe door.' *June:* 'Why didn't you take your dressing-gown off?' *Dick: (pause)* '... Well, I'll be blowed. Of course!' *June:* 'I can see you're just as on edge as I am.' *Dick:* Look, I'll amuse you. I'll make you laugh. Look, I'll stick my tongue through the hole in my mint-with-a-hole-in-it.' *June:* 'Oh, Ron, I wish I could have your gift for adapting yourself to circumstances.'

By 1950 *ITMA* had gone and *Take it from Here* was the most popular comedy show. By 1951 it was still the favourite, but as one of a handful of successes. The mild-mannered domestic comedy which always had been a reliable drawer was still holding its own with Ted Ray's *Ray's a Laugh* and *Life with the Lyons*, with Ben Lyon, Bebe Daniels and their two children. The kind of comedy written to serve a comedian's personality was blossoming splendidly in the scripts Eric Sykes was writing for Frankie Howerd. From the north came Al Read. In his sideline as radio comedian he specialised in colouring and sharpening the unconscious humour he heard around him in his main occupation of selling cooked meats. He boasted that he never used a gag, but could not say the same of the catchphrase; his 'Right monkey' swept the land like a sharp epidemic of Asian flu, numbering among those who picked it up millions who could not have said what it meant if their homes and jobs depended on it. The most improbable and fruitful of the new hits was *Educating Archie*, built round the dummy created by the ventriloquist Peter Brough. On the face of it an act that depended entirely on the audience's ability to watch a man talk without moving his lips seemed preposterous for radio, but Brough had not been a disciple of the American Edgar Bergen and his dummy Charlie McCarthy for nothing, and guessed that if the show worked well the listener's ear would turn Archie into a creation on two levels – one as a ventriloquist's dummy made of wood, the other as a character separated from and independent of his manipulator. In the event Archie shot to the top with unprecedented speed, winning the 1950 *Daily Mail* award for radio variety after four and a half months on the air.

There were two crucial ingredients in its success. One was the luck of getting Sid Colin and then Eric Sykes as script-writers. The other was the format devised by producer Roy Spear. It surrounded the dummy with strong individual talent. It seems to have been a lucky show from the start, for no comedian who appeared in it failed to make his name. The first series had the successful stand-up comedian Robert Moreton as Archie's supposed tutor, the young Max Bygraves as the odd-job man, the younger (13) Julie Andrews in the singer's spot, and Hattie Jacques from *ITMA* as two or three other comic characters. Later series brought in Tony Hancock, Beryl Reid and Harry Secombe; all of them promptly found themselves commanding star billing in the variety theatres. It was *Educating Archie* that expanded Harry's professional career by letting him sing a snatch as a serious operatic performer, a thing that the BBC had set its face against on the ground that his voice was all very well on the halls but. . . . To celebrate the programme's second *Daily Mail* award Harry discharged 'On with the Motley', ending by transposing the last note into the upper register – a feat which so far as I was concerned (I was in the audience) confirmed the BBC's judgement. Harry excused himself as a musician at the party afterwards on the ground that his audience expected these transports. I expect he was right.

Roy Speer had picked Hancock out of *Variety Bandbox* because he divined that he had the makings of a comic actor. Sykes's script cast him as a teacher who disliked his charge and felt that the business of being tutor to a wooden dummy was beneath him: so the beginnings of the great Hancock creation, with his seedy grandiloquence and unavailing pretensions, appeared in this series and – you see here the tree putting forth another shoot – struck an instantly harmonious chord in Ray Galton and Alan Simpson, a pair of young script-writers who shoved radio comedy in a new direction as power-fully as Muir and Norden had done. They had met as patients in a sanatorium to be cured of tuberculosis, a bit of luck which preserved them from the call-up and gave them time to read and listen to the radio from the point of view of a shared interest in comedy. Somebody put them on to Thorne Smith's Topper books. They went on to all of Damon Runyon, James Thurber, Robert Benchley and Stephen Leacock, whose name turns up as an impregnating influence on almost every writer of broadcasting comedy. They set up as professional writers supplying gags to the comedian Derek Roy at five shillings each. They worked from eight in the morning thinking of jokes around a particular subject – fat girl jokes, wife jokes, etc. – until they and it were exhausted, and one day heard with misgiving their first broadcast joke. 'Jane Russell pontoon?' 'Yes; it's the same as ordinary pontoon but you need 38 to bust.' Thereafter they fed streams of gags and patter to most of the radio comedians. (It used to take thirty-five to forty jokes to hold up an act for five minutes.) Their first complete show was *Calling All Forces*, which they took over from Bob Monkhouse and Dennis Goodwin. In it they began to write for Tony Hancock.

Hancock in real life was a serious, untidy, introspective, doom-haunted person of much but singularly haunting charm; he had a marvellously mobile face that seemed to contain the comic and tragic masks both at once, and an unappeasable turn for self-criticism. As a comic actor rather more than a comedian he was the right man for what Galton and Simpson and Tom Ronald, their producer, wanted to try: comedy about characters, without jokes, funny voices or catchphrases, and sustained for half an hour without interruption by guest stars and singers. Until then the only half-hour situation comedy on either side of the Atlantic was *Life with the Lyons*, but it relied very much on gags and the American formula of casting the husband and father as the lovable goofball.

Hancock's Half-Hour began in 1954, when its writers were still only twenty-three. It began more traditionally than they had hoped. It was usual to have a foil for the comedian to play against, so they got Sid James as a shady character who stole lead and promoted fantastic confidence tricks. (Once he sold Hancock Lord's cricket ground for development as a farm, throwing in Hyde Park as a tea plantation.) The ever dependable Hattie Jacques was Hancock's supposed secretary and housekeeper. Bill Kerr, the Australian comedian, played an out-of-work actor; Kenneth Williams played everybody else. Hancock was supposed to be a striving actor, in a shifty and vainglorious way. They all lived in a house in East Cheam because Galton and Simpson were tickled by the name. They were fascinated by the history evoked in such street names as Railway Cuttings, Station Road, Mafeking Terrace. (Their most famous place-name, Oildrum Lane, was derived from Pumping Station Lane, a road near Chertsey.) They found they could not altogether renounce the catchphrase and the funny voice because the certain laughs they brought were simply not to be done without and Kenneth Williams did them so well. But the show from its first series contained all the basic qualities that made it a milestone in radio. The Sid–Tony relationship quickly moved from straight man–comedian into a collision between two opposites. Sid's character was crude, materialistic and defiantly short on culture. The Hancock character had visions of nobler things but was thwarted by his natural bad taste and indolence. He was the perpetual looker-on who would never make it into the world he envied; this element deepened as the series ran on. The essence of Galton and Simpson and Hancock is in an extract from a 1958 script. He was replying to the vicar, who had asked if he could smoke his pipe. 'Oh, yes, of course, please do. You won't knock it out on the fireplace, though. Some of the tiles are a bit loose. You'll have the whole lot round your gaiters if you're not careful.' And if you hear an echo of Will Hay you are not far wrong, for his brand of resourceful seediness was an admitted influence on them.

This script was untypical of the later ones inasmuch as it had a fantastic plot. Hancock was leading a mission behind the German lines. 'I've just taken my suicide pill and nothing's happened.' 'I see. You're immune. You'd better take the box. There's a hundred there: if you're caught, take three after each meal in a glass of water. That should do the trick.' Galton and Simpson believed what they called the 'plotty' Hancock scripts were the least successful; the best of all their scripts for radio, because virtually nothing happened in it, was about a boring Sunday, full of sighs, yawns and silences. But the radio comedy was always slightly surrealistic because the listener's imagination, so much more responsive when it did not have to slow down to the pace at which the corporeal eye and ear can absorb, needed something faster and more bizarre than reality, like the old silent slapstick films. It was only when Galton and Simpson and Hancock turned to television that they achieved the true naturalistic character comedy they had been moving towards.

Fantasy in the *ITMA* strain threw up the no less original *Goon Show*. Created by the experienced Jimmy Grafton and the rising Spike Milligan, and supported in the beginning by script contributions from Eric Sykes, Michael Bentine and Larry Stevens, a highly creative comedy writer who died young, *The Goon Show* was written through most of its nine years from 1951 to 1960 by Spike. It achieved a cult success in a way that *Take it from Here* and *Hancock's Half-Hour* never did. It owed a lot to the perennial strain of nonsense comedy that has always cheered people up. Its literary ancestors included Lewis Carroll, Stephen Leacock, S. J. Perelman and the *Daily Express*'s funny man, Beachcomber (his gift for inventing names such as the Rev. Arthur Ennymoor-Emtiss and Mrs Florence McGurgle, the seaside landlady, sent generations of schoolboys into stitches). Its inventive use of radio effects owed much to *ITMA*, but it went much further with them; its sound images were like cosmic disasters. Their explosive and bloodless violence reminded me of the slapstick silents but also of the Popeye film cartoons in which childlike anarchy was overlaid with a whiff of something less innocent. I felt the creators of Popeye were reflecting a desire to blow things apart, and I felt the same about *The*

Goon Show. (The title was derived from the Popeye cartoon, where the word 'goon' described a huge loony character with hair all over its face.)

How far Spike Milligan's scripts extended radio fantasy can be tasted by this extract from one of his burleques, a murder mystery which supposedly opened in the library of Sir Mousetrap Cheese's luxurious country seat not far from the Cheddar Gorge. *Harry:* 'As I stood there mulling things over –' *Effects:* Bubbling cauldron. *Harry:* 'Mm, delicious – a flash of light caught my eye.' *Effects:* Swoop – clop! Splash, expiring guggle. *Harry* (indulgently): 'Butterfingers. A face had appeared at the great milliganed window. With feigned nonchalance (chuckle) I edged towards it across the luxurious pile carpet. At that moment, a thought struck me.' *Effects:* Musical thud, off key. *Harry:* 'Ow! You've knocked me flat!' *Peter* (Grytpype-Thynne voice): 'Moriarty always plays a blunt instrument, dear boy.' *Harry:* 'Well, look sharp and get it tuned. Where was I?' *Announcer:* 'Knee deep in luxurious pile carpet.' *Harry:* 'Yes – and it's growing up round me at a rate of knots. But what's this bristling monster creeping towards me? (panic) Nearer . . . nearer. . . .' *Effects:* Rustle of parted grasses, heavy breathing. *Peter:* 'Major Dennis Bloodnok, at your service, sir. There's not a moment to lose. I've spilt my hair-restorer on the luxurious pile carpet.' *Harry:* 'Sapristi!' *Peter* (Bloodnok voice): 'No: GroBristli. Ten and six a bottle at all good chemists and free at your local barber's. . . .' *Harry:* 'It was the work of a moment to shin up a nearby Bokhara rug and seize a pearl-handled paperknife. Then for fourteen days and nights we hacked our way through the impenetrable Wilton broadloom.' *Effects:* Sounds of tropical vegetation, panting, stumbling trudge of feet. *Orchestra:* White man's ordeal music. *Peter* (Bloodnok voice): 'Onward, lads, to the thin red lino . . . I say, do you hear what I hear?' *Harry:* 'What-what-what?' *Peter* (Bloodnok voice): 'It sounds like a motor boat. No! It's a motor mower. We're saved, lad!' *Effects:* medium pitched buzz continuing. *Harry:* 'It sounds like a bluebottle to me. Yes – it's –' *Effects:* Buzz stops with screech of brakes and rattling crash. *Peter* (Bluebottle voice): 'Hello. I have mowed my way across the sward to rescue you. Smiles modestly and falls off mowing machine.' *Effects:* Soft thump and boing. *Peter* (Bluebottle voice): 'Oh – I've fallen in the Wilton.' *Orchestra:* Closing theme, fading under *Announcer:* 'That was Strewth, or Who Killed Sir Mousetrap? And the answer is: nobody – he's alive and well and living in Gorgonzola.'

The impression is of a kind of self-absorbed, concentrated fantasy that when it was coming easily must have bubbled out of Spike like spring water. The stars were Peter Sellers, Harry Secombe and Milligan. Michael Bentine had been in the early shows but was too much of a writer himself to be able to work long with another writer. Harry played Neddy Seagoon, a simple lad derived (a long way back) from some clean-limbed Victorian yarn for boys. Peter Sellers's Major Bloodnok was an echo of Dickens's Major Bagstock. His Grytpype Thynne had a suave Foreign Office spokesman's voice. Moriarty was derived from Conan Doyle's Napoleon of crime. Eccles and Bluebottle were pure cartoon characters (Eccles talked like Disney's Goofy). Sellers and Milligan also played Henry Crun and Minnie Bannister, who used to exchange strange, inconsequential lines in gently quavering voices, Bluebottle was a kind of Boy Scout whose confidence was always being betrayed by some explosion after which he would say: 'That was a rotten trick. You have deaded me!'

I suppose it does not look funny in print. And as it is impossible to like all brands of comedy equally I have to admit that I was never on such close terms with *The Goon Show* as with the other two series. For me the fantasy floated too free. I thought Spike's humour was one of the rare examples of fantasy radio comedy that was improved by being transferred to television, where it appeared in 1956 when Rediffusion, the London ITV company, put on *Idiot Weekly Price Twopence* with Sellers, Milligan and Valentine Dyall. The discipline and slowing of pace forced by the camera seemed to me to give Milligan's invention at least the touch of a foot on the earth.

For radio there were still to come the huge hits of *Beyond Our Ken* and *Round the Horne*, hung by Barry Took, Marty Feldman and others on the expansive and benevolent Kenneth Horne. But the big audience had gone to television; and thither the comedy writers began to follow it, inflicting on themselves and their audience some pretty dismaying strokes. Their difficulty was that they had mastered radio comedy at the moment when radio was about to decline and were not quite sure in what ways television was different other than being obviously slower. Ronnie Waldman believed that television comedy needed actors more than funny faces, and a style of writing that stopped and looked at what it was about. But it seemed that writers had to learn this for themselves. One curious trick they had, repeated so often I thought of emigrating to get away from it, was to think themselves right back to the ancient comic literary convention of domestic comedy. They held up accepted situations about bullying bosses, burly wives, meek husbands, bashful suitors, shy brides and so on in a manner that reflected the thirties more than the fifties and played in a style that only said: 'For God's sake like me, I'm likeable.' They were stone dead, and the funniest faces ever pulled could do nothing for them.

A lot of good comedians broke their shins on this sort of thing in television; the only sitcom shows to see the possibility of success, albeit as a dim speck on some unreachable horizon, were *Dear Dotty* and *Friends and Neighbours*, with Avril Angers and Peter Butterworth; they were terrible, but an improvement on the ghastly. The first real comedy hit of the time was Arthur Askey's *Before Your Very Eyes*; it was very cleanly and sharply directed by Bill Ward and the script translated the superhumanly likeable personality of Arthur. It also had the inducement of Sabrina, a model with breasts of such opulence that they made her famous overnight.* The script strung together two or three sketches in the summer-concert-party, low-comedy vein that Askey put across so well. One of them had Arthur and Sabrina, dressed as apes, chasing one another in and out of doors, tripping over buckets of whitewash, and so on; it produced the loudest concerted laughter ever provoked in Britain by television up to that time.

Ted Ray had quite a good run in a series based, like Arthur's, on the elongated music-hall sketch. And since 1952 there had been the steadily developing Benny Hill, perhaps the first of the truly original comedians of television though his originality soon took him outside the frame of situation comedy. The first man to make sitcom work was Bob Monkhouse, in a 1954 series called *Fast and Loose* to which Waldman had allocated the hitherto unattempted length for a comedy show of forty-five minutes. Although it was mainly a revue-type programme it embodied enough long sketches to show that Bob and his script partner Dennis Goodwin had got hold of the essence; they developed situation through character. Unluckily for Bob he had worked himself to a frazzle, collapsed after the performance and the show had to be taken out. The glory of achieving the breakthrough was reserved for Galton and Simpson, whose *Hancock's Half-Hour* moved to television in 1956 and opened up a brilliant period of BBC comedy. It retained the James and Hancock characters, planting them in a run-down house in Railway Cuttings, Cheam. At first much of the action went on outside it, but as Hancock's great talent continued to respond to television the scripts became quieter, funnier and deeper. A lot of the time the two just talked across the table, Tony in his continuing role of yearning and pretentious striver, Sid as his low and dodgy deflater. Hancock's face, which seemed to fill in and illuminate thought, was a perfect instrument for the comedy of longing and failure that was, and is, Galton and Simpson's chief inspiration. It added depth to the smallest joke because the jokes were always coming out of character – as when in one script he was sorting out his shareholdings, all of them ridiculous (they were in Royal St Petersberg Tramways, Trans-atlantic Balloon Transportation, etc.) and doomed but representing an in-extinguishable hope. In the end there was so little physical action going on that when Pye records issued some of the TV shows they needed only to edit some pauses out of the sound track.

The series ran until 1961, and was if anything better at the end than the be-ginning. Thereafter things began to go wrong for Hancock not because, as the myth has it, he grew too vain to want to share a reputation with anyone, but because of a fundamental misreading by himself of the kind of per-

*Her nickname in TV was 'the hunchfront of Lime Grove'.

former he was and his dependence on the right script. He insisted that there was nothing left to say about the James–Hancock characters or Railway Cuttings. He did not want James and Hancock to be inextricably linked like Laurel and Hardy. He thought it was time he developed by himself; the myth says out of arrogance but it was really a response to the awful itch all performers have to stretch their talent. His producer Duncan Wood, who had nursed the series from the beginning, agreed as reluctantly as Galton and Simpson to let him try. Sid was guaranteed his own Galton and Simpson series (it was called *Citizen James* and did not catch on) and he and Hancock parted on the friendliest of terms. According to the myth Hancock's decline dated from that hour, but you have only to recall 'The Blood Donor', 'The Lift' and 'Alone' (in which he was alone on screen for a full twenty-five minutes) to acknowledge that the myth as usual is talking through its hat. 'The Blood Donor' had him complacently learning that his blood was a very rare group, insulting the doctors and nurses to whom he had consented to give a pint, quailing as the needle went in, conducting a fatuously learned conversation afterwards with Hugh Lloyd, and finally gashing himself on his breadknife and having his blood put back. Pretentious, stoical and growingly truculent, the complete Hancock creation was in it.

He made his first feature film, *The Rebel*, with a Galton and Simpson script. He could not make up his mind about their second script for him, and after waiting six months for a decision they had to look for more TV work. They contracted to write ten Comedy Playhouse scripts for the BBC. The fourth, called 'The Offer', was about two junk men named Steptoe and Son. Their relationship was a more realistic reworking of what James and Hancock had enacted, deeper because it was played by actors. The son was another doomed striver, the father a combination of protector, evil genius, and ball and chain. Neither could get away from the other; a situation that would have been unbearably heartless as comedy had the characters been mother and daughter was given an irresistibly comic twist by making them father and son. With Harry H. Corbett and Wilfred Brambell to play the parts the demand for a series could not be denied. By then Hancock had found Philip Oakes to help him write *The Punch and Judy Man*, and Galton and Simpson had become immersed in *Steptoe and Son*. Hancock made a disastrous series for ATV, a few single appearances elsewhere on ITV, completed *The Punch and Judy Man*. But he was more of an interpretive comic actor than a creative comedian, and though Galton and Simpson might not have developed without him they did not depend on him as he on them. Private disaster and public disappointment in the end got on top; he took himself out of it with an overdose of drugs and alcohol in an Australian hotel in 1968. The myth that he called in his writers and sacked them is probably indestructible, but the truth is that there never was any quarrel.

They parted because they were moving in different directions. That the parting destroyed Hancock was an unlucky accident. Fate would have been kinder if it had arranged to run him over; his fall was the crueller for being long drawn out and conducted in the glare of full and sympathetic press coverage.

The biggest influence of his success was on the character comedy series, for it showed that there was a better answer to the demand for output than American TV was making. The Hancock shows were very carefully scripted and produced with very good-quality actors backing the star. The ingredients, including Hancock, were there to serve the writers. The writers brought to them their original view of life; and though they wrote only six at a time so much was compressed into them that the life of each series could be doubled, even trebled, by judiciously placed repeats. Their special quality was a fundamentally serious attitude. They respected the truth of the situation they invented, and created a school of like-minded comedy writing. Without Hancock there would have been no *Steptoe and Son*; without *Steptoe and Son* there would have been no *Till Death Do Us Part*, Johnny Speight's funny, hard and uncompromising attack on prejudice, intolerance and ignorance as vested in the person of his monstrous dockland Cockney, Alf Garnett. The gentler comedy of Richard Waring's *Marriage Lines* and *Not in front of the Children* and Jimmy Perry's *Dad's Army* owed even more to this encouragement of respect for truth, for they belonged to areas of middle-class romance and service comedy hitherto ruined by secondhand sentimentality almost as a tradition of their survival. They looked at what they were about instead of trying to reflect the audience's expectations. They got rid of the clichés. They were by writers who happened to choose the comedic form.

Till Death Do Us Part pushed it as far as it has so far gone, for Speight used comedy for a very sharp attack on a single target. It came directly out of his attitude to his own boyhood as the child of poverty in the East End in a Roman Catholic home where the mother preached a humble, to him detestable, acceptance of the evidence that other people were their betters. As for many of the same background the war did him a good turn, for it took him out of dockland and enlarged his expectations. His life turned again when one day after the war he came upon Shaw's novel, *Immaturity*, in the local library. Shaw was so old and famous that for newspapers to ask him for a comment on any subject whatever was almost part of their daily procedure, like telephoning the AA for a comment on the traffic. Speight admired the vigour of Shaw's remarks but supposed him to be a comedian like Tommy Trinder. On learning that he wrote books and plays as well Speight devoured the lot, discovering as so many other young ones had done that the thoughts he had half-formed for himself had a powerful and articulate clarifier and protector.

The beginnings of Alf Garnett were in *The Arthur Haynes Show* for ATV. The formula consisted of sketches in which the Haynes character knocked down the puppets set up for him, invariably characters representing conventional middle-class authority; for nine years it never varied. Speight also wrote for the BBC two short plays which treated the Haynes situation without the jokes; in them the humiliation of authority was nighmarish, the revenge on it unpardoning. He probably needed to write this strain out of his unconscious, for when he came to write *Till Death Do Us Part* he had learned the trick of being cruel and funny with it.

Garnett was a dock worker, presumably retired. He lived in a little house with an outside privy with his resigned wife, his daughter and her husband, an out-of-work layabout from Liverpool. The strife was between young and old, a dead marriage and an ardent fresh one, half-baked Socialism and the crudest kind of old Toryism, the new permissiveness and the old working-class prudishness. Alf symbolised the qualities Speight most disliked, but he had learned to revenge himself through wit. On one level the joke was the vulgarity of Speight's shouting dockland world of family rows, booze-ups, fights, maudlin reconciliations, chamber pots, long underwear and the *News of the World*. On the deepest level it was a very artful and recognisable caricature of an English type. Alf was a diehard Tory who believed in the royal family, the British Empire, the Church of England and the natural order of things which put the rich man in his castle and the poor man at his gate. He was also self-righteous, arrogant, bigoted, vengeful, obsequious, narrow-minded, stuffed with half-digested misinformation and a natural-born dupe. He was soon in trouble for the violence of his language, but Speight's fiendishly ingenious twist was to show that Alf was vehemently on the same side as many of the viewers who complained about him. They too believed in corporal punishment, the iron disciplining of the young, the deportation of all wogs, wops and coons, and inveighed against permissiveness as depicted in the BBC's Wednesday plays and satire shows; Alf keenly supported Mrs Mary Whitehouse's movement for cleaning up TV, but he would have had her go further and clean up the whole country by ridding it of all the coloured immigrants. To mock in this merciless way and provoke a national storm of laughter at the same time was a very rare feat of comic writing for which you have to go to Dickens and Shakespeare to find comparisons; and one of the best jokes was that some of the series' critics, unwilling to believe that Speight was letting the healing light of laughter into some dark corners of human prejudice, preferred to believe that the huge public took Alf to its heart because they regarded him as the spokesman of their own violently intolerant views on coloured immigration, the young, etc., etc.

Speight wrote twenty-six scripts before his inspiration and material began to quail and the hate began to glare out again.* By then Alf had become the most famous fictional character of his day. He stands level with Hancock as the closest television has yet come to creating an immortal.

* As this book was going to press the BBC announced a further series of *Till Death . . .* for the autumn of 1972.

6

FROM CALAIS TO THE MOON

Now with faltering steps I approach the impossible job of condensing into a chapter the shape of television from the Coronation onward. Searching for a thesis to hang a narrative on, I submit that the two most significant factors were the dizzying speed of its development and the changes brought to bear on it from outside. To humanise the story, it is less than twenty years since David Attenborough, the boy producer, watched in comic despair his carefully contrived close-up of Alan Lomax the folk-singer blow up in his face; just as he had manœuvred his ponderous camera close enough the singer leapt up in a seizure of exuberance, crying: 'Everybody dance!' Now Attenborough, who appears to have aged about five years in the meantime, holds electronic thunderbolts in his left hand and whirlwinds in his right, and as Director of Programmes for two BBC TV channels is one of the most powerful impresarios in the world. The rise of his chief, Huw Wheldon, is even more spectacular, if you consider his beginning in television as press officer as the equivalent of Dickens's term in the blacking factory.

Another way to look at it is in terms of money spent on programmes. In 1953 the amount was £3,992,000. In 1971 it was £67,500,000. The drama series department alone was spending £4,500,000, and the BBC's total revenue was £95,630,363; you can compare this sum with the £179,788 that sustained the early wireless during the fifteen months beginning December 1922. From a local and national medium of sound communication which was marvellous and cheap the BBC grew in fifty years into the largest and most influential, admired and envied broadcasting organisation in the world and its largest dispenser of entertainment. The electronics industry altered TV from a local and national affair running between wire and microwave links into an interspace communicator linking the countries of the earth and their attendant moon. In the summer of 1951 outside broadcasts brought the first television pictures from Calais en fête. In 1956 they brought the winter Olympics from Cortina d'Ampezzo. *Saturday Night Out*, a programme created solely by the appeal of showing something happening far off, went to Paris and Antwerp. The same year Eurovision realised one of the dreams that had inspired its creators and engineers; from La Scala, Milan, we saw Act Two of *Tosca*. Watching the longed-for marvel we could only ask ourselves in awe and wonder what it might lead to.* By 1959 six countries

* One thing it led to was the Eurovision Song Contest.

were permanently connected to the Eurovision link and the next year the in-heritors of the civilisation of Rome watched, live as it was happening, Abebe Bikila, the Abyssinian winner of the Rome Olympics marathon, racing in triumph towards the arch of Constantine. In 1961 Europe saw Gagarin, the first man to look on the earth from outside it, arrive in Moscow. Telstar brought the first live transatlantic TV. The same year (1962) saw the biggest TV outside broadcast so far – 200 million people watched a 21-minute pro-gramme linking fifty-four cameras in Europe, Canada, the United States and Mexico. Like all such demonstrations of a longing for unity between the contentious tribes of mankind it was sententious and uplifting in about equal parts; two years later the funeral of President Kennedy, watched by more people than had ever watched anything together up to that time, made it clear that satellite television was only another of the means by which man told himself the things he did, of no more moral significance than a sky-scraper.

Until 1965 the earth-orbiting Telstar satellites were serviceable only during those times when the signals they received and sent were within line of sight from the sending and receiving stations. Then the Americans launched Early Bird, the first of the satellites to orbit over the Equator at a height and speed, relative to the earth's rotation, that made them appear to be stationary. It was Early Bird that introduced the complications of time changes: Sonny Liston's defeat by the then Cassius Clay for the heavyweight championship of the world was a sporting event of unparalleled magnitude in terms of its potential audience; but to watch it in Europe you had to stay up until 3.30 am. (Seven million did.) The end of that year some 350 million watched the funeral of Sir Winston Churchill, and saw television catch that most extraordinarily dignified and imaginative moment when the tall cranes alongside London's river as it were bent their heads as the body was borne to Waterloo Station in its barge. In 1968 this event was superseded as the biggest ever outside broadcast by the Olympic Games from Mexico – in colour.

Within most of these technical developments a continuous process of im-provement and miniaturisation was going on. For the cameras of 1951, single-lensed and about as manœuvrable as tanks, there were in 1972 cameras that could be held easily in the hand and get a close-up of a man smoking a cigarette a hundred yards away with no more lighting than he could provide by striking a match. Consider the speed of improvements to video recording, the most important single invention next to the camera and microphone, for it made television flexible within time, able to store and collect programmes and suit the convenience of its performers. At first it was impossible to edit; then possible but difficult, then not so difficult; within five years editors were slicing and splicing tape as easily as they could push a button, and could offer viewers an instant replay of a high moment in sport and in slow motion, thereby promoting television to an electronic referee compared with which its human counterpart's ability to judge whether a ball was in or out was that of a person stumbling in the dark. The dreadful risk of the 'dry' was cured by the teleprompter, a device that projected your speech on to a screen so that you could actually read it while appearing to be looking straight into the camera lens in the manly, unaffected fashion of a man about to try to borrow a fiver. When Peter Dimmock used it first in *Sportsview* it was a complicated device about the size of a small sitting-room which Dimmock did not so much use as enter. It is now no more complicated than a typewriter and a pair of reading-glasses.

Taken together the teleprompter and video-recording machines have decisively changed the studio current affairs programme, the extended interview and the chat show. With recording the strain of appearing on the box diminished and a wider variety of faces began to appear, accompanied by the statistical probability that sooner or later most of the people in the British Isles would show up. But one curious effect has been to reverse the order in which such a show was put together. When it was live it was a matter of trying to create a shape in advance. A recorded show is put together afterwards, by cutting out the dull or superfluous bits. On the live show a speaker was within reason master of his material and could say what he wanted, if he could remember what it was. When he was recorded control passed into the hands of the producer, not always to the speaker's advantage. I once recorded an interview for *Panorama* on the cult of the Western, in the course of which I spoke of the appeal to urbanised man of this anarchic world in which all needs were simple and physical and there was a simultaneous satisfaction of the opposed needs for disorder and for law, and all that stuff. I dare say I did not put it very well, but I put it. Unknown to me the eminent Dr Stafford Clark, the psychiatrist and a formidable TV person of the day, had said much the same thing. So they cut my amateur motivational research, leaving in a few obvious remarks about the wide open spaces which must have left many viewers reflecting that they were nothing to the wide open spaces inside my head. I did not blame the producer; but it is a very good idea, if you have something you want to be sure of saying, not to be recorded saying it. Another consequence of recording has been the disappearance of the gaffe. There was once an item in a children's programme which introduced an American red-tailed hawk as the most savage carnivore in the bird kingdom. 'But', said the presenter, 'savage though he is, this bird does have one little friend from whom he is inseparable.' A hand brought into the picture a mouse and laid it on the table. The hawk glared down at it, glared left, glared right and closed a talon on the unlucky mouse with the most indifferent ferocity. When the recording was transmitted it was a little different. 'Savage though he is, this bird has one little friend from whom he is inseparable, but', went on the presenter, 'who unfortunately is not with us this afternoon.' And it is a long while since directors had to deal on the run with live contributors who turned out to be drunk. Brendan Behan, the Irish playwright, arrived to appear in *Panorama* in a noticeably elevated condition. It seemed probable that he would become the first man to use a four-letter word (the accepted euphemism for one of the sexual oaths) on television and there was much careful discussion about whether he should appear. It was at length agreed that he should, but Malcolm Muggeridge, then *Panorama*'s linkman, was begged: 'If he says ——, for God's sake don't laugh.' As it happened by the time of transmission poor Brendan had declined from the jocose and bellicose into the comatose stage of intoxication, and his answers to Muggeridge were reassuringly incoherent.

The most remarkable speed was in the spread of colour, though here the BBC like all other television organisations rode on the back of the pioneer work and accumulated experience of the Americans. It was introduced on BBC 2 during the 1967 Wimbledon tennis championships. I recorded the criticism that though a bottle of lime juice looked green, the grass did not particularly. Colours at first were decidedly variable, and though this did not matter much when the audience did not know what colour a thing really was and so had nothing to compare it with, a fault in anything as familiar as a face was sure to excite hostile comment. We were advised to tune the colour control until the faces looked natural; but having got them that way was no guarantee that they would stay. I remember an episode of an early serial of *Vanity Fair* when a ghastly greenish pallor fell upon the guests at the Duke of Richmond's ball, as though they had just heard of Napoleon's crossing of the Sambre. I had more exercise trotting to and fro adjusting these changes, or the sudden access of salmon-pink flushes that suddenly overwhelmed a face, than I had had since the old Brighton days. By 1972 it was so long since I had called in the servicing engineer I had forgotten his phone number; yet colour had been on all channels only three years. Another curious thing about colour was the speed at which it outgrew its status as an expensive novelty and settled down as the natural standard of television. The moment people saw it, they wanted it. The fact was that everything looked not only natural in colour, it looked a lot better. In colour even the rainy back streets of Belfast, as depressing a prospect as the eye could rest on in the seventies, acquired a golden tone; the cameras turned the grey stone the colour of honey. Cricket matches looked as though the players strove under the skies of a sunlit afternoon. It was only when you noticed that the sweater-clad players cast no shadows, and the cameras dwelt upon the mackintoshed, dejected and stoical spectators, that you saw that summer still held the land in its iron grip.

Broadcasting, like architecture, is an art that is steered as much by its engineers as by its artists. Nobody can foresee where technical developments may lead it. Things happen because a tool is made. A complete new dimension of film happened when somebody thought of strapping a camera to a helicopter; the result was the beautiful *Bird's Eye View* series. Television began to create operators who learned to be more at ease among the fascinating gadgetry. In such soil ideas grew into programmes propagating and mutating in a kind of explosion of talent. Yet the first generation of television men that went into it in the forties is still there, far from used up, and programmes have developed so thickly that you can only descry a pattern in them by trying to step outside the seventies and looking back. Then you see that the story of television from 1946 to 1972 was one of programme people working over new ways of doing things better, or discovering new things to do as technical advances and social change made new things possible and desirable, and programme needs demanded technical refinements.

Tonight, Sportsview, Panorama, Monitor, Maigret, Z Cars, Look, were themselves innovators but owed something to what had gone before. *Tonight* did things with magazine journalism that had hitherto not been imagined. It was like a newspaper run by the journalists; it begat Alan Whicker (himself a whole department of TV), Trevor Philpott, Kenneth Allsop and Cliff Michelmore; it helped to beget *Twenty-Four Hours*; inasmuch as it was the first news magazine to contain ribald references to news events written by journalists it can be said to have fathered the satire movement which in turn sired *Not Only But Also* . . . and *Monty Python's Flying Circus.* Yet the father and mother of *Tonight* were Cecil Madden's *Picture Page* and Joan Gilbert's *Diary.* It became what it was because Donald Baverstock, its producer, one of the great originators of television, had grasped that TV journalism must be harder and faster and was a young man of exceptional vision, drive and tenacity, well able to get what he wanted. (I was talking in the BBC Club one night with Alasdair Milne and Cliff Michelmore when Baverstock suddenly appeared in the doorway, looking as he always did like a handsome and aggressive young bull about to charge. At his imperious beckon Milne and Michelmore downed their glasses and ran to his side; so did half the people at the bar, including myself and an old producer of classic serials, who had nothing whatever to do with *Tonight* but could not resist the force of Baverstock's personality.)

Monitor began in 1958 as an obvious filler of a gap. BBC TV had *Panorama, Tonight* and *Sportsview* and there ought to be some kind of magazine about art. The need to begin it was accelerated in order to defeat proposals from Broadcasting House to transfer sound radio's *The Critics* to television following the successful transfer thither of *The Brains Trust.* Leonard Miall's Talks department thought it silly to attempt to deal with visual arts through talking heads, refused to take *The Critics,* and invented *Monitor.* Under Huw

Wheldon's editorship it became more than that. The key to its achievement was his commitment of policy and his personal control over the able people he picked. He had not wanted a programme of art criticism; he had not wanted simply to show the artist at work; it had to be something between criticism and creation, something between the topical and the lasting, in which an item on Shelagh Delaney and an item on Rembrandt would be equally acceptable. He did not want himself or the BBC to be the creature of any kind of art establishment, he wanted them to be the creatures of their own interests. It boiled down, as creative television always does, to what interested its producer personally. He was given as much freedom as he wanted and all the resources he could reasonably ask; he set about creating a permanent unit of men and women who could work with him and each other; and no line of commentary, no sequence of film, was ever put out without having passed through Wheldon's hands 'with knobs on', as he put it.

In those days there were no colour supplements or art supplements in the newspapers. There were only Lord Kemsley's *Sunday Times* and the *Observer*. Wheldon guessed that quite a large public would be well disposed towards a programme about art, but was equally certain that they could not be defined in terms of their education. It would be a programme for the interested. This eminently sane and practical decision brought him extraordinarily bitter personal attacks from highbrows who could not stand being told what they knew already, even in the artful way the programme used to put it across. Once *Monitor* came across some fascinating old film of Tolstoy's last days, enough to make a little documentary. It was then necessary to draft a commentary to fill in what the film left blank, specifically the row between Tolstoy and his wife over his renunciation of worldly goods, in such a way that it would remind those who knew of this act and inform those who not only did not know but would have been hard put to it to arrange Tolstoy and J. B. Priestley in chronological order. So the commentary began the relevant passage: 'When Tolstoy made his famous renunciation . . .'. It could hardly have been done any other way, but this sort of thing roused a curious frenzy among some of his audience. No doubt it had something to do with Wheldon's hypermanic performance. The cameras stimulated him, as they did so many others, into producing a kind of cartoon of himself that had no existence outside the programme, a Wheldon that might have been created by some malicious prosecuting lawyer and gave an already powerful personality such a boost that he appeared to be talking when he was really listening. But the bulk of *Monitor*'s audience was not so foolish as to mistake the shadow for the substance, and the programme became a prime source of a range of programmes among which were some of the BBC's most lustrous achievements. It produced the art and music documentaries that led to *Omnibus*, *Master Class* and *Workshop*, brought John Schlesinger and Ken Russell into television (where they made such names for themselves that they were lured out of it again by the cinema), and fathered Lord Clark's *Civilisation* and John Berger's *Ways of Seeing*. Yet when you look back along its ancestry you see Mervyn Levy and his successor Sir Gerald Kelly, the peppery academician who gave a series of illustrated trips round the galleries. He caught the ear of a surprisingly large number of the public, perhaps because the affectations of manner he had carefully contrived for himself matched the popular expectations of how a bohemian artist ought to carry on. I thought him a vain and silly old man, but may have been prejudiced against him by the troubles he brought me one night by becoming the first person to swear on television. 'Bloody marvellous!' he exclaimed, pretending to be moved beyond the power of normal speech to express. The news desk telephoned to ask me to ring him up and ask him what he meant by it, a humiliating task for a critic.

Another acorn from which oaks were to sprout was *At Home*, a series of outside broadcasts to the homes of the famous which offered a mixture of guided tour and revealing interview. It was of its time, respectful and even flattering, the BBC turning the light of its countenance upon such as Dame Megan Lloyd George, Humphrey Lyttleton, the jazz trumpeter, and the Duke of Norfolk, before whom Richard Dimbleby passed into such an ecstasy of reverential regard that he appeared to achieve weightlessness. The programme was too bland to last in such a form, but stripped of its good nature it moved on to become *Face to Face*, a series in which John Freeman embarrassed the nation by asking poor old Gilbert Harding a question about his mother that made him cry.

As for the art of televising music at concerts, it has not changed in essence since Philip Bate and Christian Simpson (a very gifted producer of early ballet who died too young) began to do it. They evolved a kind of visual grammar that accompanied the music: a close-shot for a soloist, an angled shot for a row of instruments, a long shot for the big orchestral blasts. Today the camera's mobility greatly increases the variety of shot; Patricia Foy's opera productions can move the equipment round the singers instead of the other way round. But the grammar has not altered. It is done better because with modern equipment the director can call the shots precisely on the beat instead of a fraction of a second before or after it. Sport too has been wholly conditioned by technical improvements. I hesitate to declare that the commentaries have improved, partly because I could never hear much wrong with them; but whereas the nonpareil Henry Longhurst once had to frighten his friends by climbing a forty-foot ladder after lunch in a high wind in order to tell what he could see of the golf, now towers manned by remotely-controlled cameras, radio cameras aimed at players striving in bunkers, and microwave links feeding banks of monitors let him describe the play over

ten acres of golf course without getting his feet wet or raising his pulse beat
by a single tremor. Programmes developed because of developments inside
the techniques of television. Programmes changed because of events outside
television.

7

THE DEATH OF AUNTY

The mature and opinionated comedy series was a response to what was happening outside, exemplified by the sudden rediscovery of their native land by writers in such novels as John Braine's *Room at the Top* and Alan Sillitoe's *Saturday Night and Sunday Morning*, in television by Alun Owen's *No Trams to Lime Street*, and in the theatre by John Osborne's *Look Back in Anger* and the revue *Beyond the Fringe*, which introduced the enormously influential quartet Jonathan Miller, Dudley Moore, Peter Cook and Alan Bennett. But the most important event in its consequences for the BBC was the ending of its monopoly in 1955 and the arrival of a commercial competitor. From then on the BBC had to do what it would do within the terms that the competitor had shown the public wanted: that is to say, after losing two-thirds of its audience it was forced to adopt the commercial pattern of placing its popular programmes at peak times and its programmes for minorities at times where they would not cause more of a national loss of audience than the BBC could afford to accept. The ITV companies had taken this pattern from American television; by 1972 it was standard round the world even, in modified forms, in Communist countries where the television service was an instrument of dictatorship.

The Americans had taught ITV that audiences the world over liked familiarity; far from resenting the fact that the police series *Dragnet*, a great favourite of the late 1950s, came on at the same hour of the same night every week, they welcomed it and were far from grateful when the networks felt obliged to interrupt the routine with some important news broadcast. What was more they welcomed the familiarity of the characters. They liked to hear Sgt Friday say week after week, 'My name's Friday. I'm a cop.' They would have written letters to complain if he had left it out, just as radio's wartime listeners protested when Jack Warner dropped his 'Mind my bike' catchphrase from Garrison Theatre. It is curious that television planners should not have learned this lesson from radio, but they did not; perhaps they did not want to, for in the early days of television one of the anxieties was that watching might become down-graded by habit. Cecil McGivern sought to preserve the quality of surprise and sense of occasion by trying to arrange schedules that did not look the same week after week.

That the audience liked its television in indefinitely repeated slots was the lesson the BBC had to learn from ITV; but though it caused some sad casualties among the shows that appealed to a very small audience, some of them, such as astronomy, managed to survive late at night – a convenient hour for such a subject, after all; having imbibed Patrick Moore's effervescent tour of *The Sky at Night* the fans could go out and look at it for themselves. With the coming of BBC 2 in 1964 and its gradual spread across the kingdom BBC 1 could afford to grow more assertively competitive; but until then it retained an exhilarating flexibility and boldness. When I look back on what was done on the single channel between 1956 and about 1966, when BBC 2 was becoming a national network and complementary planning between One and Two was operating, I seem to be looking back upon a golden time: I think of *Look, Zoo Quest, Monitor, Sportsview, Portraits of Power, Men in Battle*, the Richard Cawston film documentaries, 'The Pilots', 'On Call To A Nation', Peter Watkins's extraordinary reconstruction of the dedicated horror of Culloden, which told the audience more about Scottish nationalism in an hour than most of them would have picked up from a hundred books; the Rudolph Cartier productions of *Carmen* and *A Tale of Two Cities*; the rise of the high-quality drama series such as *Maigret, Dr Finlay's Casebook, Mogul*; the adventure of *The Age of Kings*, which presented the Shakespearian historical plays as a thirteen-part serial. It was the decade of the great democratisation of the BBC, when it stopped being Aunty and became a man and a brother; and I am in no doubt about the programmes that emphasised the change; they were the mature comedies, the Wednesday Play, *Z Cars* and *That Was The Week That Was*.

A fairly constant proportion of opinion leaders would restore the monopoly tomorrow if they could, but one gift the coming of commercial competition conferred on the BBC was well worth what it cost. It freed it from the weight of paternal responsibility it had acquired through being the only source of broadcasting in the land. If part of the price was that it must do much of what ITV did, another part was that it was freer to do it better and to do what ITV did not do. I do not want here to go into the politics of the coming of ITV – for anyone who wishes to read about it, plenty of books* are available. But that the BBC had been set free to mirror the changing times was the fact Sir Hugh Greene grasped when he was appointed Director-General in 1959; and in implementing this freedom he presided over a period in the BBC's history which I enjoyed and admired and respected more than any other.

To say that the BBC was a kind of PRO to the establishment until Greene arrived is not altogether true, but it would take so many pages to do justice to the fine shades of argument to the contrary that it is convenient to admit that, broadly speaking, such was the case so far as the leadership was con-

* I recommend my own: *The Mirror in the Corner* (London, 1972).

cerned, particularly where it saw a danger of offending political pressure groups. That mysterious influence known as the establishment, made up of the leaders of politics, the church, the law, industry and science, felt they could count on the BBC as an associate member. It became apparent that the new regime did not mind including politicians and similar symbols among those who could be offended if the need arose. The detonator of this explosion was not, in my view, the satire series that began in the autumn of 1962 but the great drama fiction series, *Maigret* and *Z Cars*. Suddenly we had conventional fictions that broke out of the conventions.

Maigret was fashioned by Andrew Osborn out of the detective tales of Georges Simenon. Its immediately apparent virtue was its respect for the quality that lifted Simenon's work out of the rut; it was about real people in real trouble. Technically it was beautifully done, for Osborn and his directors, mixing film with studio more successfully than had so far been achieved, brought back a deeply satisfying whiff of Simenon's France, in which his detectives, crooks, tarts, landladies, pimps, maniacs, country squires, waiters and dockers laboured away at the sins and pleasures of the flesh with an authenticity never before seen in a crime series. It established the important principle that series drama could and must be as truthful about its subject as a one-shot play was supposed to be. (It made a huge TV star out of Rupert Davies as Maigret; at the height of his success he commanded £10,000 to make a commercial advertising Dubonnet, though against this profit he had to set the penalty of becoming inextricably associated with the character; when the series ended he fell upon lean times.) Claiming as always to represent the nation the Puritan fringe protested against its frankness and as usual was backed up by a few MPs and newspapers that thought they might extract some benefit thereby. The continued success of *Maigret* made it obvious that they represented only each other, but with the first *Z Cars* in 1962 uproar broke out compared with which the storm over *Maigret* was a gentle breeze.

This famous series was the first to come from the new line of competing harder against ITV with series that would go on and on, binding the audience's loyalty to them week after week. To that extent it was a straightforward adaptation of American techniques as displayed in the Hollywood-made film series, such as *Bonanza*, which were beginning to sweep across the television screens of the western half of the world. These were tooled up and assembled like the process of creating a new automobile in Detroit inasmuch as the shape in response to known audience tastes was worked out before a line was written. *Bonanza* was the first western where the heroes stayed in the same place, at the time a novel concept, for unless they were town marshals the heroes wandered across the west on their own as in *Shenandoah* and *Wells Fargo* or led a train of settlers as in *Wagon Train*. *Bonanza*'s family stayed put. To maximise audience identification, as the jargon has it, the physical characteristics were as different as was plausible. The father was a rich, strong autocrat. The eldest son was handsome and reliable; the giant second son was kind to animals; the youngest was small and quick-tempered, though fundamentally sound. To explain their markedly dissimilar looks, the scripts let the audience know that the father, Ben Cartwright, had been married three times – to an Anglo-Saxon girl from Boston, to a big Swede from Nevada, and a Creole from New Orleans. To avoid alienating ortho-dox church opinion it was emphasised that all these wives had been res-pectably killed, by illness or Indians, before the stories began. This type of elaborate technical structure was now brought to bear upon *Z Cars*.

The artistic genesis of it was a single documentary called 'Who, Me?', written by Colin Morris and produced by Gilchrist Calder. It showed the police methods of breaking down suspects by superior intelligence and practical psychology, and went down so well with the police that several regional forces asked if they could show it as part of their training exercises. Among them was the Lancashire constabulary. Elwyn Jones, then assistant head of drama, took the recording to Liverpool and conceived the notion of making a police series there instead of London. He invited the young writer Troy Kennedy Martin to go to Liverpool to reconnoitre. As usual with newcomers from the south his first impression could be compared to the sensation of having received a blow between the eyes from a mailed fist. He was fascinated by the ugliness and vitality of the place. The new towns, built as dormitories without the smallest regard for cultural or social needs, seemed to him to contain the rawness and tensions that frontier towns in the old American West must have had. It was a man's country where closing time in the pubs normally started fist-fights and husbands knocked their wives about.[1]

Elwyn Jones had laid down that the series must have a minimum of six heroes, so that if one of them wanted to leave, or took sick and died, they would still have a series.* Kennedy Martin constructed a format: the Liver-pool suburb of Seaforth became Seaport. Kirby New Town, a hideous, soul-crushing community outside the city, became Newtown. Four young constables patrolled in their crime cars, also called Z cars, reporting back to Newtown police station where they were chivvied by Inspector Barlow and Detective Sgt Watt. And here the borrowing of American techniques ended, for what *Z Cars* achieved was a marriage of complicated series pro-duction methods with the BBC's tradition for documentary realism, as applied to a modern fictional police series – though where fact and fiction began and ended was hard to tell, for the original of 'Who, Me?'s detective,

* A few months after *Z Cars* began Leonard Williams (the desk Sergeant, Twenty-man) died of a heart attack between one episode and the next.

Sgt Bill Prendergast, supplied the case material round which the stories were written. The creative dash of Kennedy Martin and Allan Prior, who wrote eleven of the first thirteen scripts, was tempered by the hand of the documentary specialist Robert Barr as executive producer; the combination produced the series' richest quality; it seemed as though the programme had hewn out a huge area of Lancashire and set it under glass with all the people moving about it.

Topped and tailed by a lugubrious north-country folk song speeded up to the pace of a jaunty march, the first programme went out in January 1962. An audience that had derived its picture of the police force from Robert Barr's sober documentaries, Ted Willis's *The Blue Lamp*, and Willis's re-incarnation of the policeman who met his death in that film, *Dixon of Dock Green*, learned that policemen were human, came mostly from the same class as those they protected, and displayed no better social habits than some of their charges. Lynch (James Ellis) made his first appearance as a young constable sticking his head through the window of the cars he was shepherd-ing to ask who had won the 2.30. Steele (Jeremy Kemp) was seen rowing with his wife, who had evidently sustained contusions and bruises from an earlier argument; a stain on the wall marked the spot where he had thrown the previous night's hot pot. The newspapers next morning printed columns of complaint from viewers who disliked its proposition that policemen were human. The chairman of the Police Federation said it injured police status to represent them as wife-beaters and gamblers and, some other critic added, disgusting eaters. The chief constable of Lancashire, whose force had co-operated in the production, announced that he was on his way down to London to have the series stopped; but he was met by the BBC's controller of programmes, Stuart Hood, who assured him that to suppose the series would be abandoned was to suppose that the Romanovs might be restored. As it happened the Chief Constable was on shaky ground, for he had not seen the programme and was relaying the indignation of his wife; police wives led most of the first wave of protest, no doubt seeing the programme as injuring their neighbourhood standing. Hood had not seen the broadcast either but he had in his pocket perhaps the most unanimously laudatory reviews the newspaper critics had ever given a new television series. The officer had to retreat. The end of his protest was the withdrawal of the credit thanking his force for its co-operation.

Technically and artistically the early *Z Cars* represented the professionalism of live TV at its summit. It amounted to the presentation week after week of a fast-moving feature film in fifty minutes flat with no retakes, their only cushion against disaster two recorded programmes. With something like 250 changes of shot in each episode, an average of five a minute, the actor's hardest problem was to remember which scene he was in. Even when you knew how it was done you could not believe it. And the technical artistry was serving a very fine artistic creation which transcended the crime series and offered a vivid social and moral comment on a vast slab of life. It was the first television series not to reflect back to its working-class audience a flattering, fundamentally insulting picture of itself as making the best of things. The undercurrent was one of protest. The scripts showed people who had enough to eat (and usually more than enough to drink) but were pitiably and needlessly shut off from the graces of life. Culturally they were as deprived as the victims of nineteenth-century industrialism had been starved physically, their affluence channelled into beer, bingo and betting shops. It offered, to quote a good phrase from Peter Lewis, 'a dry-eyed lament for life as it is messily lived in affluent 1962';[2] among the life moved the police, tough, impatient professionals prowling round their charges like cynical sheepdogs.

As the audience figures climbed, from nine to fourteen million in the first eight weeks, it was clear that the BBC's inspired guess was correct; the public was good and ready to accept that the police were not all fatherly Dixon types who helped old ladies across the road and always had a sweet for a lost child. The intended first run of thirteen was extended to thirty-one. After a six-week break a further series began. *Z Cars* became as permanent a fixture as *Panorama*, following the careers of Barlow and Watt as they rose up the Force in a new series called *Softly, Softly* and reproducing itself as the old *Z Cars* with a second-generation cast moving through the old setting. Elwyn Jones believed that some of the scripts were as good as the best that anybody was writing in the single play shot. It offered a format that was at once disciplined and free; a writer could say almost anything within it. It became a true source of new writers; Alan Plater, Keith Dewhurst and John Hopkins were three who learned their craft writing for it.

By showing the truth as it saw it *Z Cars* widened the gap through which new forms of television might pass; this is why I allot it some of the parentage of *That Was The Week That Was*, which opened in November 1962 and immediately plunged the BBC into the hottest controversy the Greene revolution provoked. Unlike most new ideas this one came from the top. Hugh Greene thought a show on the lines of the very free pre-Nazi Berlin cabarets might suit the times. Kenneth Adam, the Director of TV, favoured something like the sophisticated Gate Theatre revues of the thirties. Their decision from which all followed was to ask Current Affairs to create the programme instead of Light Entertainment, which they believed might be too soft and conventional. Thus the project fell into the hands of Donald Baverstock, Antony Jay, Alasdair Milne and Ned Sherrin, of the old *Tonight* group. Sherrin condensed its brief into a sentence: 'To discuss anything that people might talk about on Saturday night.' Aimed at an irreverent minority it was cast as a late show for Saturday nights, but within a few weeks was reaching a regular audience of ten million and had become the most talked about television programme in the world. It was as though a great bulk of the people had been waiting for a current affairs show that represented their own well-founded scepticism about their rulers. The visual presentation was skilfully casual. One saw camera booms and microphones as often as performers. But though it appeared to be put together by amateurs (even some of the professional critics, who should have known better, mistook the casual air for sloppiness) its guides were steely professionals whose sharp understanding of what they were about included the knowledge that there would be indefensible errors of taste and judgment. The very flexible format included some major setpieces by professional scriptwriters and uncovered a rich mine of new talent among journalists working for the mass circulation dailies in Fleet Street; they rushed to satirise themselves with the eagerness of men hungry to get their own back. It was all put together throughout Saturday in a studio at the TV Centre which as the series grew took on the air of a huge, friendly club of like-minded people.

The novelty was its catholic audacity. It mocked everybody, not just the traditionally safe targets that do not sue, such as British Rail and the Post Office. It brought the television equivalent of the newspaper cartoon to bear on anyone who roused its sense of mockery. It was the first journalistic programme to let it be known that it wanted no part of the principle that dog will not eat dog. The rabble-rousing columnists, the half-baked political soothsayers, the editors who peddled pornography and pretended to be defending morality, could be sure of a bad time; as a journalist I found it extraordinarily satisfying to see this quite new degree of honesty at work in a mass medium speaking in tones that anyone could understand. It plugged a hole in communications that had been left open too long. Its attitude was fundamentally serious and much more carefully thorough and analytical than its manner let on. Its programme in mourning for the murdered President Kennedy was the only one that seemed to speak for the non-political for whom his assassination was the worst public event in their lives, who had felt instinctively that his presidency had let light and hope into the grim round of international politics. It sought to carry controversy into all areas where argument was possible. But it expressed itself as wittily and cheekily as it could, venturing into territory hitherto signposted as unsuitable for jokes, such as racism, patriotism, religion, royalty, bull-fighting and Northern Ireland. It was never out of the headlines. On Monday morning the papers published the number of telephone calls dealt with by the BBC as though they were cricket scores (there was a curious echo here of the Battle of Britain), and the news pages described the awful details as frankly as their conventions allowed. Fleet Street on the whole fell into its traditional error of supposing that the writers of protesting letters represented the bulk of its readership. It continued to send feature writers out to attempt a hatchet job on David Frost long after he had become accepted as one of the most popular entertainers in the business.

One's attitude toward *TW3* was emotional rather than reasonable, an opinion about life rather than a TV show. Its fans knew that it was often uneven, crude and pointlessly smutty. Sometimes it was sour and cross instead of witty, and sketches spluttered angrily to an end instead of rising to meet a punch line. It was often unfair. But they recognised its freedom from cant and from the kind of grey clouding over of serious subjects that hung over public argument in Britain. They felt it represented themselves laughing at the bullies, the con men, the pushers around. It was, said Greene, firmly on the side of the angels. To those who took a contrary view everything about it was an affront. It provoked an ecstasy of rage among people who sincerely believed that it was wrong to encourage argument about subjects hitherto taboo and to raise doubts and disbelief in heads that if left to themselves would never have harboured them. Some of them tried to maintain an outwardly reasonable critical stance. They insisted that while not opposed to satire as such they could not accept as proper targets for it religion, politicians, the royal family, the RSPCA, or any other opinion or organisation that they took seriously themselves. The words 'jackanapes', 'juvenile wit', 'undergraduate humour', 'schoolboy smut', freely accompanied these reflections. Youth leaders said the show was sapping the moral fibre of the younger generation. Publicans said customers were leaving half an hour before closing time to reach home before *TW3* went on the air. Some of the public, not necessarily those that had seen the show, could hardly contain themselves on hearing authority mocked and tabooed subjects talked about. A Tory MP wanted to have the BBC impeached on a charge of holding MPs up to ridicule, but as the item in question had mocked only the Tories he failed to carry the Socialist side with him. Some of the clergy displayed an un-Christian virulence; the Rev. John Culey, a holy man from Cheshire, used his parish magazine to stigmatise the studio audience as 'rabble' (most of them, to judge from what the camera showed, looked curiously middle-class and respectable) and Bernard Levin as 'a thick-lipped Jewboy'. (Levin's spot in the show was as the uncompromising interviewer of some person or group who represented something he felt should be challenged.)

The style of the company was a further aggravation. They were not, as writers to the *Daily Telegraph* supposed, a bunch of undisciplined amateurs. The resident singers, Millicent Martin and David Kiernan, came from the musical theatre and the movies. Roy Kinnear came from Joan Littlewood's Theatre Workshop, Kenneth Cope from *Coronation Street*, William Rushton from *Private Eye*, Lance Percival, Eleanor Bron and the young compère

David Frost from clubs and cabaret. Timothy Birdsall, the gifted and charming young cartoonist whom everyone liked (he died of leukaemia within the year) was a brilliant and thoroughly professional illustrator. Frost had made one previous appearance for Rediffusion in a programme about the twist, a fashionable ballroom gyration of the time. Devised as an outside broadcast nearly everything went wrong, but he amazed all beholders by carrying it off with the nerveless calm of a man for whom these disasters were all in the day's work. They were, however, undeniably young and classless, years away both from the respectful young persons of the general knowledge shows who spoke when they were spoken to and the bright ones, imitatively upper-class, who manned the smart West End revues. Like *Tonight* it achieved a style, accent and manner that was neither artificially posh nor patronisingly plebeian. This too was sharply resented, and provoked many personal comments on Rushton's untidiness, Kinnear's stomach, and Frost's front teeth. Nor were its defenders spared. Like all the critics who fought for it from the start I received violently abusive letters; one of them denounced me as a homosexual atheist of negroid-Jewish ancestry, but mitigated this diagnosis by supposing that I was the same age as Frost, the demon boy.

Sir Hugh Greene summed it up in a lecture to Birmingham students in 1968. He thought the BBC's output, the vein of programming which *TW3* influenced, brought into the open one of the great cleavages in British society. 'It is of course a cleavage which has always existed: Cavalier versus Roundhead, Sir Toby Belch versus Malvolio, or however you like to put it. But in these years was added to that the split between those who looked back to a largely imaginary golden age, to the imperial glories of Victorian England and hated the present, and those who accepted the present and found it in many ways more attractive than the past. It was not a split between old and young or between Left and Right or between those who favoured delicacy and those who favoured candour. It was something much more complicated than that, and if one could stand back for a bit as the brickbats flew it provided a fascinating glimpse of the national mood.'

The whips and scorns of satire continued to divide and scourge the nation in *TW3*'s successor, *Not so much a Programme, more a Way of Life*, but the sparkle began to dim when Baverstock, Jay and Frost and then Sherrin left and the sharpness of the jokes became blunted by the growing influence of sabotaging infiltrators from *Private Eye*, for whom any kind of success, worthy or not, was to be lacerated. It petered out rather sadly; one felt it had become a liability which the BBC was glad to wind up. What was best in it was transplanted into David Frost's *The Frost Report* and went on to fertilise *Monty Python's Flying Circus*. The style Frost had mastered as compère of sharp discussion became the base of his talk shows for Rediffusion. The popular image of the BBC was finally broken. It left her standing on the corner outside Broadcasting House in her black bombazine wondering what was to become of her. (Some say that she was whisked away in a taxi to the ITA's headquarters in Knightsbridge.)

Sir Hugh Greene was vilified for his part in all this as few figures in British public life have been. He claimed that the BBC had done a great service to the country by widening the limits of discussion and challenging old taboos. I ardently agreed. If, as I most devoutly believe, the chief job of television is to make the popular stuff better, *Z Cars* and *That Was The Week* were the most significant programmes of the Greene years. The BBC is still moving under the impetus of that time. But it owed more than its new freedom to the creation of ITV; it was the success of this commercial competitor that helped the BBC to win what it had sought since 1946, the second channel that would let it plan a true alternative service arranged in harmonious contrast with the first.

The case that only thus could the BBC offer in television the same breadth of service it had achieved in sound was energetically lobbied in the early fifties as a powerful argument against the introduction of a commercial channel. It was defeated by the Churchill government's insistence that the principle of competition, which brought so many benefits to the people when they went shopping, would be equally beneficial in the field of entertainment. Thus Captain Gammans, Deputy Postmaster-General, presenting the second reading of the 1954 Television Bill to the Commons. But in 1960 the Pilkington Committee, examining Gammans's view in the light of four years' experience of commercial competition, agreed with the line the BBC had laboured away at during all its brilliant presentations to the committee; that it could not adequately perform its job on a single channel. Having got permission to create BBC 2, it set about the hard part – the building of programmes – which would carry out the easy part – the broad intention.

It was always clear what had to be done. The second channel had to offer choice. It would be planned in co-operation with BBC 1 but had to be at once identifiable as sufficiently new and different to persuade millions – not just thousands – that the new 625-line service, requiring a new television set and an aerial that could cost up to £15, was something they ought to have. It had to restore to television the expansion of programme range that the need to win back the BBC's share of the audience had curtailed. There had to be more programmes for minority audiences about subjects that had not found a place, such as a magazine about motoring, or had been squeezed out by competition, such as opera, archaeology and the classic serial for adults. It had to offer these programmes at peak hours, and encourage by planned repeats the civilised notion that a good programme might be seen twice. But how to do it? The problem for Michael Peacock, appointed Controller of BBC 2, was like that of a railway engineer who has to lay a track through the mountains and can see three different ways to go. He can find the best route only by choosing one. His choice was the ill-fated Seven Faces of the Week, designed to give each evening its characteristic flavour. Saturday offered classic serials and documentaries; Sundays, important plays, opera and ballet, foreign films and a current affairs series. Monday was light entertainment night. Tuesday was consecrated to life-enhancing education. Wednesday offered repeats drawn from BBC 1 as well as BBC 2. Thursdays offered the major programme for the minorities, plus series about hobbies. Friday was drama night. There was nothing wrong with this plan except that the audience didn't like it; and though it helped the BBC to conciliate the demand for a service that would widen the range of mass audience's interests, it did nothing for the BBC's need not to frighten the mass audience away from BBC 2, or the manufacturing industry's natural desire to see the kind of programmes on Two that would make the big audience rush to buy the new sets.

The Peacock plan was quietly shelved, but a structure as huge as television is like a giant ocean liner in that it is an appreciable time – in this case it was about a year – before changes signalled from the bridge are apparent in the altered course. Peacock returned to run BBC 1 in the spring of 1965, following a shake-up which displaced Donald Baverstock as Controller of BBC 1 and brought up Huw Wheldon two moves at a time from Head of Documentaries and Music to Controller of Programmes. A little later Wheldon persuaded David Attenborough to assume executive office and run BBC 2, an inspired appointment (though an eminently sane and practical one) that put the right man in a job for which his whole experience, interests and temperament fitted him. But it was September 1965 before BBC 2 was finally free from the wreckage of its start.

I must not leave the impression that Peacock botched it. What he did was what was wanted from him; it was only the way he arranged it that failed. His plan left much that lasted, notably in the look of the weekend and the vast expansion of music. It was a wonderful luxury, the kind you gloated over before, during and after, to be able to look at Klemperer conducting Beethoven's Choral Symphony and Benjamin Britten his *War Requiem*, slap bang in the middle of Sunday evening. Even better, because they were true television creations that could not have been done in any other medium, were the programmes about music. I never enjoyed anything more than *Workshop*, which followed a work from the composer's notebooks through to performance – unless it was *Master Class*, in which teachers and virtuosos such as opera's Carl Ebert and Yehudi Menuhin took professional pupils through a work; or *In Rehearsal*, of which the title is self-explanatory.

These programmes for minorities basked in general approval because the majority did not mind not being able to see them. Peacock's popular successes, the first of them the brilliant 26-part compilation of battle film, *The Great War*, brought the BBC a new source of complaints. Viewers who couldn't get BBC 2 were enraged by the thunderous critical acclaim for something they couldn't see, and the BBC's very practical plan for building audiences for Two by publicising its attractions on One brought the red mist of fury floating before their eyes. There was something undoubtedly and specially provoking in exhorting them to watch programmes they would have liked to watch but could not; the BBC had to deal with much hostile criticism on the lines that it was not entitled to put out popular programmes on a channel that comparatively few people could receive. It had to yield to the pressure, and in October 1964 began to repeat *The Great War* on BBC 1 before it had completed its first run on Two. There was no significance in the overlap, but there was in the precedent. It seemed to be saying that viewers need not put themselves out to buy BBC 2 since anything outstandingly successful would be shown on BBC 1 later on. A similar concession was made after the enormous acclaim that greeted Donald Wilson's 26-part adaptation of *Forsyte Saga*. Wilson's lavish and masterly reconstruction of Galsworthy's world, materially so secure and emotionally so unstable; Eric Porter's aloof, unlucky, drily endearing Soames; Kenneth More's Bohemian but at bottom respectable Jolyon; Nyree Dawn Porter's beautiful, enigmatic and some said inadequate love goddess Irene; Susan Hampshire's impetuous and resolute Fleur: proliferating through the Edwardian and Georgian past the intertwined relationships of the clan captured the imagination and sympathies of the loyalest audience BBC 2 had won up to that time. The clamour was irresistible for an early showing on BBC 1, where it became instantly the most successful serial ever made by any television anywhere.

In short the most intractable difficulty that held back the growth of BBC 2 was simply its novelty. It presented television and its audience with new conditions that needed time to absorb. The ideal BBC 2 programme, said Attenborough, would be like a word in a crossword puzzle; it had to make sense horizontally in terms of an evening's programme in its own right, and vertically in terms of what was on BBC 1. It had to offer viewers an alternative programme. It therefore had to create time junctions with BBC 1 so that choices could be made before two programmes began. But it could not have too many of them, for this would mean that BBC 2 programmes would have to be the same length as BBC 1's. (Attenborough's compromise was a minimum of three time junctions in an evening.) It also had to decide what was a proper alternative. To the audience this was easy; it was a programme they wanted to see put against one they didn't; but for television it was a problem that could only be settled in favour of annoying as many people as possible as little as possible. Until BBC 2 arrived the alternative had been settled by competition into what some termed a 'clash': *Panorama* against *World in Action*, feature film against feature film, news against news, etc. Logically this was better than it sounded, for when both channels were showing the same kind of programme was the only time the viewer could make a rational choice. To choose between a panel game and a police series involved irrationality, swiftly accompanied by perplexity and exasperation; but when Attenborough commissioned a little survey to see if it could discover what he called a 'preference quotient' it could only give him the answer he knew already and could not incorporate into his programme planning: that the only way to reduce conflict among his audience was to put a popular programme against an unpopular one. Anything else was another compromise. But his survey also suggested that a good possible compromise was to pair programmes not according to their high or low cultural appeal but according to their difference in kind, e.g. *Call My Bluff* against *Softly, Softly*.

The third novelty, perhaps the knottiest, was that the BBC now had to inculcate a great reversal of viewing habits. Before BBC 2 the whole of BBC and ITV scheduling had been arranged as cleverly as experienced professionalism could devise to discourage audiences from switching channels. Now they were being encouraged to do just that. And I believe it was this pressure suddenly put upon them to make a second choice when they had previously been urged to stay where they were that frightened many of the potential audience from BBC 2, though they rationalised their unwillingness to face this new situation by claiming that BBC 2 was 'highbrow' and 'not for us'. But time passed, the network of BBC 2 transmitters covered the land, the old 405-line receivers wore out and were replaced by the uhf models that transmitted BBC 1, BBC 2 and ITV on 625-lines and, from 1969, all of them in colour.

The switching habit spread. By 1971 thirty-two million people could watch BBC, and some of its programmes (mostly the westerns and comedies of the type available on BBC 1) claimed regular followings of five million. On Monday nights, when BBC 1 and ITV were showing *Panorama* and *World in Action*, the BBC claimed an audience of ten millions for its BBC 2 western, *Alias Smith and Jones*. But the three declared functions of the planned alternative were working far better than this statistic might suggest. BBC 1 remained the channel catering to the huge audience in competition with ITV. BBC 2 offered the balanced alternative to what BBC 1 was showing and specialised in providing the sort of television BBC 1 and ITV did not do. It opened up new fields of television, in golf, motoring, archaeology, finance, science, folk music, acting as an art, sociology, foreign films and Rugby League, the last clinching humorously and irrefutably Atten-borough's declaration, 'the illusion that a minority programme is the same thing as an intellectual programme is nonsense'.[2]

The arrangement of proper alternatives was as contentious a subject as ever, but greatly alleviated by repeats. By 1972 it was common practice for a popular series either on One or Two to be exchanged. The quaint idea that a programme should be thrown away after one showing persisted among a sub-stratum of viewers who felt obscurely that they were being done out of part of the licence fee unless everything they saw was new. Some of the newspaper critics continued to attack repeats, but that was because repeats seemed to threaten the supply of raw material they needed for reviewing; they had nothing much against them on principle. The combination of planned programmes and repeats gave the BBC a very powerful extra arm, for it allowed them to reap the reward on One of its successful ad-ventures on Two, such as the renowned *Six Wives of Henry VIII*. The width of selection offered by the two channels could have eaten into ITV's share of the audience as voraciously as ITV had grabbed the BBC's back in 1955–8. The BBC, taking one of those characteristically right decisions for which I honour it, attempted no such thing. The BBC's share of the audience re-mained what it had been, roughly 50–50; for as Attenborough declared, if its share ever rose above sixty to seventy per cent or beyond it would signal failure, not triumph. It would mean that the BBC was failing to take ad-vantage of its freedom to balance its output between serving minorities and majorities. 'It would be clear that the schedules were not enterprising enough to devise innovations which initially might be unpopular, nor daring enough in its catering for minority tastes.'[3] His successor as head of BBC 2, Robin Scott, planned his programmes to reach an average of fifteen per cent of the total audience, and knew that he could not get higher than that over the year without accepting a destructive change in the character of the channel.

Despite its failures – it has so far developed no way of presenting pro-grammes about literature, done nothing to combat the national dread of Shakespeare, and been no more successful than BBC 1 and ITV in its pre-sentation of politics – BBC 2 proved a significant liberator of TV from the tyranny of the mass market, bearing in mind that in television, as in the motor industry, minorities are a few hundred thousand and never a few hundreds. It has made the BBC the most democratic system of TV in the world. But neither David Attenborough nor anyone else ever solved to everyone's satisfaction the question, 'What was a proper alternative?' and hooting letters to *Radio Times* on the theme 'Is the BBC Mad?' continued to air the injuries suffered by the fact that only viewers with three heads could watch all of everything.

8

THE BIGGEST ASPIDISTRA IN THE WORLD

Somewhere in the course of finishing this book I notched up twenty years in my curious occupation. Had it not been for eighteen months out in 1963–4 I would have a record of unbroken watching for money that most must wonder at, if few will envy. I have seen the BBC grow in fifty years from a most cheap and wonderful local and national sound medium into a keenly embattled competitor within and without its own island (in 1971 it exported £3·2m of television programmes to eighty-seven countries), a giant communicator which had became a secondary, electronic super-state in which nearly all the goings-on in the bigger world were faithfully mirrored. It was now a medium in which one man, David Frost, could make a million pounds as a performer and impresario before he was thirty; another, Graham Kerr, could earn himself world fame and a fortune out of processing Philip Harben's old craft of cooking in front of the cameras into an international distraction; in which it was possible to lead a happy and fruitful life of adventurous scholarship, like the natural history film makers for whom the BBC has been such a beneficent patron; which had created on the other hand wizards of the medium of such brilliance that they seemed to operate as humanoid extensions of the apparatus, like David Dimbleby and David Coleman. And everyone in the BBC worked in the knowledge that he could go somewhere else if he did not like it. The ease with which producers slipped from working for the BBC to ITV and back indicated how competition had blurred an image of the BBC that the public used to think of as hard and clear even when they could not have defined it more exactly than by preferring to watch Christmas and the Queen on its service.

The BBC had accepted a commercially structured schedule for BBC 1, compensated for by the opportunity for stretching TV on BBC 2. But though Paul Fox, who succeeded Baverstock and Peacock as Controller of One, was as sharp and ingenious a competitor as anyone on the opposite side, he was also a very conscious inheritor of the BBC's traditional obligation to offer the audience better than it thought it wanted. BBC 1 kept a far wider definition of what was mass entertainment, particularly in the field of what the very early BBC used to call 'variety'. I must call here upon an analogy I have used elsewhere, because I do not believe a better one exists. Television is like a restaurant that imposes a minimum charge per person (in 1972 the full licence fee was

£12) but where most of the customers must be carefully tempted to ask for their money's worth, to try new dishes in addition to their favourite egg and chips, sausage, beans and chips, tomatoes, beans and egg, and suchlike delights. I would not say that all BBC 1's dishes were better cooked than ITV's, but the range of the popular menu was incomparably wider than its rivals' set dishes of quizzes, serials, drama series and comedy series based on the appeal of the gormless.

The dominance of television, the decline of radio as a mass medium and the change in listening conditions produced by the development of the transistor had led to a new type of listener, most of whom used radio by day as an accompaniment to driving the car, doing the housework or turning something in a factory, and were more unwilling than they had ever been in their lives to search the dial for what they wanted. If it was not there, off went the switch. The listener who wanted more could still find his way about the programmes; but the division into Radio One, Two, Three and Four surrendered the remnants of the old Reithan principle of giving help to the listener who needed it most, whether he wanted it or not. Consequently where there had been one BBC there now appeared to the public to be three or four quite separate BBCs. For Radio One listeners the Corporation had become a barmy teenage twit, endlessly playing gramophone records of pop music and chatting up the housewives in a frightful Americo-Australio-Cockney-fied-Liverpool jargon that seemed to rise from some international sub-world. For Radio Two listeners it had become a kind of meals on wheels service, nourishing the old folk with selections from Ivor Novello and the Grand Hotel Orchestra. Frequently two Corporations appeared to exist within the same programme; the *World at One* harboured the old-style BBC news-readers in the same bulletins as the new-style reporters who sounded as though they were shouting their reports through hollow tubes of cardboard in a language with which they were unfamiliar. Similarly BBC TV could plunge from the pinnacle of *The Six Wives of Henry VIII*, which bounced firm and hard off the deepest traditions of BBC broadcasting, into the abyss of *The Generation Game*, a 1971 quiz show permeated from head to foot with the image of commercial television in the fifties.

Some said that these separate BBCs, already existing *de jure*, should exist *de facto*. The BBC had grown too big for its system of self-government to be able to control. As a matter of fact it was not all that big. It was about the same size as the Metropolitan police with which, in its proportions of active practitioners to administrators, it could well be compared. As for being out of control, it was responsible to a very elegantly designed structure of checks and balances which had at its apex a Board of Governors whom the professional broadcasters of the Board of Management were bound in theory and practice to obey, on pain of forced resignation. It was also answerable indirectly to Parliament inasmuch as its Board felt constrained to answer a complaint raised by that body. Its advisory councils numbered seven hundred souls, no one of which was behind any of the others in expressing its views about how broadcasting should be run; and they were drawn from a huge range of professions and jobs. Along with these there was the ceaseless, suspicious and basically hostile scrutiny of broadcasting by the newspapers, who could be relied on to make as much of any apparent lapse by their rival as they could. And this hostility reflected, not quite accurately but with more exaggeration than distortion, a curious healthy suspicion and want of affection among the public. In programmes like *Talkback*, and in the letters in the newspapers and *Radio Times*, the prevailing note was one of honking disapproval and carping over detail. The writers were often, they admitted, sick and tired, and suffered from boiling blood. 'As a lifelong fan of the steam engine I must protest against the unrealistic sound effects employed in *The Archers*.' 'Does not the BBC realise that to present a play like *Cathy Come Home*, with its skilfully slanted attack on Britain's housing conditions, is to play into the hands of our country's enemies?'

It was always easier to abuse than to praise, and perhaps watching television invited a negative and passive response. One was aware that *Dad's Army* was a great comedy show, but did not go on to say: 'What a fine institution the BBC must be, to be able to preserve such high quality in a comedy series aimed at the likes of us.' One wrote a letter to say that much as one might have enjoyed the show one's pleasure was ruined by the fact that Capt Mainwaring's form of reply to superior officers on the telephone was contrary to the correct procedure as practised daily by the writer for four years in the Home Guard at Wisbech, Cambs.

Through all its fifty years broadcasting has been a medium whose faults got the attention. Nor lagged the public critics behind the individual ones; they not only complained of what they disliked, but argued therefrom that the BBC be divided into groups which by being smaller would be more controllable, and less likely to do things offensive to them; and behind their complaints lurked a wish to limit the BBC's freedom by some sort of censorship. Peregrine Worsthorne, the *Sunday Telegraph*'s chief soothsayer, managed to argue himself into a position from which he could claim that the BBC's status as a body financed by the public ought to bar it from engaging in programmes that it knew would provoke large numbers of that public. He said this in a *Talkback* programme with Charles Curran, the Director-General, whose rebuke was concise and crushing. 'Are you suggesting that no public body can ever tell the truth about this country? If so, I think that is one of the most corrupt doctrines I have ever heard.' Malcolm Muggeridge, who had been one of the doughtiest of fighters for broadcasting freedom in the fifties, by 1972 was demanding restrictions on it which were only a stage away from the burning of books, in the name of the new morality he had espoused in his old age: 'Where the persuasion to turn away from what we believe to be the true morality is intrusive it should be restricted.' As always the complaints were not against the great enemies of television, blandness and banality, but against those programmes that introduced some abrasive element. It always seemed to me that this simple fact put the critics in their proper place, but in 1971 the Government went as far as challenging the BBC's right as a communicator to mount a discussion on the rising in Northern Ireland, and in October the BBC's governors thought it expedient to set up an independent complaints commission before which Muggeridge, Worsthorne, Lord Longford, Mrs Mary Whitehouse, and other deafening propagandists on behalf of what they called the silent majority, could join the public in laying charges of unfair treatment in radio and TV programmes. This shrewd stroke neatly pre-empted what might otherwise have occurred, the establishment of some authoritative supervisory body from outside which would have eroded the freedom, which I prefer to call the responsibility, of broadcasters, and thereby permanently damaged the BBC; it demonstrated too the subtlety with which the BBC always gauged the moment at which to appear to surrender a fragment without really giving away a thing.

I think the British tend to get bored with the BBC from time to time, as people get bored with anything that has been around a long while; without having any rational reason for it they feel it would be rather fun to burn it down and start again. In a way the Greene regime did burn it down and start again, but the danger of any fresh attempt to do it is that the shape of the new structure would almost certainly contain a reaction against what Greene did and towards less self-government for the BBC.

Undoubtedly the BBC is too big in the sense that everything else is too big. There are too many people, too many motor cars, too much noise; the fact of size seems in itself oppressive and menacing and ungovernable. Nearly everybody would prefer to live in small independent communities building motor cars out of wood for an employer who knew their wives and families and called them by their first names. Huw Wheldon must inevitably be as personally unreachable to a studio assistant as Field-Marshal Montgomery was to Wheldon; and though David Attenborough may shine like a star he is seen from roughly the same distance. The question is not whether this is desirable, for clearly it is not; and obviously the sense of person-to-person command that runs through some of the ITV companies could be restored to the BBC by splitting it into separate compartments of the same size. Those who want to divide the BBC because they think it would be easier for them to bully five parts than one whole are quite right; it would. The more honourable belief that it would produce better programmes is, however, in my opinion not on. It is pleasant to imagine a structure of British television in which BBC 1 and BBC 2 and ITV 1 and ITV 2 planned four complementary schedules in obeisance to a single broadcasting authority, but that prospect was closed for ever in 1955 when television became a medium in which a public service and a commercial service competed for audiences. A dismantling of the BBC would produce some form of two national networks supplied with programmes from various smaller, independent sources. But because television is so costly they would not be small. We would have something like a second ITV without the fish fingers and sliced bread. As this concern would still be in competition with an ITV system that was sustained by the advertisers' demand for big audiences we would end up with much the same kind of service as we have now, but without the strong, unified chain of command and flexibility of action that the present structure gives the BBC.

Size favours better broadcasting in so far as it safeguards producers' freedom, but it endangers responsibility. The most important question the BBC had to answer was whether the famous BBC ethos, the spirit guide that had accompanied it for so long, could be transmitted through such a large and complicated structure. Sir Ian Jacob, Greene's predecessor, was inspired to define its message in words which have become part of the tablets of the law. 'It is a compound of a system of control, an attitude of mind, and an aim, which if successfully achieved results in a service which cannot be given by any other means. The system of control is full independence, or the maximum degree of independence that Parliament will accord. The attitude of mind is an intelligent one capable of attracting to the service the highest quality of character and intellect. The aim is to give the best and the most comprehensive service of broadcasting to the public that is possible. The motive that underlies the whole operation is a vital factor; it must not be vitiated by political or commercial considerations.'

Its essence is that it put responsibility into the hands of the producers. Whatever the job was the person doing it was expected to get on with it, taking whatever decisions had to be taken and referring upwards only when in doubt. The point about broadcasting, as Reith saw from the beginning, was that no management could work fast enough to control everything that goes out; all it could do was to create a climate of opinion which guided the people who made the programmes. The result was a degree of self-responsibility that staggered outsiders but it was practical, idealistic and worked well. In the nature of things its inevitable clangers made more noise than its triumphs, but nearly all of these were accidents rising out of technical limitations, e.g. the need to edit, or were intrinsically trivial and silly, springing from the offended vanity of politicians. It was not so much in what went on the air as in who did not get on it that the system of producer's responsibility was most open to abuse. A producer who wished to pursue private grudges had match-less opportunities to do it and was virtually invulnerable, since it was im-possible for the victim to prove that he should have been on a programme and had been kept off it by malice. But the freedom the system conferred im-measurably outweighed the abuses of it. It produced what people remembered best: *Civilisation, The Great War, Forsyte Saga,* the great comedy series, the long, long line of achievement stretching back to the headphones of the twenties. That the BBC was run in this way from the bottom was a great source of its strength. It ensured a seething, yeasty liveliness of thought and made it tolerably certain that the Huw Wheldons, the Attenboroughs, the Paul Foxes and the Robin Scotts would be the kinds of person who ought to be at the top and would have risen there through the ranks after bearing the burden and heat of the day. It was a powerful sustenance to the morale of a newcomer who pitted himself against the others in the jungle to know that he carried the insignia of a Director-General's knighthood in his briefcase and that his chance of getting to wear it would not be thwarted by someone on the board who wanted to find a place for his wife's brother.

The BBC's power to absorb and make over newcomers was admirably demonstrated at the very top when Lord Hill stopped being chairman of the ITA's governors to become chairman of the BBC's. To quote one of David Attenborough's jokes, his appointment seemed as bizarre and indigestible to the BBC as the replacement of Montgomery by Rommel would have struck the Eighth Army in 1943; but in no time at all Lord Hill was defending the faith as ardently and sonorously as any before him; and one would have had to dislike him very much to find any significant evidence that his regime had harmed the BBC. But since Jacob wrote his celebrated definition its purity had become ineradicably tinged by competition. The ethic was a splendid spur when the BBC was recovering its audiences by beating ITV at its own game. Obedience to it was harder when beating ITV became part of the game and a generation began to move into the BBC that had never seen it as anything but the public service half of competitive broadcasting. However realistically it accepted this in private, in its public attitudes it seemed to be seeing things not as they really were, on one hand playing down the inevitably powerful influence of competition upon it, on the other justifying some changes in radio by pointing to competition which did not exist. Its habit, that had exasperated its friends for fifty years, of talking as though everything that happened was for the best, that whatever it did it had always intended to do, began to spread. One example was its claim for the drama series. It could not do without these, they were television's most characteristic form of fiction. A successful series was the most valuable com-modity in the industry, and when one came along every facet of skilled professionalism was brought to bear to make it run and run. There was nothing wrong with this; at their best as in *The Trouble Shooters, Dr Finlay's Casebook* and *Z Cars* they could achieve something like the depth of Conan Doyle's Sherlock Holmes stories. On the other hand it was a self-deception to claim, as the chiefs of the BBC claimed from time to time, that in the course of these series, during which the original creators perforce hand over their characters to half a dozen other writers, by sheer length of run the series produced characters as rounded and fully examined as anything in Balzac. The claim was made because they wanted it to be true, but it was a dangerous delusion because of its propaganda value against the single play, the only form that offered the writer full freedom and which in the nature of television, a medium that relied almost wholly on the series, was already highly vulnerable.

Similar self-deception clouded talk about co-productions. This was a means of financing expensive programmes by sharing the cost with some other organisations; it was also a useful way of securing overseas distribution and enlarging exports. Sometimes the latter merely put up part of the stake in return for a showing of the programme; they had no share whatever in the artistic side of production. This worked very well and produced among other splendid things the Benjamin Britten opera *Owen Wingrave*. But the public remained anxious and worried when the co-production was between the BBC and American commercial television manufacturers and a conflict of styles could occur. In Christopher Ralling's *The Search for the Nile* the Americans insisted on having James Mason as narrator and carried the day; he did his stuff in the ballooning, overblown style that the Americans prefer and the British had to put up with it. The BBC insisted that it retained complete editorial control of these co-productions, but one way of retaining control was to agree with what the other fellow proposed. It was dangerous to pretend that these disadvantages did not exist.

The fall in standards of home news reporting was in obedience to the notion that radio news was competitive; it ought to address a mainly working-class audience in a style that made them prick their ears; what a man said became more important than how he said it. The result was an awkward squad of reporters that mangled its mother tongue, reading in a grinding, apprehensive monotone as though fearing to be tripped up by some hard word. A slipshod habit spread of omitting the verb from a sentence. Standards of pronunciation were left to the individual. Yet the BBC had inherited most of the responsibility for the care of the spoken language. To downgrade the art was to throw away fifty years of its own craft.

Lord Hill, in an address to one of the newspaper associations in April 1972, justified the occasional trivialisation as better than some academic selection of news values. But the right choice lay in neither extreme; and when he justified the popularisation of news programmes on the ground that they competed in popular journalism one might have asked him where, in radio, was the opposition it was competing against and why popularising required the trivial and silly approach. An embarrassing example of the latter occurred over the story of Pauline Jones, who in 1971 kidnapped a baby following her own miscarriage. Her cause became celebrated because of the harshness of the sentence of three years' imprisonment passed on her by Mr Justice O'Connor. It was reduced on appeal, and she was sent to work off most of it in an open prison from which she absconded one day with a fellow prisoner. She was clearly disoriented mentally, but the BBC's bulletins could not have made more of her flight had the wretched girl got hold of a Thompson gun. To defend this overloading of a minor news item on the ground of following the standards of commercially based newspapers, and not to perceive that it damaged the public's confidence in the BBC's news, was the most curious example of the kind of split thinking that endangered the survival of what Sir Ian Jacob was talking about. It was as if the BBC could not bring itself to admit that it did certain things when it could not admire its motives.

I think the spirit guide will always be listened to when it is pronouncing on something that the BBC's deepest instinct holds to be vital. An example of this occurred in January 1972, when BBC 1 proposed to televise a special programme about Northern Ireland, 'The Question of Ulster – An Enquiry Into the Future'. It invited Lord Devlin to chair it and representatives of the rival factions, but excluding the IRA, to talk on it. The ill-advised Home Secretary, Mr Maudling, contended that the broadcast would be inflammatory and irresponsible. But the BBC's guide evidently urged on Lord Hill, Charles Curran and Huw Wheldon that it was neither logical nor proper for the government to condemn television for arranging what would have been praised as responsible and enterprising journalism had it been done by the *Sunday Times*, and that it would be unwise for the BBC to accept the notion that television was a specially potent instrument and should not expect the same freedom to probe for truth that the press had won. The broadcast duly went out and was, to tell the truth, amazingly dull, the chief effect of Mr Maudling's intervention being to refrigerate the discussion down to a degree where emotions hardly existed. Still, the principle was worth upholding.

But for the reasons I ventured upon earlier the spirit guide might find it lost the attention of its adherents when it submitted advice in the parts of television most affected by competition. Partly because television had grown so expensive that it was a heavy undertaking to scrap a series once it was committed to production, partly because a high rating was easy to justify as creating a big audience for the following programme, the BBC was increasingly tempted to declare that a popular programme was a good programme. It did not believe it. (Another of its exasperating quirks was never to agree with its critics in public while being exactly of their mind in private.) But the risk must increase that one day it would believe it, and it was a bigger threat to its future than those that came from outside. On the other hand the type of man who sought executive power within the BBC would always be the type who by character and talent was drawn to serve the ethos. Those who had reservations about it might do much good work but they would never get their hands on the tiller.

Robert Robinson said to me once that as far as he could tell the BBC did the right thing by tradition and instinct. The wrong thing was an unlucky accident. It was a neat way of putting a lot of truth. The BBC has a number of highly exasperating qualities. It is capable of a stony cruelty to people it has decided are no longer valuable. They are un-personed, like the victims of Big Brother in Orwell's *1984*. Few organisations produce as many masters of the art of suddenly letting their glance focus just past an approaching person whom it would be inconvenient to notice. It honours in theory the principle of equality between the sexes, but is in practice a masculocracy. Only two women in television, Grace Wyndham Goldie and Joanna Spicer, have reached positions of real authority. It courts its enemies and despises its friends, on whom it heaps the crudest and most insulting flattery. You can be close to the BBC for twenty years and suddenly find it turning upon you the face of a secret society that you realise you know nothing about. But I believe that its inner artistic integrity is as good as incorruptible when it comes to the pinch, and I end up as every commission who has ever investigated ends up, by regarding it as an enormously valuable national possession which we are lucky to have and would be insane to spoil.

Miss Marghanita Laski once amazed a session of the discussion programme *Any Questions?* by declaring that the BBC had been the greatest single influence for good upon the life of the nation since the decline of the Churches. Considering this proposition not by comparing broadcasting with other influences but by measuring what the BBC has put into the nation's life that would not be there without it, the people whose story it had accompanied for so long would have admitted that she was quite right.

REFERENCES

PART I

Chapter 1

1 J. C. W. Reith, *Wearing Spurs* (London 1966).
2 Reith, *Broadcast over Britain* (London 1924).
3 A. R. Burrows, *The Story of Broadcasting* (London 1924).
4 *BBC Handbook 1928*.
5 *Ibid.*
6 Light Programme, January 1952.
7 C. A. Lewis, *Broadcasting from Within* (London 1924).
8 *Ibid.*
9 Vol. I, no. 1, November 1924.

Chapter 2

1 W. J. Baker, *A History of the Marconi Company* (London 1970).
2 Lewis, *op. cit.*

Chapter 3

1 S. A. Moseley, *Broadcasting in my Time* (London 1935).

Chapter 4

1 L. Sieveking, *The Stuff of Radio* (London 1934).
2 *Squirrel's Cage* (London 1931).
3 Val Gielgud, *British Radio Drama* (London 1957).
4 Moseley, *op. cit.*
5 Eric Maschwitz, *No Chip on my Shoulder* (London 1957).
6 Gielgud, *op. cit.*
7 *Ibid.*

Chapter 5

1 *BBC Handbook 1938*.

Chapter 6

1 Burrows, *op. cit.*
2 Reith, *Broadcast over Britain*.

3 Lewis, *op. cit.*
4 *BBC Handbook 1928.*

Chapter 7

1 *BBC Year Book 1933.*
2 M. Gorham, *Sound and Fury* (London 1948).

Chapter 8

1 Reith, *Broadcast over Britain.*

Chapter 10

1 Gorham, *op. cit.*

PART II

Chapter 1

1 *BBC Handbook 1942.*
2 Asa Briggs, *The History of Broadcasting in the United Kingdom,* Vol. 3 (London 1970).
3 Published in *Delight* (1949).

Chapter 2

1 H. Thomas, *Britain's Brains Trust* (London 1944).

Chapter 3

1 Stephen Potter, *The Sense of Humour* (London 1964).

Chapter 4

1 Harman Grisewood, *One Thing at a Time* (London 1968).

Chapter 5

1 D. G. Bridson, *Prospero and Ariel* (London 1971).
2 *Ibid.*

Chapter 6

1 Bridson, *op. cit.*

PART III

Chapter 1

1 R. Heppenstall, *Portrait of the Artist as a Professional Man* (London 1969).

Chapter 2

1 Gorham, *op. cit.*, p. 69.
2 *BBC Year Book 1950*, p. 19.

Chapter 4

1 G. Webb, *The Inside Story of Dick Barton* (London 1950).
2 G. Baseley, *The Archers* (London 1971).
3 Wilfred Pickles, *Between You and Me* (London 1949).
4 Bridson, *op. cit.*, p. 301.
5 Douglas Cleverdon, *The Art of Radio in Britain*.
6 *BBC Year Book 1951*.

Chapter 5

1 Eric Barker, *Steady, Barker* (London 1956), p. 225.

Chapter 7

1 Peter Lewis, 'Z Cars', *Contrast* (summer 1962).
2 Lecture on BBC 2, March 1966.
3 *BBC Handbook 1972*.

SOURCES

PART I

BBC *Year Books*, annual reports and *Handbooks*, 1928–40.
Baily, Leslie, and Brewer, Charles, *The BBC Scrapbooks* (Hutchinson, 1937).
Baker, W. J., *A History of the Marconi Company* (Methuen, 1970).
Briggs, Asa, *The History of Broadcasting in the United Kingdom*, Vols. 1 & 2 (Oxford University Press, 1961 & 1965).
Burrows, A. R., *The Story of Broadcasting* (Cassell, 1924).
Eckersley, Peter, *The Power behind the Microphone* (Cape, 1941).
Evens, E., *Through the Years with Romany* (University of London Press, 1946).
Gielgud, Val, *British Radio Drama, 1922–1956* (Harrap, 1957).
—— *Years in a Mirror* (Bodley Head, 1964).
Gorham, Maurice, *Sound and Fury* (Percival Marshall, 1948).
Guthrie, Tyrone, *Squirrel's Cage* (Cobden-Sanderson, 1931).
Hall, Henry, *Here's to the Next Time* (Odhams, 1956).
Henry, Leonard, *My Laugh Story* (Paul, 1937).
Hibberd, Stuart, *This – is London* (Macdonald and Evans, 1950).
Hulme Beaman, S. G., *Tales of Toytown* (O.U.P., 1928).
Knox, Collie, *It Might Have Been You* (Chapman and Hall, 1938).
Lewis, C. A., *Broadcasting from Within* (Newnes, 1924).
Maschwitz, Eric, *No Chip on my Shoulder* (Herbert Jenkins, 1957).
Miall, Leonard (ed.), *Richard Dimbleby, Broadcaster* (BBC, 1966).
Moseley, Sydney A., *Broadcasting in my Time* (Rich and Cowan, 1935).
Payne, Jack, *Signature Tune* (Paul, 1947).
Pedrick, Gale, *These Radio Times* (a Light Programme series, 1951).
Reith, J. C. W., *Broadcast over Britain* (Hodder and Stoughton, 1924).
—— *Into the Wind* (Hodder and Stoughton, 1949).
—— *Wearing Spurs* (Hutchinson, 1966).
Sieveking, Lance, *The Stuff of Radio* (Cassell, 1934).
Stone, Christopher, *Christopher Stone Speaking* (Mathews and Marrot, 1933).

PART II

BBC *Handbooks*, 1941–6.
BBC War Correspondents, *War Report* (O.U.P., 1946).
Bridson, Geoffrey, *Prospero and Ariel* (Gollancz, 1971).
Briggs, Asa, *History of Broadcasting in the UK*, Vol. 3 (O.U.P., 1970).
Gilliam, Laurence, *BBC Features* (Evans, 1950).

—— and McGivern, Cecil, Christmas Day Broadcasts, 1939–45.

Kavanagh, Ted, *Tommy Handley* (Hodder and Stoughton, 1949).

McGivern, Cecil, Home Service scripts of 'Battle of Britain', 'Bomb Doors Open', etc., 1941–4.

Miall, Leonard (ed.), *Richard Dimbleby, Broadcaster* (BBC, 1966).

Priestley, J. B., *Delight* (Heinemann, 1949).

—— *Margin Released* (Heinemann, 1962).

—— *Postscripts* (Heinemann, 1940).

Thomas, Howard, *Britain's Brains Trust* (Chapman and Hall, 1944).

Train, Jack, *Up and Down the Line* (Odhams, 1956).

Worsley, Francis, 'Anatomy of ITMA', in *Pilot Papers* (Pilot Press, 1946).

PART III

BBC Handbooks, 1947–72.

Barker, Eric, *Steady, Barker* (Secker and Warburg, 1956).

Baseley, Godfrey, *The Archers: A Slice of my Life* (Sidgwick and Jackson, 1971).

Black, Peter, *The Mirror in the Corner* (Hutchinson, 1972).

Brough, Peter, *Educating Archie* (Paul, 1955).

Cleverdon, Douglas, *The Art of Radio in Britain, 1922–1966* (monograph for UNESCO).

Edwards, Rex, *The Dales* (BBC, 1969).

Greene, Sir Hugh, *The Third Floor Front* (Bodley Head, 1969).

Grisewood, Harman, *One Thing at a Time* (Hutchinson, 1968).

Harding, Gilbert, *Along my Line* (Putnam, 1953).

—— *Master of None* (Putnam, 1958).

Heppenstall, Rayner, *Portrait of the Artist as a Professional Man* (Owen, 1969).

Nathan, David, *The Laughtermakers* (Owen, 1971).

Pickles, Wilfred, *Between You and Me* (Laurie, 1949).

Webb, Geoffrey, *The Inside Story of Dick Barton* (Convoy Publications, 1950).

Wheldon, Huw, *Monitor* (Macdonald, 1962).

I am grateful to Mr Frank Cobb for letting me borrow his collection of material stored from his years as a BBC press officer, to Mr Ralph Wade for letting me see his manuscript account 'Early Life in the BBC', and many individuals who sent me anecdotes and memoirs. I am especially indebted to Mr Leonard Miall, who read the proofs and provided me with much useful information. The *Radio Times* files yielded much good stuff. A lot of material was absorbed by me in talks over twenty years with more people than I can possibly list; my final and lasting debt is to the *Daily Mail* for giving me a platform from which to sound off for so long.

INDEX